Noisy Island

But, though I have been thus for my whole life a devoted lover of music, and more particularly of the melodies of my country – which are, as I conceive, the most beautiful national melodies in the world – neither the study nor the practice of this divine art has ever been with me an absorbing or continuous one, or anything more than the occasional indulgence of a pleasure, during hours of relaxation from the fatigues of other studies, or the general business of life.

George Petrie (1855: vi–vii)

Noisy Island

A Short History of Irish Popular Music

Gerry Smyth

CORK UNIVERSITY PRESS

First published in 2005 by
Cork University Press
Youngline Industrial Estate
Pouladuff Road, Togher
Cork, Ireland

British Library Cataloguing in Publication data
A CIP catalogue record for this book is available from the British Library.

ISBN 1 85918 387 5

A CIP record for this publication is available from the Library of Congress.

Typeset by Redbarn Publishing, Skeagh, Skibbereen, Co. Cork
Printed by ColourBooks Ltd., Baldoyle, Co. Dublin

www.corkuniversitypress.com

CONTENTS

Acknowledgements

My thanks to the following people who in one way or another have contributed to the writing of this book: Stuart Borthwick, John Braine, Sean Campbell, Catherine Casey, Lucy Collins, Mike Collins, Cork Campus Radio, Gerald Dawe, Tom Dunne, John Fisher, Ian Gallagher, Mark Kavanagh, Francis Kennedy, Colm McAuliffe, Bernard Mac Laverty, Martin McLoone, Jonathan Moore, Stephen Moulton, Ron Moy, Killian Murphy, Tony Murray, Deirdre O'Byrne, Mick O'Keefe, Martin O'Neill, Ondrej Pilny, Francois Pittion, Bill Sweeney, George Smyth, Kevin Smyth, Caroline Somers, Ray Tierney, Billy Webster, Paul Webster, Sara Wilbourne. Thanks also to the academic and administrative staff in the School of Media, Critical and Creative Arts at Liverpool John Moores University.

Introduction

'The Isle is Full of Noises'

Contemporary Irish popular music represents a set of enormously successful cultural and economic practices. Much in the way that Irish literature was felt to have produced an inordinate number of geniuses throughout the last century, so the island seems capable of issuing forth an endless supply of successful pop and rock acts. At the top of the pyramid, of course, is U2, which has sold well in excess of 100 million albums; after that one finds acts such as The Corrs, Enya, The Cranberries and Sinéad O'Connor who have also sold records in large amounts and who possess established international profiles. Pop acts such as Boyzone, B*Witched, Westlife and Samantha Mumba have had unprecedented success in Britain and Europe. At the same time, performers such as The Saw Doctors, JJ72, The Frames, Ash and Therapy? are all widely respected in the independent rock world, while many lesser known artists also continue to perform successfully around the world. While all this has been going on, second-generation British musicians such as John Lydon, Kevin Rowland, Johnny Marr, Stephen Morrissey, Noel and Liam Gallagher have all emphasized an Irish heritage as a significant factor in their musical identity.

As may be seen from the artists name-checked so far, there is no one dominant trend within contemporary Irish popular music. From the punk-metal hybrid of Therapy? through the teeny pop of Westlife, and on to the classic rock of U2, latter-day Irish artists have engaged with a wide range of contemporary popular musical styles and genres. Besides the ones already listed, there's also a vibrant hip hop scene, a punk-retro scene, and an incredibly dedicated clubbing scene that encompasses the vast array of contemporary dance music styles. What we find under the banner of 'contemporary Irish popular music', then, is an enormously diverse, critically acclaimed and economically successful array of practices – as one commentator rather gushingly put it at the height of Celtic Tiger fever, '[the] worldwide Irish musical renaissance is upon us' (Walsh 1996: 78). Apart from the nomenclature indicating a specific national provenance, however, on first appearance there would appear to be no one single factor linking this range of popular musical practices.

Amongst other things, this book represents an attempt to consider the 'Irishness' of 'Irish popular music', more specifically, of 'Irish rock music'. Such an

1

analysis encompasses many complex issues concerning national identity, globalization, cultural nationalism and various related matters which we shall be encountering in due course. I'd like to begin, however, with an extract from a speech to the Irish Music Rights Organisation (IMRO) from 1998, in which the Taoiseach Bertie Ahern affirmed the role of music in Irish cultural history:

> Music and writing have always played a central role in the social and cultural life of Ireland. Not alone as a source of entertainment, but also as an effective way of recording Irish history and communicating its stories widely throughout the country and the world. In addition to the historical function of music and song, they also play an important role in defining the identity of a nation and its people. They help to tell us who we are, to express our hopes and aspirations, our trials and tribulations, in a way that makes us uniquely Irish. Internationally, the Irish nation is perceived very much through the medium of its music.[1]

A number of interesting points are raised in this passage. The first thing worth noting is that the Taoiseach invokes *music* alongside *writing* as both having 'played a central role in the social and cultural life of Ireland'. This is certainly true in some respects; since the earliest records, Irish cultural history reveals a recurring fascination with both modes of expression – the organization of sound into music, and the reproduction of verbal language in some form of written sign system. It's also the case, however, that the latter discourse has tended to dominate considerations of Irish 'identity' (a trendy theoretical concept to which Ahern also alludes), especially during the twentieth century when such considerations began to take institutional form (White 1998: 151–9). The discipline of Irish Studies that emerged during the latter decades of the twentieth century was one organized predominantly around the written word, either in the form of the imaginative produce of individual talents, or as primary source material in which historical agents recorded their experiences and motives.

The study of Irish music began in earnest during the First Celtic Revival of the eighteenth century, when historians and scholars such as Joseph Cooper Walker and Charlotte Brooke were concerned to vindicate an ancient Irish culture in support of a politically valid modern nation (Smyth 1998). Since then, the formal study of music in the Irish academy has tended to focus on either the European-based art tradition or the indigenous folk tradition, and much interesting and important work has been done in assessing the contributions of these traditions to Irish cultural life (McCarthy 1999; Pine 1998; White 1998). The art tradition is predicated upon the emergence of discourses of authority, creativity and interpretation that have their bases in an international (although predominantly European-American) bourgeois world view, either in its Romantic (classical) or post-Romantic (modernist) mode (Brackett 1999). Although the field is thus implicitly cosmopolitan in orientation, one dimension of Music Studies in the Irish academy is concerned with domestic engagements with this world view, especially in the areas of composition and consumption: what is peculiar about the ways in which Irish people make and / or use art music?

Study of the indigenous folk tradition, on the other hand, tends to be animated by an understanding that views culture as a more or less unmediated expression of the 'spirit' or 'soul' of the people. Technical analysis (in the adjacent fields of sociology and history, for example, as well as within musicology itself) is not eschewed – it is, after all, an incredibly complex form of music – but such analyses are invariably underpinned by a more or less unreconstructed belief in the power of music to reflect a wider social and historical 'reality'.

Even as the study of Irish music has tended to be overshadowed by the study of Irish writing, the former field has itself been dominated by the twin pillars of the art and the folk traditions. This means that the study of other forms of musical practice – popular music, for example – will be doubly marginalized, once in terms of the object of study itself (music) and once in terms of its socio-cultural orientation (neither art nor folk music). Like the art tradition, modern popular music is international in origin, but, unlike the former, it's widely regarded in scholarly discourse as a debased cultural form, formulaic and manipulative, possessed of nothing original or beautiful to say about the *human* condition. Similarly, modern popular music is (like the folk tradition) ostensibly 'of' the people, but is seen by most commentators as a hopelessly corrupt cultural practice, lacking a mandate from national history, and possessed of nothing original or beautiful to say about the *Irish* condition. If the Irish scholar *must* study music, then let it be 'real music', or better still, 'real Irish music', not the decadent, inane noise that passes for music amongst the culturally impoverished.

In short, there exists no dedicated critical language or tradition for the formal study of popular music as a significant dimension of modern Irish experience. Such studies as have appeared tend to be predominantly journalistic in tone and tenor.[2] When it's not being condemned or dismissed, the music is invariably celebrated in accounts which, interesting or suggestive though they may be, can offer no systematic analysis of the form's role within Irish history, and can tell us little or nothing about the ways in which popular music has engaged with wider issues of Irish identity during the modern era. One of the intentions of the present volume is to redress both the negligence and the misrepresentation suffered by Irish popular music, and to open to scholarly analysis a crucial aspect of the island's modern experience.

This analysis is expedited by the emergence in recent years (from a number of disparate sub-disciplines, including cultural studies, popular culture, sociology, semiotics and popular history) of Popular Music Studies as a fully fledged intellectual discipline. In methodological and theoretical terms, the field appears to be splitting along three recognizable lines: those favouring a musicological approach (the dynamics of composition, performance and recording); those adopting sociological perspectives (the function of popular music in relation to certain salient theoretical categories such as youth and capitalism); and those pursuing an ethnographic methodology (the consumption of popular music and the socio-political formation of its various audiences). In relation to Irish popular music, such dedicated in-depth studies lie in the future; here, I merely wish to introduce what I consider to be a crucial aspect of modern Irish experience, and to indicate in fairly broad strokes some of the ways in which analysis of that practice might contribute to an understanding of the Irish historical condition.

To return to the Taoiseach's speech, it's important that it be considered in the context of the revival of Irish economic fortunes during the 1990s, and the concomitant recognition of music's role in, and contribution to, that revival. This is something Ahern alludes to when he draws upon an implicit binary in which music is apparently both 'a source of entertainment' and at the same time fulfils a recognizable 'cultural' function is so far as it's capable of telling 'stories . . . [which] play an important role in defining the identity of a nation and its people'. Such a division partakes of an established trope whereby music's economic role is invariably marginalized or downplayed in relation to its supposed affective capacity. One of the ironies of the Taoiseach's comment is that it was delivered to a forum wherein the former commercial function is actually emphasized over and above the latter cultural function. Modern Ireland is in fact awash with societies, boards, organizations and fora wherein the many economic dimensions of music (incorporating all the different aspects of production and consumption) may be finely calibrated.[3] The title of a 1996 report (prepared by a specially appointed task force named FORTE) to the Minister for Arts, Culture and the Gaeltacht, for example, says a lot about how music was increasingly coming to be perceived in Ireland during the period of its economic expansion: *Access All Areas: Irish Music – An International Industry.*[4]

The development of the modern Irish popular music industry was predicated on the relatively huge international success achieved by Irish artists, especially during the 1990s. Musicians such as Van Morrison, Rory Gallagher, Thin Lizzy and The Boomtown Rats had established international profiles in a variety of subgeneric forms, although their success remained 'unusual' insofar as Ireland's popular music tradition (such as it was) could never hope to compete with those of the UK or the US. The prejudice (both internal and external) towards Irish popular music began to change, however, with the emergence and sustained success of U2 during the 1980s. Thereafter, 'success' and 'Irish popular music' became less of an anomalous coupling, and the 1990s witnessed the emergence of high-profile international artists such as Sinéad O'Connor, The Cranberries and The Corrs, as well as a host of less familiar, more sector-specific names which we shall be encountering during the course of this book.

These achievements could not be ignored by a society (both in the Republic and in Northern Ireland) that, after years of stagnation and underachievement, had launched itself on a programme of representational reform. In short, Irish popular music offered economic opportunities that were too good to miss. Such economic considerations led to the industrialization of the practice, which has in turn led to the development of an increasingly formalized infrastructure designed by a loose affiliation of government and industry personnel.[5] To twist the metaphor slightly, in Ireland during the 1990s the cultural lamb lay down with the economic tiger, and this has resulted in one of the most active – as well as one of the most managed – popular music scenes in the world. These developments have had profound effects upon both the *amount* and the *kind* of music produced in Ireland, as we'll see throughout the course of this study; in the meantime, it's worth noting that even as popular music has continued, by and large, to be ignored in Irish intellectual-institutional discourse, it has emerged as a flagship industry of the new Ireland, locked in to other key areas of national development such as tourism, media production and leisure management.

The methodology favoured in this book is one in which neither the 'economic' (entertainment) nor the 'cultural' (stories) dimensions of music predominate, but are rather seen to inform each other at a number of interrelated levels, all the way from the lowliest singer-songwriter to the biggest popular music star, from the most casual CD purchaser to the fiercest industry player. To a greater or lesser extent, we all know that popular music comes into the world as the result of largely non-musical decisions, and that it manages to circulate by means of a network of multinational cluster corporations; some of us suspect that popular music is perhaps the most 'managed' of the modern entertainment media. At the same time, we all appreciate to a greater or lesser extent the ability of popular music to map our lives, to speak to us – to speak directly to me – of the fears and desires that order my experience of the world. As Simon Frith writes: 'Music constructs our sense of identity through the direct experience it offers of the body, time and sociability, experiences which enable us to place ourselves in imaginative cultural narratives' (1996: 124); as Ahern has it, of communicating stories about who we are.

So, popular music (like all culture) is caught up in both economic and interpersonal discourses, played out in the space that emerges between structure and agency. It's this recognition that determines the subject matter, the tenor, and (as remarked above) the methodology of this text; for I believe that neither structure nor agency should prevail as categories for the analysis of cultural phenomena, and that the musical meanings to which analysts address themselves are in fact produced by the friction that results when structural and affective discourses are brought into contact with each other. Accordingly, this study combines analyses that emanate from a variety of discursive fields. Depending on the context and the material under discussion, I have regularly brought (for example) sociological, historical and semiotic interpretations into creative juxtaposition, allowing the language and the assumptions of these different discourses to interrogate and mitigate each other. The result is hopefully both elucidating and enjoyable.

The final thing worth noting at this stage about Ahern's comments is the claim (clearly related to those addressed above) that '[internationally], the Irish nation is perceived very much through the medium of its music.' It's certainly true that the Irish have traditionally enjoyed a reputation as a musical race; but this begs a number of questions which, to my understanding, have not been adequately addressed. These questions included a) how this reputation as a musical race emerged; b) how it has been maintained and deployed during the era of mass popular culture; and c) what kind of 'music' is particularly associated with Irishness. 'Irish popular music': every term of that phrase is loaded with difficulties and ambivalences that complicate the task of analysis; when combined, they present a dauntingly complex network of affiliations and prejudices with which any critic is obliged to engage.

The quality of 'Irishness', for example, was extremely strained in the period leading up to and overlapping with the emergence of rock 'n' roll; indeed, it had been a site of intense cultural battles during the island's revolutionary phase, with ideologues such as Pearse, Yeats and de Valera producing interventions that set the agenda for the consideration of modern Irish identity, north and south, at home and abroad. I think it's fair to say that the version of 'Irishness' that dominated the post-revolutionary island, and that was still in sway during the 1950s when rock 'n' roll was emerging, was one that was generally unsympathetic to international cultural trends, and generally unsympathetic also to the age group (young adults) who would come to identify so closely with the music and its various generic offshoots. The concept of a modern 'Irish popular music', therefore, was loaded from the start with all manner of ideological implications that impinged upon the practice at many different levels, from production through creation and on to dissemination. Another way of saying this is that the dialectic of *international / national* haunts both 'Irish popular music', and, as a consequence, this book also. It's something to which we shall find ourselves turning again and again in our consideration of modern Irish popular music practices.

The institutional and methodological narratives introduced in the previous paragraphs are animated to a large extent by the work of Theodor Adorno. This imposing intellectual figure produced one of the most influential twentieth-century accounts of cultural production, and we shall be encountering variations on his thought at various points throughout this study. In theoretical terms, Adorno's pessimistic view of modern popular culture (especially popular music) received an immediate rejoinder from his fellow Frankfurt School critic Walter Benjamin who argued that, rather than signalling the termination of progressive cultural politics, modern mechanical production possessed a deeply subversive potential which it behoved progressive critics to explicate and exploit. Benjamin's work has played an important role in the emergence of Popular Music Studies, as it provides for serious scholarly engagement with cultural material all too readily dismissed (in Adornian terms) as the damaged product of a damaged world order.[6]

One problem with Adorno was that, despite his avowed Marxian proclivities, he accepted more or less unconditionally the established bourgeois classification of sound into 'music', on the one hand, and the great amorphous mass of non-musical 'noise', on the other. Not only did this implicitly support the bourgeois ideology of art to which Adorno was ostensibly opposed; it also begged a number of crucial theoretical questions: how did 'music' and 'noise' get to be classified as such? What differentiates one from the other? And what licensed individuals and / or institutions exist to make these decisions?

This brings us to the work of the great French music theorist Jacques Attali, whose work provides in large part the theoretical animus for this study. At the opening of the study entitled *Noise*, Attali wrote:

> For twenty-five centuries, Western knowledge has tried to look upon the world. It has failed to understand that the world is not for the beholding. It is for hearing. It is not legible, but audible.
>
> Our science has always desired to monitor, measure, abstract, and castrate meaning, forgetting that life is full of noise and that death alone is silent: work noise, noise of man, and noise of beast. Noise bought, sold, or prohibited. Nothing essential happens in the absence of noise.
>
> Today, our sight has dimmed; it no longer sees our future, having constructed a present made of abstraction, nonsense, and silence. Now we must learn to judge a society more by its sounds, by its art, and by its festivals, than by its statistics. By listening to noise, we can better understand where the folly of men and their calculations is leading us, and what hopes it is still possible to have (1977: 1).

Attali is one of the most important theoreticians of music to emerge in recent times, for two reasons: firstly, for his challenge to the established categories of music and noise; and secondly, for the pre-eminent role he assigns music in the analysis of modern life. With regard to the first, 'music' can no longer be narrowly defined as the intentional human organization of sound into a variety of established forms (although it is that as well); rather, it embraces the entire sonic continuum which begins in the womb and ends only with death. Whereas Adorno hoped to identify the radical potential *within* established musical discourse (hence his championing of serialism, for example), Attali rejected the established categories as culpably partial (incomplete *and* privileged) and insisted on the necessity for changing the *object for*, as well as the *mode of*, analysis. After Attali, the first issue the analyst must address always concerns the political organization of any society's sound ratio into categories of 'music' and 'noise'.

Attali's second contribution to the theory of music is even more radical, for music, he claims, 'is prophesy. Its styles and economic organization are ahead of the rest of society because it explores, much faster than material reality can, the entire range of possibilities in a given code' (1977: 12). This amounts to a claim that music is the most sensitive indicator of social change, that it's in advance of all other cultural forms as a gauge of the factors and tendencies that function in the present to order the future. Music does not 'predict' what will happen in some kind of warped variation on old-fashioned vulgar Marxism; rather, because of its intensely dialectical nature – in which economics and aesthetics are so closely enmeshed – music registers and engages change before other aesthetic forms; its dilemmas will be ours, so too its negotiations and compromises. In this way, Attali shifts music, and more importantly the analysis of music, to the centre of the academic stage, for it's there that the future is in a sense already taking place.[7]

If Attali's theories regarding noise and music are correct, then the marginalization of popular music within Irish Studies is unacceptable, for it's with the wide range of practices that are developed in relation to late twentieth-century popular music – creative discourses, policy decisions, consumption trends and so on – that modern Irish identity has been, and continues to be, most actively negotiated. As Iain Chambers writes: 'Sounds migrate. Music wanders without a fixed address . . . In its ambiguous power, music always represents an elsewhere, an interruption, a stepping out of time that displaces the particular world we have inherited and permits us to catch snatches of what politics fails to hear' (1996: 247). The island is full of noises, and it behoves the Irish critical community to begin listening seriously to them, and not only to the noises that are 'sweet', but also the ones that we are routinely encouraged to believe are not. This book, then, represents a first tentative step in the direction of a serious scholarly engagement with modern Irish popular music as a crucial site for the representation and continuing negotiation of Irish identity.

Finally, with regard to my own place within the critical-cultural matrix of Irish popular music, the following passage from Simon Frith (who, as one of the founding figures of Popular Music Studies, should know a thing or two about it) strikes me as apposite:

> [The] cultural study of popular music has been, in effect, an anxiety-driven search by radical intellectuals and rootless academics for a model of consumption – for the perfect consumer, the subcultural idol, the mod, the punk, the cool commodity fetishist, the organic intellectual of the high street who can *stand in for them* . . . [What's] at stake in such writings are what it means to be male, to be white, to be middle class (1992: 180, original emphasis).

Like all criticism, in other words, *Noisy Island* is as much a coming to terms with the self as it is an ostensibly objective response to some arbitrarily delimited set of practices and relationships. This relationship, which is at once political and existential, obtains in all discourse: the describing subject constructs itself as a function of the material that is being described. It may be the music itself, or it may be its ubiquitous presence in our lives, but it seems to be the case that modern popular music offers a particularly resonant instance of this universal phenomenon. As Martin Stokes writes: 'Music is very clearly very much a part of modern life and our understanding of it, articulating our knowledge of other peoples, places, times and things, and ourselves in relation to them' (1994a: 3). Generation and gender certainly play a part in this process, as many commentators attest, and as we shall see at length in the coming pages; whether class and nationality do (or at least whether they do to the same extent) is perhaps the key issue to which this study is addressed.

1

From Hucklebuck to Horslips
The Roots of Irish Rock

INTRODUCTION

Ireland during the 1960s was an isle full of noises of various kinds. Many different popular musical styles had emerged as a response to major changes in the post-war world (including quite centrally the rock 'n' roll revolution of the previous decade), and had begun to compete with each other for the ear of the population. These traditions were recognizable enough in their ideal forms, although in practice they often overlapped and blended into one another. My intention in this chapter is to describe some of these musical trends in terms of their sonic forms, stylistic characteristics and ideological assumptions, and to observe the ways in which, despite critical and institutional attempts to demarcate discrete musical practices, such trends frequently met and overlapped in precisely those terms (that is to say, form, style and ideology).

If Ireland underwent a musical revolution during the 1960s, this was a reflection of the wider cultural and political situation. Events such as the Vatican Council, the beginning of domestic television broadcasting, and the visit of US President John F. Kennedy were only the most visible signs that some kind of change was in the air (Tobin 1984: 9–94). The island north and south had been traumatized by the revolutionary activities of the early twentieth century, and the attitudes and practices caused by that trauma persisted more or less down to the decade in question. When Sean Lemass took over from Éamon de Valera as leader of Fianna Fáil and Taoiseach in 1959, however, he adopted a modernizing, liberalizing agenda and began to look for ways to move beyond the policies that had characterized the southern state during its first four decades (Bew and Patterson 1982; Lee 1989: 371–408). Economically, this meant an end to protectionism and the opening up of

9

the economy to foreign capital.[1] Culturally, it meant (re-)engagement with a range of concerns which had been categorically off-limits during de Valera's long reign. Politically it meant a mitigation of the obsessive nationalism which had persisted after the revolution it had helped bring about. Lemass's credentials were the best (he had been in the GPO in 1916 as a teenage volunteer with Pearse and Connolly, and in the Four Courts with Rory O'Connor six years later), but during his time in office he pursued a pragmatic line of co-operation with Terence O'Neill, his Northern counterpart, and dragged his party and his country with him.

The Lemass era, in other words, ushered in the age of revisionism in Irish life, one aspect of which was a somewhat belated revolution in youth culture. This revolution was monitored at the time by one of the island's most active revisionist agents, *The Irish Times*. 'Young people of today are', proclaimed one of its editorials from October 1965,

> in their own phrase, tough-minded . . . Young people coming up, no matter what allegiance their fathers had, can look at the evolution of other countries from the British Commonwealth and wonder honestly if 1916 was absolutely necessary. They can ask if, with Home Rule on the statute books, we would not today have a united Ireland, with or without some tenuous links to the British Commonwealth.

Another editorial from January of the following year, the fiftieth anniversary of the Easter Rising, asserted:

> Young people want things in a hurry, and want to forget the past . . . The young man sees himself appearing in the pages of *Paris Match* or *Life* magazines . . . Without any trammel of the past, whether Protestant/Catholic or Separatist/ex-Unionist, the differentials are disappearing in our country. Our young people want to forget. Boys in Dublin gravitate towards coffee-skinned girls . . . The past is not only being forgotten by the young; it is being buried with great relish, and even with disdain (quoted in Fennell 1993: 88).

Now, *The Irish Times* may (as the stridently anti-revisionist journalist Desmond Fennell suspects) have overstated the case somewhat, trying to *instigate* the kind of attitudes that it purported to *reflect*. 'The past', which the editorial regarded as ready for the grave, was in fact alive and well and living in Derry City; at the same time, the Catholic Church continued to exercise a powerful influence on life and thought south of the border. Indeed, conservative forces of various kinds continued to influence every aspect of life on the island throughout the 1960s. Nevertheless, economic prosperity (relative though it was) made a clear social and psychological impact as the decade progressed. A new atmosphere, youth-oriented and at odds with received notions of national identity, was abroad throughout the land. 'Atmosphere' is a deliberately nebulous term chosen to describe the array of changes – some blindingly obvious, some more subtle – that took place in the way in which Irish people perceived themselves and their country during the 1960s. Nowhere were those changes more apparent nor more influential than in the sounds produced by that society, and in particular in the different sounds that emerged from the field of social activity that became *the* key emblem of modern international youth during the post-war period: popular music.

I don't want to labour the matter here, as much of the import will emerge in relation to the specific texts and practices described throughout the course of the chapter. But just to reiterate the point made in the introduction: it's my conviction that the musical-cultural and socio-political revolutions that overtook Ireland during the 1960s are interdependent. I argue that each – in some aspects and to some degree – both *anticipates* and *determines* changes in the other and that, as a consequence, the appropriate methodology for a study of the popular music of the period is one that attends to the interplay between individual agency and institutional structure; between the interpersonal construction of 'texts' on the one hand, and the institutional manipulation of 'trends' on the other. With that in mind, let's try to interpret some . . .

SHOWBAND DREAMS

In the beginning . . . there are no beginnings. No aspect of human endeavour (and certainly no music-making, of any quality or variety) takes place in a vacuum. In stories about contemporary Irish popular music, the showbands invariably function as a point of departure (Clayton-Lea and Taylor 1992: 7; Prendergast 1987: 11–12; Rolston 2001: 51). Such indeed is the function they serve in this book. But it's important to acknowledge before we get going that the showbands also had an inheritance, and that there existed a complex, island-wide, popular music-making culture throughout the twentieth century from which emerged the values and practices that came to be associated with the showbands. This prehistory comprises an uncertain and overlapping mesh of *ceilidh* bands, dance orchestras, and the odd jazz combo which no one, to my knowledge, has as yet adequately described.[2] But while some aspects were obviously inherited from existing practices, some aspects of the showband scene – orchestration, performance and marketing, for example – were clearly, radically novel. And it's this sense of a watershed in modern Irish cultural history that makes the emergence of the showband scene such a useful place to begin to tell the story of Irish popular music.

Insofar as they were primarily oriented towards established dance genres, the earliest Irish showbands owed much to existing values and practices. The Clipper Carlton (formed in 1950 in Strabane, Co. Tyrone) is usually considered to have been the first. It entered a world in which transport and electricity were limited, the power of the Catholic clergy was extensive, and the musicians who made up the 'orchestra', led by figures such as Mick Delahunty, Maurice Mulcahy, Johnny Quigley and Brose Walsh, dressed in black suits and stayed largely hidden behind their music stands (Wymbs 2003). They exchanged the black suits for some natty blazers, ditched the music stands and began to move to the rhythm of the music as if they were enjoying it, not just reproducing it for the purposes of dancing. They also demanded (and received) a percentage of the door takings, rather than a flat-rate fee. Most significantly of all, The Clipper Carlton also extended its musical range; recently unearthed recordings include examples of most of the popular genres of the day: skiffle ('Rock Island Line'), show tunes ('New York, New York'), country (a Jim Reeves medley), calypso, Bill Haley era rock 'n' roll, light jazz instrumentals, a Shadows' medley and various 'Irish' ballads and tunes, all performed to a high musical standard.

The Clipper Carlton acted as a kind of mirror to international popular music. With animation and no small degree of musical skill, it could reproduce at the local ballroom whatever was big in Britain or the US that year. In these terms alone, its appeal may be readily appreciated when set within the context of the island's social and infrastructural limitations. The band's most significant innovation, however, and what really set The Clipper Carlton and the bands that followed in its wake apart from the dance orchestras, was the introduction of the 'Juke Box Saturday Night' feature, during which dancing was temporarily suspended and the crowd was encouraged to approach the stage to gaze upon the band going through various comedy routines and personality spots. This association of music with spectacle represented the most significant contribution of the early showbands to the emergence of a new dispensation in Irish popular music-making practices.

In keeping with pop music scenes in many different parts of the world, however, what really fired the showbands was their engagement with the phenomenon of American rock 'n' roll, which began to make an impact during the middle part of the decade. Considered in terms of ethos and sound, the two were in fact obviously linked during their early stages. They were also linked by the fact that the music produced by each was considered to be little more than 'noise' in the prevailing critical orthodoxies of their respective societies. Whereas in the US (and to a certain extent in Britain), early (pre-1960) rock 'n' roll was vilified by an older generation in reaction to the perceived dangers of the Cold War, in Ireland the early (pre-1960) showbands were regarded with suspicion by an ultra-conservative establishment determined to resist any 'foreign' cultural influences that might threaten what it considered to be the core 'Irish' values. It's hard to credit in retrospect, but in the latter part of the 1950s the showbands were, if not exactly hip, then certainly in the vanguard of those who were agitating for a new Ireland, one less in thrall to the past and more open to the values of the wider world.[3] In this respect, the showbands might be considered *the* typical cultural expression of the Lemass era in Ireland; like his administration, the showbands still ostensibly serviced the local community, but both were determined to re-introduce into that community the values and possibilities of a modern world which had been shunned by the prevailing powers (an assortment of protectionist politicians and Catholic clergy) since the earlier part of the century.[4]

But there were also significant differences between these Irish and American popular musics. For one thing, the showbands were not necessarily youth-oriented, as was rock 'n' roll. Whereas the latter fetishized socio-cultural (and soon economic) categories such as the adolescent and the teenager, the former, reflecting the peculiar social culture that had evolved in Ireland since the famine of the mid-nineteenth century, tended to attract people to their live performances from across the age range. No doubt different age groups responded to and used the music in different ways; no doubt (as we'll go on to see shortly) significant sections of Irish society condemned the showbands on a variety of grounds, one of which would have been its damaging effects upon the country's youth. Whereas rock 'n' roll developed a specific (albeit international) audience defined in terms of a relatively confined age group, the success of the showbands depended at least in part upon their appeal to an audience characterized by a much broader age range.

There were other differences. In terms of orchestration, whereas rock 'n' roll began to evolve almost immediately the classic format which has remained the basis of rock music ever since, the showband represented a transitional stage between the orchestras and bands that preceded them and the groups that followed. Although formed around a core rhythm section (comprising drums, bass and guitars), brass and keyboards were still important components, and the average band size remained at about eight throughout the showband era. More fundamentally, whereas the dissemination (and subsequent success) of rock 'n' roll was founded on the availability of relatively cheap vinyl recording, the music of the showbands, at least in their first generation, could only be experienced in the form of live performance. Indeed, the impact of the 'music' depended in large part on the context of the 'show': in 1963, the journalist Adrian Cronin went so far as to define the showband as 'a musical ensemble that performs with actions whilst playing' (quoted in Kennedy 2003). In this respect, you could say that the showbands remained true to one of the core values of rock 'n' roll – live performance – long after rock 'n' roll itself had sacrificed that value in favour of the much more lucrative formats of vinyl recording and (in Elvis's case) movie-making. It's true that by the time something like a rock (as opposed to a rock 'n' roll) aesthetic began to make itself felt in Ireland, the showbands had started recording. But the basis of their appeal and their continued enormous success throughout the 1960s remained live performance.

The audience numbers for which the top acts performed on a regular basis during their ascendancy between 1960 and 1965 were extraordinary in the context of the small, relatively low-income communities on either side of the border. (During Lent, when they were not allowed to play, many showbands toured Great Britain, Europe or North America.) It's difficult to know, and probably useless to speculate upon, who was leading whom, but it would seem that, despite the conservative ideologies promulgated both north and south, Irish people were growing less concerned with their official cultural inheritances, and more determined to embrace the modern world in one of its most exciting forms. And once the appeal had been confirmed, an entire infrastructure emerged to service it: management, adapted and new-build venues, instrument and hardware provision, accommodation and travel provision, media coverage (advertisements, dedicated journals, radio and eventually television time) and so on. Moreover, given the significant financial rewards, the job of showband musician became a highly attractive career option for young, working-class boys from low-income backgrounds throughout Ireland.

The impact of the top-range showbands can never be fully appreciated because there's limited opportunity to hear them (and none to view them) in their natural milieu, the large purpose-built ballrooms that were regularly packed with anything up to 3,000 people. The records and radio shows that these musicians began to make from about 1962 can't really do them justice. (The first pop music chart, compiled by Jimmy McGee, was broadcast on Radio Éireann on 2 October 1962.) For one thing, showband musicians were stage- rather than studio-oriented; the musicianship (in terms of technique, attack, control and so on) required by the former location was significantly different from that required by the latter. Moreover, Ireland's recording industry was still very much in its infancy during the early 1960s, and it's clear that neither the technology nor the expertise existed at this time to capture the show-band sound in all its vibrancy and excitement. But if you had to pick one song that summed up the ethos, the appeal and the limited ambition of the showbands, you could do a lot worse than 'The Hucklebuck', released for the first time by Brendan Bowyer and the Royal Showband during the scene's heyday in 1964.

Although it had its competitors in the premier league of showbands – Dickie Rock and the Miami, Joe Dolan and the Drifters, Butch Moore and the Capitol, Billy Brown and the Freshmen, and so on – Waterford's Royal consistently dominated the scene throughout the 1960s and is widely acknowledged to have been first among equals when it came to showband heroes.[5] From the time the band turned professional in 1959 to the time it officially disbanded on Bowyer's departure in 1971, the Royal ruled the roost, not because its musicians were necessarily better or more charismatic or more attractive or more ambitious than the others, but because they possessed all the right elements in the right combination. What with winning prestigious entertainment awards in England, rubbing shoulders with the likes of The Beatles and Elvis, and having television programmes made about them, Bowyer and the boys had come to represent a form of Irishness – internationalist, modern, successful, market-oriented – that was more or less a direct cultural counterpart of the political and economic policies (foreign capital, dismantling of protection, free trade) pursued by Lemass and his inheritors.

All these elements were perfectly distilled on the Royal's biggest hit, 'The Hucklebuck', described by the journalist John Waters in the course of a revisionist appraisal of the showbands as 'a blistering three minutes as good as anything since' (1994: 96), and by the generally unsympathetic Mark J. Prendergast as 'one of the classiest number one singles' of the period (1987: 12). The song was picked up by Bowyer during one of the band's American trips, and entered the Irish charts in January 1965 where it stayed for twelve weeks, including seven at number one.[6] Although a minor chart hit in Britain also, 'The Hucklebuck' failed to provide a platform for the mainstream international success clearly desired by Bowyer and the Royal at this stage in their career. At home, however, it provided the soundtrack for Ireland in 1965 and encapsulated the showband scene at more or less the peak of its popularity. Musically, it clearly belongs to the rock 'n' roll end of the showband spectrum, a spectrum which, as it developed over a number of years, was large and diverse enough to encompass a wide range of sub-traditions in which different individuals, bands and band-families specialized.[7]

'The Hucklebuck' was a dance-craze number, a subgenre that peppered the popular music charts in the US and Britain during the decade after the inception of rock 'n' roll. Which is to say, unlike the love / loss songs that have traditionally made up the bulk of the popular music canon, it's a hymn to the dance floor, specifically directed at the live audience that constituted the showbands' principal constituency. If this makes 'The Hucklebuck' a paradoxical *recording* success (although it was in fact recorded more or less live like all showband discs), it's also what renders it emblematic of the entire showband ethos. Clearly involving elements of 'the twist' and traditional jiving, it also invites the listener / dancer to 'wriggle like a snake' and 'waddle like a duck'. The dancer is encouraged, in other words, to join a community that seeks pleasure in sonic / bodily practices – such as loudness, repetition, wriggling, waddling and so on – located at some remove from everyday, 'normal' activity. Musically, also, 'The Hucklebuck' demanded an active bodily, rather than a passive listening, response. In structural terms, the songs was a standard blues work-out in the uplifting key of G major, although it had none of the blues elements (apart from some 'bent' notes during the saxophone solo) that might darken its otherwise bright, positive connotations. All in all, it provides us with one of the most characteristic sonic representations of Lemass-era Ireland, a record with an energy and a rawness that does as much as any record probably could to reproduce all the camaraderie and the possibilities of the Saturday night dance floor at that particular time and in that particular place.

If the showbands are routinely (and mistakenly) invoked as the *ex nihilo* point of departure for the story of Irish rock, they are also invariably represented, implicitly or explicitly as the case may be, as the problem that rock thankfully solved. Since the late 1960s the rock fraternity – represented by the likes of Rory Gallagher, Brush Shiels, Eamon Carr, Philip Lynott, Bob Geldof and Bono – has been more or less united in its antipathy towards the showbands. Much in the way that a co-opted American rock 'n' roll came to be seen as 'square' by post-1960 generations, so the showbands have been, and by and large continue to be, regarded as representatives of a benighted past which modern Ireland in all its sophistication has happily left far behind.

But why have the showbands been so unfashionable and so unpopular in Ireland for so long? People like to party, musicians like to play; much of the time, people like to party to the live sound of their favourite bands, even if that sound is reproduced (sometimes to a startlingly high quality) by musicians other than those who composed it.[8] Given the relative lack of sound media in Ireland at this time, there were considerably fewer opportunities for people to hear their favourite songs than there are now. But the best showbands played your favourite songs, they played them well and they played them on your own doorstep. In a very real sense, these groups were more important than the hopelessly remote originals they were aping. So, what's the problem with a group of musicians getting out there and giving the paying punters what they want?

Two reasons, one musical, the other socio-political, suggest themselves. Firstly, it's clear that the rock music that began to emerge in Ireland during the early 1960s was aesthetically opposed to the values upon which the showband scene had evolved and thrived. It's also clear that the same rock music has coloured all subsequent interpretations of the showband phenomenon. There are many ways to describe the differences between the two musics, but perhaps the easiest is to say that whereas the latter was organized as a business (and soon as an industry), the former had, from its inception, artistic – specifically, romantic – aspirations. Rock music, that is, invited its adherents to invest in discourses of *expressive originality* and *authenticity* that were fundamentally opposed to the showband values of *accuracy* and *entertainment*. 'Showbands were not seen as purveyors of originality', as Robert Ballagh, bass player with contemporary beat group The Chessmen, maintained: 'They were purveyors of entertainment. In fact, the public didn't like to hear original music' (Power 2000: 413). There's no reason why Bowyer shouldn't have written a song like 'The Hucklebuck'. He didn't, however, and the reason is probably less to do with talent than with the general musical context within which he and the other showband musicians were operating.[9]

The showbands, then, provided the soundtrack for the Lemass era, an era of comparative colour and fun after the grim days of the 1950s with its seemingly endless cycle of economic underachievement and emigration. In fact, far from being *essentially* conservative or *essentially* regressive, the early showbands (as Noel McLaughlin and Martin McLoone suggest) 'brought to the youth of rural and provincial Ireland the same kind of liberating hedonism that was associated with other imported forms of popular culture (2000: 188). That particular aspect of the showband scene was overlooked by those who came to maturity after that era, however. Nowhere is the arrogance of the present more visible than in the disdain shown towards the showbands by subsequent generations, those who didn't have to contend with the 1950s, and who came to regard the colour as *kitsch*, and the fun as infantile. Added to this is the fact that rock music is primarily an urban phenomenon; the people who make it, attend its performances, listen to it and comment on it are those who, whatever their origins, have by and large materially affiliated with the city, and who tend to regard the culture of the hinterlands as seriously deficient in any number of ways. Ireland underwent a period of significant urbanization in the latter part of the twentieth century (Redmond 2000: 14–16), and this only contributed to a general scepticism towards cultural forms that had their bases in a rural context.

The showbands had broadened Irish musical horizons; now they were being rejected by a rock community (and, indeed, a folk community, on somewhat different although related grounds) who had come to regard itself as more mature, more modern and more musical. At the same time, Irish society during and after the Lemass era evolved in such a way as to leave it generally unsympathetic towards the showbands. John Waters has speculated that the showband scene came to be seen as 'an unconscious expression of the post-independence failure to reconstruct an indigenous culture on solid footing' (1994: 93). This is another way of saying that disdain for the showbands was (and to a significant extent still is) an important part of the way in which modern Irish society stratified itself in terms of cultural value. As Pierre Bourdieu writes, 'Art and cultural consumption are predisposed, consciously and deliberately or not, to fulfil a social function of legitimating social differences' (1984: 7). In other words, disliking the showbands on aesthetic grounds – a clear instance of what Bourdieu calls 'disgust at the facile' – is one way in which an aspirationally middle-class, internationalist, urban community could confirm its taste, and hence its identity, in contradistinction to a lumpen working-class / rural community it had come to regard as an embarrassment.[10] As Irish culture materially improved from the 1960s, and as it 'matured' towards standard international middle-class values, it turned its back on the pleasures, now regarded as coarse and callow, that characterized its first brush with the modern world.

It's ironic (although not at all unusual) that ideological enemies should gang up on a third party in this way. The fact is that the rock and acoustic-based music which began to emerge in Ireland during the 1960s made common cause with the Dublin-based bourgeoisie in their shared antipathy towards the showband scene. It's also ironic that rock should indict the showband scene, and the enduring tradition of Irish pop which it helped to foster, on grounds of commercialism, when it's clear that, despite decades of claims to the contrary, rock has always been as goal-oriented as pop, and those goals, no matter how they are romanticized or disguised, are invariably materialist in essence. Condemnations based on aesthetic criteria are equally misconceived, as even a cursory familiarity with the history of rock music reveals that no popular cultural tradition in history has produced more disagreement about what constitutes quality, nor more diverse criteria upon which to organize discourses of value and taste. As Theodore Gracyk writes: 'Music's aesthetic value is a function of its use by appropriately knowledgeable listeners' (1999: 215). Those who inhabit the worlds of art, folk and rock music clearly do not constitute 'appropriately knowledgeable listeners' when it comes to the music of the showbands. Or to put it another way, each of these different worlds has invested its cultural capital in significantly different stock, and as a consequence is ill-disposed to appreciate the value, or indeed the meaning, of each other's activities.[11] We shouldn't be surprised at disagreements between classical, rock, folk and showband music on aesthetic grounds, but we should endeavour to understand the cultural and socio-historical provenance of such judgements.

Added to all this is the fact that music migrates and mutates, insinuates and influences. All noise, even that we are disposed to consider objectionable on one or another set of aesthetic criteria, contributes to musical possibilities in both the present and the future. Routine condemnation of the showbands is thus either disingenuous or ignorant; when you denounce the music, you denounce, whether or not you know it, part of yourself. I'd like to suggest that the dismissive reflex be abandoned, and the music in all its many styles, genres and standards, should instead be considered for what it was: a highly popular set of cultural practices that first anticipated, and then accompanied, a period of significant social change in modern Irish history.

IRELAND UNPLUGGED

In attempting to trace the emergence of an Irish rock tradition *and* to identify any distinctive qualities, sonic or otherwise, which such a tradition might possess, we are obliged to take account of the great wealth of acoustic-based music that was produced in Ireland during the 1960s and the early 1970s. There were in fact two main sources from which all the other tributaries of acoustic-based music flowed during this time. The first was the international vogue for folk music, a phenomenon that in turn gave rise to an enduring figure of the contemporary popular musical world: the guitar-playing singer-songwriter. The second was the rejuvenation of Irish traditional music and its subsequent re-orientation within the Irish sonic landscape. I want to spend a little time mapping these two streams, before going on to speculate upon the nature and extent of the influence they exercised upon Irish rock music.

Folk music became an important aspect of North American progressive politics during the 1950s as part of a radical response to Cold War politics, as an expression of disillusionment with national life after The Second World War, and as an investment in an alternative, apparently more authentic, era (Laing *et al* 1975: 7–43, *passim*). One strand of Irish acoustic music during the 1960s and 1970s was deeply influenced by this American folk revival.[12] This is ironic, of course, insofar as the American folk revival was itself at least partially influenced by older Irish and British traditions, or at least looked to those traditions as examples of the musical authenticity it valued so highly. Trying to sort out who or what inspired what or whom in this story is a difficult task (and a full-time career for many dedicated musical historians, both amateur and professional).[13] What does seem reasonably clear is that there was already a significant 'Irish' element to American folk and country music (including the music of The Carter Family and Woody Guthrie) which in turn became a major influence upon Bob Dylan, who in turn became the fountainhead of the American folk revival during the early 1960s, and a 'folk' hero on both sides of the Atlantic. Dylan had also been listening to The Clancy Brothers and Tommy Makem, a group of Irish emigrants who found success in the clubs and cafés of Greenwich Village singing a form of folk music – the ballad – that was British in origin, but that in its adapted Irish form had become both extremely popular and extremely influential throughout the English-speaking world.

The number of Irish people from the period, including musicians, who claim Dylan as one of the primary sources of their interest in popular music is telling.[14] Early Dylan – the predominantly acoustic-based material from the eponymous first album of 1962 up to and including *Highway 61 Revisited* (1965) – was a wake-up call for many people. Although the things to which it woke people up were many and varied, there seems to be a general consensus as to Dylan's importance as a figure within the history of modern popular music. But what was it about his 'folk' music that made it such a fascinating experience for contemporaries, and subsequently such an influential force upon the course of popular music, both Irish and otherwise?

One deceptively simple answer is that Dylan wrote much of his own material, songs that were both ambitious and complex and that apparently expressed his own responses to both the personal and political conditions in which he found himself. If this was in marked opposition to 'traditional music', the basis of which was a more or less intact canon of tunes and forms, it also differed from what was beginning to occur within the contemporaneous popular musical genre of rock 'n' roll. Not only was rock 'n' roll a self-consciously youth-oriented music in contradistinction to Dylan's increasingly adult orientation: the fact is that Dylan *was* Dylan in a way that Elvis *could never be* Elvis. What I mean by this is that Dylan's music encouraged a close identification between singer, song and performance, whereas Elvis had begun to lose that identification at a very early stage in his career. If an Elvis performance was an *interpretation of emotion*, then a Dylan performance was (or at least was marketed as) an *expression of meaning*. And this idea of music expressing an authentic individual response to the world became one of the keystones of the international folk revival.

If Dylan apparently had a line on 'the truth' in a way that other contemporary popular musicians did not, he had also mastered the 'three chords' that would enable him to communicate that truth in as effective a way as possible. Accompanied only by acoustic guitar and harmonica, early Dylan possessed a lo-tech, yet extremely resonant, iconography. In an important sense, *he* was the meaning of the song; the musical 'texts' he produced were not answerable to the precepts of traditional musical analysis, but functioned, with relation to aspects of timbre, inflection and gesture, in a more corporeal, and more individualistic, sense. In other words, Dylan's status as a powerful artist was seemingly (although deceptively) dependent upon the force of the message rather than the quality of the medium. It's difficult to know if the power was an effect of the simplicity or vice versa; the overall effect, however, was to render Dylan one of the most irresistibly *cool* icons of the period. Not only did this have the effect of rendering cool by association the kind of musical activity (acoustic-based folk music) in which he was engaged; at the same time, it encouraged many young people on both sides of the Atlantic to aspire towards the same musical and iconographical values.

Thus was born the genre of the modern folk-inflected singer-songwriter. This figure, who unquestionably represents Dylan's most important generic legacy to contemporary popular music, has proved amenable to endless adaptation and reinvention over the years. However, what characterized the cool North American singer-songwriters who emerged in Dylan's wake during the 1960s – for example, Leonard Cohen, Joni Mitchell, Gordon Lightfoot (all Canadian, incidentally) – was the diminishing importance of any 'folk' element in their work, and a concomitant emphasis upon Dylan's notion of expressive authenticity. This particular popular musical form still owed something to the onset of the folk revival during the 1950s (Mitchell, for example, was still being described as a 'folk singer' well into the 1970s), but increasingly the musical and lyrical complexity of the material drew it inexorably away from the 'folk' values of the original revivalists.

If Dylan led the American folk revival in the direction of the singer-songwriter genre and the notion of expressive authenticity, the British folk revival leaned towards the ballad form and the notion of recovered tradition. There had been a strong folk movement in Britain throughout the twentieth century, not only in popular cultural forms, but also in some aspects of its art tradition, as may be heard in the work of composers such as Vaughan Williams, Holst and Britten (Blake 1997: *passim*; Revill 2000). Without ever rediscovering its 'lost' mass audience, however, British folk became a popular (as opposed to an élitist) force from the early 1960s, when it began to make an impression upon youth culture. Folk clubs sprang up throughout the island and a significant scene emerged, related in some ways to other movements but possessed nonetheless of its own distinctive values and practices (Laing *et al* 1975: 138–9; O'Connor 1991: 153–6). It's from this scene that enduringly influential musicians such as Martin Carthy, Bert Jansch and Richard Thompson, as well as groups such as Steeleye Span, The Incredible String Band and Fairport Convention, emerged. With these individuals and bands, British folk took up the perceived challenge thrown down by Dylan after he 'went electric' in 1965, by developing the extremely broad school that was folk-rock. Many of the sounds and images developed during this period, including the lone acoustic guitar maestro and the long-haired, hippy group, became enduring presences in British popular music, mutating in a variety of interesting ways over the years.

One thing that the American and British folk movements shared was an emphasis on authenticity – hence, their regard for African-American acoustic blues. However, whereas for Dylan and his heirs an equal accent was placed upon personal expression, for one influential wing of the British folk movement the equal accent was on technique, interpretation and the de-emphasising of personal truth in favour of the communal truth maintained in the canon of traditional song. Which is to say, whereas Dylan *was* his own style, a performer such as Carthy *developed* a distinctive, successful style that enabled him (in keeping with the alternative values of the British scene) to interpret traditional folk ballads for modern audiences.[15] In fact, Dylan and Carthy represent ideal alternative models of the different values and practices that infused the international folk revival of the early 1960s. In reality, there was extensive, intense traffic between all the different wings of the 'folk' movement, and individual musicians characteristically adopted positions (and built careers) somewhere along the continuum that ran between the ideals of the singer-songwriter and the ballad interpreter.

The British-American folk scene was one of the contexts within which Irish folk music emerged and thrived during the 1960s. Another was the indigenous 'traditional' music scene which had performed an important function in relation to national identity since the Middle Ages (Traschel 1995: 27–8), but which had been developing as a particularly significant aspect of Irish cultural nationalism since the nineteenth century (McCann 1995; McLaughlin and McLoone 2000: 181). As political nationalism moved into a position of ideological dominance throughout the part of the island subsequently known as the Republic, traditional music became (along with various other activities and pursuits, such as Irish language and sports) an important aspect of its cultural identity.[16] Although the modernizing agendas of the new state's civil servants and politicians did not immediately stretch to sponsoring *mere* cultural pursuits, many individuals throughout Ireland (and the diaspora) became concerned in the years after 1922 to preserve and disseminate what they considered to be the clearest expression of Irish musical identity. What we find occurring throughout the twentieth century is a process whereby particular sounds come to be understood as the sonic equivalent of an Irish cultural identity, and those sounds beginning to be organized (through education, social and cultural events, state-sponsored media and so on) in such a way as to represent the organic 'expression' of 'the Irish people'.

The recovery of indigenous folk music and its formal expression in state-sponsored bodies has been an important aspect of European nationalism since the mid-eighteenth century (Traschel 1995: 31). In Ireland this process was instituted in Comhaltas Ceoltóirí Éireann (CCÉ) – translating as 'The Association of Irish Musicians' – an organization with roots going back to the 1930s, although only formally instituted in 1951. This organization, based in Ireland but international in its scope and ambition, is dedicated to the promotion of Irish traditional music as part of a wider programme of Irish cultural revival. A cultural nationalist agenda, clearly indebted to a wider nineteenth-century programme of Irish cultural revival, has continued to underpin CCÉ policies down to the present day (Henry 1989).

'Trad.' was not in particularly good shape at the beginning of the 1960s. Many regarded it as part of the 'bogman' inheritance they wished to leave behind, while the minority who valued it did so, by and large, in terms that were not conducive to the long-term health of the music itself. Its recovery was aided in part by the folk boom. But CCÉ became the primary conduit through which traditional music entered the Irish sonic landscape in the second half of the twentieth century; and probably its greatest achievement was successfully to promote an interest in the music amongst young Irish people at a time when there were so many different sounds competing for their attention, and so many more media through which those sounds could be heard. The seeds of traditional music's enormous (comparatively speaking) success as a modern cultural form were sown in the 1960s, during the heyday of the showbands and against the backdrop of a burgeoning beat scene. That it managed to do so from a grass-roots level, *and* to bring government onboard (in the form of official recognition, and eventually funding) is a testament both to the power of the music and to the ability of ideologically motivated individuals to make an impact upon both the shape and the character of national culture.[17]

At the same time, the introduction of new blood fostered the kind of controversies which attend any formalized institution. A key question emerged (or rather re-emerged) between those concerned to retain the 'essence' or 'core' of the music intact and those who maintained that, to survive, the music had always adapted to changing social and cultural circumstances and must continue to do so.[18] This tension may be understood to underpin the debate that surrounds the competition structure which has been a key element of CCÉ activities for many years. For some, the idea of examining musical proficiency – and the fetishization of certain instruments, styles and materials that results from competition – is something that belongs to the art tradition and runs counter to the music's 'folk' roots. Competition, it could be argued, has come to dominate the institution's extensive Fleadh (festival) programme, replacing socialization and exchange as its principal *raison d'être*. For others, competition has contributed to the professionalism of musicians and to the improved profile the music enjoys both nationally and internationally. CCÉ, it could be argued, facilitates an absolutely vital dialectic between tradition and innovation without which the music would be liable to 'museumification', on the one hand, or complete cultural disinheritance on the other. At the same time, there have always been those who, while perhaps sharing CCÉ's esteem for the music itself, disdain its official sanction and prefer to operate outside any formal institutional framework.

A number of factors converged upon Irish society at the outset of the 1960s that provided the context for the emergence of a wide range of acoustic musical activities – what May McCann (in a slightly different context) calls a '"bricolage" of sound' (1995: 67) – and we can locate most of the acoustic-based artists and groups from this period in terms of the tendencies described above. The Dubliners, for example, was a powerful ballad group which emerged from the city's burgeoning folk scene at the beginning of the decade. This enduringly popular outfit did not write any original material, but specialized in interpreting ballads (British as well as Irish) that drew much of their resonance from the personalities of the two most prominent members, Ronnie Drew and Luke Kelly. When The Dubliners scored an unlikely Top Ten hit in Britain in 1967 with 'Seven Drunken Nights' (a version of an eighteenth-century Scottish ballad), Irish folk music acquired both a sound and an image that have remained influential down to the present day. This 'Irish' music was a strange beast, however, being neither 'traditional' (in the CCÉ sense) nor 'folk' (in the Dylan sense), although obviously related to both in some seminal aspects. Whereas the occasional 'tune' from Barney McKenna's banjo or John Sheahan's fiddle kept the band in touch with the country-wide 'traditional' revival, for example, the vocal styles of Drew and Kelly, as well as the key role played by Drew's rhythm guitar, meant that it always maintained at least some contact with the international movement that had reached its purest form in Dylan's self-penned 'folk' music.

Although there were obvious affinities between traditional, folk and other acoustic musics, and although many groups were eclectic in their choice of sound, the discipline of the single tradition was strong, and was always pulling performers back towards the idea of being purveyors of one single, identifiable style. The members of The Johnstons (including Paul Brady, a performer who, given the distribution and longevity of his musical activities, is seminal to this book) were quite conscious of the difference, so much so that they released two different albums on the same day in January 1969: one (*Give a Damn*) comprised of contemporary 'folk' music written by the likes of Joni Mitchell, Jacques Brel and Ewan McColl (Canadian, Belgian, and Scottish-English, as it happens – so much for the 'American' influence); the other (*The Barleycorn*) a collection of traditional Irish songs and tunes. This shows the extent to which some Irish artists were compelled to go to accommodate their different musical impulses: on the one hand, the traditional *Gemeinschaft* with all its powerful 'local' associations, on the other, the 'cool' Anglophone folk movement and its associations with a youth-oriented, international counter-culture.

If The Dubliners have come to represent one well-known image of 'Irish music', another band emerging at more or less the same time has come to represent another. As remarked above, The Dubliners' leanings were always as much towards the international folk movement as towards an indigenous instrumental folk tradition. From their eponymous first album of 1963, however, the music of The Chieftains has remained (despite some fascinating diversions) rooted firmly within that latter tradition. Evolving from an informal gathering of musicians associated with the composer Seán Ó Riada, piper Paddy Moloney has led the various musicians who at different times have comprised The Chieftains on a series of international musical adventures over four decades.[19] Professional yet unassuming, fully familiar with the traditional repertoire of styles and tunes yet open to diverse musical influences at the same time, The Chieftains have come to represent the acceptable face of Irish traditional music produced in a commercial context.

There was one band, however, which for a short period during the late 1960s functioned as a pool into and out of which flowed many of the musical streams that I've been discussing so far in this section: Sweeney's Men.[20] The various musicians who were involved with the band during its short life – Johnny Moynihan, Andy Irvine, Joe Dolan (not the showband singer!), Terry Woods, and Henry McCullough – have links that stretch into every corner of Irish acoustic-based music, and indeed into many other areas too.[21] Although these tremendously cool young men shared many of Dylan's concerns, it's fair to say that their musical interests (or at least the lengths to which they were willing to go to express those interests) were broader than his. These interests spanned most contemporary acoustic traditions, including the many and various styles that comprised both the Irish traditional and the international folk movements. Thus, whereas Moynihan and Irvine tended more in the direction of 'ethnic' music (including both anonymous ballads from the Atlantic archipelago and what nowadays would be called 'world music'), Woods and McCullough had closer connections with the American folk movement in both its 'roots' and singer-songwriter modes. Yet there was enough common ground between all these musicians to make Sweeney's Men, for a time at least, both commercially and artistically viable.

The range of influences shared by all these musicians may be clearly heard on the recordings produced by Sweeney's Men in 1968 and 1969. The eponymous first album introduced the British and Irish material favoured by Irvine and Moynihan, while also reflecting Woods' American interests in ballads such as 'Tom Dooley' and 'The House Carpenter'. The following year's *Tracks of Sweeney* (recorded after Irvine's departure) maintained that musical breadth. However, it also included a number of songs composed and performed in the 'contemporary' folk idiom that was indebted to Dylan. Woods' plaintive 'Dreams For Me', for example, had as much in common (in terms of style and inspiration) with the expressive originality of any of the post-Dylan singer-songwriters as it did with either the rootsy American ballads he himself favoured or the 'authentic' ethnic sounds and rhythms which so fascinated Moynihan. All in all, in the range of its reference and allusion the music of Sweeney's Men may be considered as both a form of resistance to established cultural narratives regarding the 'nature' or 'essence' of Irish music – folk, traditional, or otherwise – and an anticipation of Irish social pluralism, located in the 'liminal spaces' that emerge whenever disparate cultures encounter each other (McLaughlin and McLoone 2000: 183).

'Scenes intermingle,' as Mark Olson says, 'producing relations of mobility' (1998: 279), a claim borne out by an observation of the Irish popular music of the 1960s. I have consciously employed the metaphor of a river to try to describe the intermingling, overlapping and cross-fertilization of different kinds of noise that could be heard in Ireland during the 1960s and early 1970s. Pursuing this metaphor, it's clear that the acoustic 'stream' itself was broad and deep, accommodating many diverse values and practices. This great stream of acoustic music has had a profound influence on the Irish sonic landscape, including, as it happens, Irish rock music, even when (as during punk) this latter array temporarily turned its back on this seminal dimension of its own inheritance. If one important feature of this music was the drive to discover, practise and protect pristine examples of an abstractly defined music – 'pure' traditional or 'pure' folk, or whatever – another was the drive (fuelled in part by changes in the media and in part by changes at a national political level) to accommodate the processes of musical cross-fertilization that inevitably occurred within a single band, a single individual or, occasionally, within a single musical text.[22]

BIRTH OF THE BEAT

If the showbands and acoustic-based music were important (although frequently underestimated) influences upon the emergence and subsequent character of Irish rock music, its true roots may be found in the beat groups that began to appear, especially around Dublin and Belfast, towards the beginning of the 1960s. These bands introduced a new sensibility into Irish popular music-making, one that, despite major changes in technology, in social and political background and in the perceived role of cultural activity, has endured to the present day. This new sensibility might be described in any number of ways, with reference to any number of theoretical systems; at this stage, however, suffice it to say that in its ideal form it represented a romantic, anti-commercial, youth-oriented, music-led set of attitudes and practices, consciously at odds with dominant (showband) and other emergent (folk and traditional) forms. In this section I want to describe the origins and constitution of that sensibility.

As a description of a particular array of popular musical practices, 'beat' music first began to appear in England towards the end of the 1950s. Associated in particular with the city of Liverpool, this style of music represented a response to a number of musical, social and wider cultural factors which coalesced there in the years after the Second World War. Given both its status as a major western port and the influx of American military personnel during the war, one such factor was obviously going to be a susceptibility to the cultural trends of the US (Cohen 1991: 12). Despite this, it's clear that beat music (and Merseybeat in particular) was not an attempt slavishly to imitate an American popular cultural form, but represented a genuine adaptation of the sounds (themselves diverse in provenance) of one place to the socio-cultural requirements of another. Drawing on popular musical genres such as rock 'n' roll and skiffle, beat music emerged as not only a distinctive sound amongst the many others that were vying for attention in British popular culture at this time, but as a particular cluster of attitudes towards life in general, and towards music-making in particular. Both the musical and the attitudinal aspects were, of course, encapsulated in The Beatles.

Despite decades of official cultural embargo, cultural exchange between modern (for which read 'degenerate') England and traditional (for which read 'holy') Ireland continued to function much as it had done for centuries. When The Beatles performed in Dublin and Belfast in November 1963, the trend for 'beat groups,' as they were described in the Irish press (Power 2000: 26), was established. Just as Merseybeat represented a peculiar local response to a wider (American) cultural trend, however, so a number of local factors were also significant – both in terms of the music's particular sonic character and the kinds of attitudes and practices that animated its adherents – when Irish musicians began to play a form of beat music during the 1960s. I want to spend this section thinking about those sounds, attitudes and practices.

How to begin? The following anecdote offers a point of departure from which to start thinking about the issues raised by the emergence of beat music and its relation to other popular music styles in Ireland at this time. A friend who grew up in Dublin during the 1960s tells of the relative dearth of city venues willing to cater for new styles, and how a popular gig for new bands became the Friday or Saturday night dances run by the many tennis and rugby clubs that ringed the city.[23] One such venue was Templeogue Tennis Club, situated in a quiet, middle-class suburb of south Dublin. Despite the club's relatively small size and the somewhat sober neighbourhood in which it was located, most of the names which are now synony-mous with the emergence of early Irish rock music played there at one time or another. As a regular attender at the Friday night gigs, my friend remarked a regular ritual in which young women would approach the stage as the band came on and put to them this one key question: 'Are yez blues or commercial?'

What did they mean? What did 'blues' and 'commercial' stand for in this context? What social, cultural and / or economic considerations encouraged these young women to organize the popular music-making world into these two seem-ingly exclusive categories? It might be worthwhile taking a little time to unpack this deceptively simple question as a means of approaching the emergence of Irish beat music during the 1960s and the process of its evolution into a fully fledged, self-conscious rock scene towards the end of the decade.

The terms in question, 'blues' and 'commercial', carried both descriptive and evaluative resonances. Moreover, they were invariably defined negatively in terms of what they *were not*, rather than what they *were*: if you weren't *blues* (whatever that meant) you were *commercial*, and if you weren't *commercial* (whatever that meant) you were *blues*. As the decade progressed, 'blues' became a shorthand term for any kind of music (including Irish beat) that leaned in the direction of American and

African-American popular genres and / or their British adaptations. At a sonic level, it was a kind of music that stressed, if not fetishized, rock 'n' roll's implicit back beat, an underlying pulse characterized by energy and speed, and one that that suggested both aggressive resistance and cathartic release.[24] Attractive and threatening, this reliance on the beat also points to the music's basis in a masculine ideal: its provision of a space within which white, middle-class boys from across the western world (for which Ireland just about qualified in the early 1960s) could perform and celebrate their identities in a way that was both highly public and highly pleasurable (Hicks 1999: 27).

'Commercial', on the other hand, connoted the world of the showbands, a 'pop' world in which the music was familiar and dance-oriented, the 'scene' was official and well supported by an industrial infrastructure and the prevailing ethos was one of entertainment. The image cultivated by the showbands was 'safer', less aggressive and more directed towards 'good, clean fun' as defined in received Irish socio-cultural mores. The music they played was also more 'harmonious' – literally and figuratively – than that of the beat groups, especially with their use of brass instruments to provide a range of texture and colour that the latter could not produce, even had they wished to.[25] 'Commercial' and 'blues' also served as useful descriptions of different financial tendencies; the former (played by 'bands') were, by and large, successful, the latter (played by smaller 'groups') were, by and large, not. The financial, musical and socio-cultural discourses attending these different styles fed each other. And so, making a virtue of necessity (as invariably occurs amongst the disadvantaged in any such situation), adherents of 'blues' music claimed the moral highground and routinely disparaged the business orientation of their 'commercial' counterparts.

All in all, the showbands represented a readily identifiable matrix of sound, attitude and practice from which the beat groups were trying to distance themselves. They did so in a number of ways. For one thing, although people still danced to the music, dance was not the primary motive behind either playing or attending a performance. The music was not a means to an end, in other words, but an end in itself. This was reflected in the repertoire of music played by the beat groups (an eclectic mix of popular American styles, including quite centrally rhythm 'n' blues, soul and jazz), which was, in both commercial and artistic terms, less accessible than standard showband fare. Formed in many instances to provide 'relief' for showbands keen to cut down their hours on stage, or obliged to play in smaller (occasionally *very* small) venues around Dublin, Belfast and (later) other cities, these smaller groups were very much the poor relation. Even during the late 1960s, at a time when the showband craze was on the wane and rock music was in the ascendant amongst the country's youth, the average showband musician could expect to earn many times more than his counterpart in the beat groups (Power 2000: 26). In the face of this financial fact, the latter had to be pretty dedicated to an alternative aesthetic; as contemporary DJ Danny Hughes put it, '[the] beat scene was about love for the music' (Prendergast 1987:18).

Yes, perhaps, but we all know that the path of true love never did run smooth; and the fact is that neither the divorce from showband values nor the birth of a discrete set of beat / rock values were as straightforward as some concerned might have hoped for, nor as clear-cut as some historical accounts would have us believe. Many of the beat groups included ex-showband members, or musicians for whom a showband career was a constant temptation.[26] By the same token, just as the orchestras had been forced into crisis by the onset of the showband era, so the showbands themselves were obliged to reassess as alternative musical values began to emerge. Many 'proper' showband musicians clearly coveted (and occasionally attempted to engage with) different aspects of the beat scene – its emphasis on energy and authenticity, for example – without, however, wishing to jeopardize their financial security. Then again, few of the earliest Irish beat groups composed their own material; it was the *nature* of the material they covered, rather than the *fact* that they played covers, that differentiated these bands (in the minds of musicians and audiences) from the showbands.[27] In retrospect, it's clear that these first beat groups occupied a grey area in between the showbands they ostensibly rejected and the 'proper' beat and rock groups of the US and Britain they were looking to emulate. Hence, the great amount of dithering that was apparent throughout the 1960s as individual musicians (and sometimes whole bands) moved back and forth across the showband / beat group divide.[28]

The Greenbeats are generally acknowledged to have been the first significant Irish beat group.[29] Even before encountering the music, we can appreciate that *as a name*, 'The Greenbeats' was performing a number of important functions. On one level it obviously made intertextual reference to The Beatles, whose songs the Irish (hence 'green'?) group specialized in covering as faithfully as possible. Besides the obvious allusions, however, and in keeping with a general shift in popular band names at this time, the choice of 'The Greenbeats' was a clear signal that this group's musical values were located at some remove from those that informed the likes of 'The Royal' and 'The Capitol'. Whereas the latter, as Michael Hicks writes, typically 'tended to exalt their owners into the high life, evoking images of sophistication and opulence' (1999: 115), the former represented a calculated affiliation with a specific set of values which were lower class, marginal and self-consciously opposed to established discourses, both in terms of music and the wider lifestyle options to which the music was ineluctably bound. It was a long journey, in more ways than one, from [The] Miami to Skid Row.[30]

Besides The Beatles, The Greenbeats also covered material from a range of other performers working in different styles: the traditional rock 'n' roll of Jerry Lee Lewis, the rhythm 'n' blues of The Rolling Stones, the gospel-tinged soul of Ray Charles, as well as the occasional jazz number. Just like the showbands, in other words, The Greenbeats covered other people's songs; however, they only covered songs that they regarded as 'better' – of greater value according to the emergent beat scene's elusive and constantly refined criteria – than those covered by the former. What's more, these songs were performed and received in different ways to the songs performed and received in a showband context. In this respect, and to reiterate a point made above, the source of the beat groups' antipathy towards the showbands lay not so much in the fact that they *played* other people's songs, but rather in the material that they chose and in the way that they performed it. As Jimmy Rabbitte, manager of the eponymous band in Roddy Doyle's *The Commitments*, says to his charges: 'It's not the other people's songs so much . . . It's which ones yis do' (1992: 12).

Added to this is the fact that The Greenbeats also composed some original material (such as 'If This World Were Mine' from 1964), thereby demonstrating an ability and an ambition that the showbands, almost without exception, lacked. In any event, it was this combination of cool covers and original songs that The Greenbeats performed in their spiritual home (Liverpool's Cavern Club) in 1964. No breakthrough immediately forthcoming, they drifted back to Ireland where the energy dissipated amidst personnel changes and differences over direction. Guitarist Brian Lynch left because the brass element which the rest of the band were trying to introduce smacked of the showbands and was at odds with the beat aesthetic to which he adhered. The point is, however, that The Greenbeats and groups like them significantly broadened Irish popular musical horizons, introducing an alternative cultural capital – articulated in a range of identifiable sounds and activities – that contributed to the marginalization of the showbands whilst simultaneously enabling the emergence of a fully fledged Irish rock scene.

In March 1965, Butch Moore, singer with A-list showband The Capitol, came sixth in the Eurovision Song Contest with a song entitled 'Walking the Streets in the Rain'. It was Ireland's first time in the competition. Three months later, Dublin beat group Bluesville scored a No. 7 hit in the United States with 'You Turn Me On', a song written by their English keyboardist, Ian Whitcomb. No two events do more to encapsulate the aspirations of Irish popular music, in either its 'commercial' or its 'blues' tendencies, at this time; no two songs do more to point up the differences that animated popular music-making practices during this formative period.

Entering the Eurovision Song Contest was a clear signal of the Republic's willingness to open its doors to the modern world.[31] The act chosen to represent the country for its Euro debut had to reflect the new values with which the new Ireland wished to be identified. Enter young, handsome, sweet-voiced Seamus (christened 'James') 'Butch' Moore from north Dublin. The move from James to Seamus to Butch, incidentally, is a neat encapsulation of twentieth-century Irish history up to this point: the 'English' name is exchanged for its Irish equivalent during the period of cultural enthusiasm following the revolution, only to be ditched in turn for an obviously Anglophone 'pop' name when the revolution starts to run out of ideological steam. Although 'James' had temporarily left the building by 1965 (he would return), the fact is that 'Seamus' and 'Butch' were still locked in deadly combat for the soul of modern Ireland, and that despite their 'squareness' in the eyes of the beat groups, the showbands represented a set of values which (like the beat groups themselves) were far removed from 'traditional' Irish culture.

Although Moore and his backing band The Capitol observed the established showband tradition of covering other people's songs, they also had several Irish hits between 1964 and 1966 with original custom-composed songs, including 'Foolin' Time' from February 1964, written by Queens University student Phil Coulter. This didn't mean that they were a beat group, however, or that they ever approached (or wished to approach) the music-making values of the beat scene. Musically accomplished and entirely professional in outlook and organization, Moore and The Capitol in fact epitomized the ethos of the showband scene in all its commercial aspirations and populist orientation. These were the values that would represent Ireland at Eurovision, and that would in time evolve into a fully-fledged 'pop' aesthetic. Ireland's remarkable record in Eurovision (seven victories in thirty-three entries), as well as the string of successful pop acts the country has produced since the 1960s, is evidence of the force with which that pop aesthetic, rooted in the show-band scene, has impacted upon the Irish popular musical imagination.

Bluesville, on the other hand, was a typical group from the Dublin beat scene that had been developing since about 1963. The band's name was a clear signal which side of the 'commercial' / 'blues' divide it was on. With six members, it was somewhat over-staffed for a beat group; nevertheless, the music it played, and the attitudes and values that informed it, placed Bluesville firmly within the beat camp, while leaving them fundamentally at odds with the showband scene and *nearly* all it stood for. The one thing they shared was the desire for a hit record in Britain and / or the US, which was exactly what Bluesville achieved with 'You Turn Me On'. While The Capitol and The Royal had minor hits in Britain, the beat group's achievement must have left the showbands somewhat confused: after all, *they* were supposed to be the populist, commercial acts, *they* were supposed to be in it for the money, whereas the beat groups were supposed to be in it for the love of the music. Bluesville's achievement was to demonstrate that beat music and commercial success were no longer mutually exclusive, and that a fundamental shift, reflecting a shift that had already occurred elsewhere, was just about to overtake Irish popular music-making practices.[32]

By 1965, as Fergal Tobin puts it, '[life] in the Republic began to manifest the strains of a transitional society' (1984: 120). These strains could be observed in many different areas of Irish life, but nowhere more markedly than in popular music. Slowly, imperceptibly, the balance shifted during the middle years of the 1960s. The showbands peaked in 1966, but the industry was becoming saturated and the socio-cultural factors that had provided the context for its emergence were in the process of disintegrating. During this same period, some bands (The Chess-men, The Strangers, The Vampires, The Impact) existed in a sort of no-man's-land located somewhere between the opposing ideals of the showband and the beat group. The latter still played covers and aspired to the professionalism and success of the top showbands – some even appeared on RTÉ's *The Showband Show*. Many showbands, meanwhile, continued to covet the hipness of the beat groups and recognized the advantage, both professional and personal, of being able to perform original material.

By the second half of the decade, however, it was clear that the tide had turned. The beat groups had appeared towards the beginning of the 1960s, right in the mid-dle of the showband phenomenon. They had done as much as they could to resist the values and practices which were dominant at that time, and to pave the way for an alternative model of popular music organized around romantic discourses of authenticity, identity and personal expression. A new generation, perhaps half a decade younger than these first beat musicians, embraced this latter model whole-heartedly, and saw no reason why it should have any truck with showband values at all. The showbands would fend for themselves, and the 'pop' ethos that animated them would survive (indeed, thrive) in other forms. For the large numbers of young people who were increasingly tending towards a beat sensibility, however, the time had come to acknowledge the demands of the music, and to take the short but decisive step over the imaginary divide that separated one form of music-making practice from another. Thus it was that in or around autumn 1966, Irish rock music was born.

PIONEERS

This, then, was the context within which Irish rock emerged, one rich in musical sounds but rich also in the diverse array of meanings attached to those sounds by variously motivated agents. For the remainder of this chapter I wish to introduce some well-known pioneers from the field. I do this not with the intention of adding anything particularly new to the vast amounts of interpretation their careers have already attracted; rather, I want to indicate how, on the one hand, the music made by these people, and the ways in which they thought about it, engaged with some of the issues that have been introduced in the opening sections of this book; and on the other, to describe the kinds of practices and sounds that characterized Ireland's first rock generation, so that the practices and sounds of those who followed on may be all the more fully appreciated when we come to address them in their turn.

We start with Them, a group which would have played an important part in Irish rock history even if it hadn't functioned as one of the staging posts through which Van Morrison moved on his way towards international fame. But then again, it's unlikely that there would have been a Them without Morrison (or at least unlikely that it would be widely known) for he it was who raised the group's ambitions above local scene heroism. Without Morrison, Them would have been like The Greenbeats or Granny's Intentions or a host of other Irish groups of the 1960s – academically 'influential' yet unheard (of) except by the very few.

'Them' was a well-chosen name. Not only does it create grammatical anomalies (such as the one in the previous sentence) that reflect the group's recalcitrant attitude towards cultural orthodoxy; it also serves as a suitable description of the fluid, not to say chaotic, personnel roster that represented the band throughout its career. 'Them' was in fact a musical ideal to which many different musicians subscribed – at least temporarily – over an extended period of time. Even more than their American contemporaries The Byrds, Them were not so much a 'group' in The Beatles tradition – a tight, organic unit comprised of a relatively small number of friends – as a space through which a pool of performers constantly moved in the service of a musical ideal represented by the band name. Other writers have attempted to track the many comings and goings that characterized Them, and I have no desire to replicate that work here, or to attempt to come up with a definitive list. That kind of activity is beyond the scope of this book; in any case, how can historians be expected to know the truth of the matter when much of the time the band members weren't sure about who was in and who was out? In this context I'm more interested in some of the theoretical issues thrown up by the band's career, and two in particular that I want to mention briefly here: i) exactly what kind of music did Them believe they were making? ii) what ideas and values are invested in the debate surrounding the issue of who played guitar on the band's seminal first release, 'Baby, Please Don't Go' from November 1964?

With regard to the first issue, it's probably easier to start off with what Them knew it was *not*. First and foremost, of course, it was most definitively *not* a show-band – the name alone was enough to make that clear. Before forming Them with guitarist Billy Harrison late in 1963, the teenage Morrison had played with The Monarchs, a band which had followed the showband trail somewhat against the will of (at least some of) its members. Again, the choice was between a romantic tendency towards various marginal contemporary styles, and a professional tendency towards the financial rewards offered by the showband scene. Like a number of other Irish musicians of the period, The Monarchs attempted to find a compromise between these tendencies. Eventually, however, the tension proved too great, and so Morrison and his like-minded band members made an irrevocable break from the showband world and everything it stood for.

But if Them had turned its collective back upon the showband scene, neither was it reducible to mere 'beat group' status. As we've seen in the previous section, the Irish beat scene was comprised of a number of different musical impulses, some of which were just as offensive to Morrison and his fellows as were the showbands. The Beatles may have written their own material; they may have been a genuine group as opposed to an idea manufactured to exploit new markets; they may even have been talented and attractive. It was clear, however, that their primary influences were the African-American commercial artists of the 1950s (such as Little Richard and Chuck Berry) and their white imitators (such as Elvis Presley and Buddy Holly) who together had been responsible for the advent of the popular musical form known as rock 'n' roll. For Morrison and like-minded musicians throughout Britain and Ireland, rock 'n' roll was *already* exploitative to a degree; it had *already* contributed to the adulteration of the 'real thing' – the 'real thing' that they were so concerned to access. Although clearly removed in both influence and impulse from the showbands, the commercial success of white beat groups such as The Beatles was nonetheless evidence of their susceptibility to a similar 'pop' aesthetic; and the attempt on the part of various Irish musicians to recreate the sound (not to mention the success) of The Beatles rendered them culpable in the eyes of Morrison and like-minded others.

So, if Them was neither showband nor beat group, what was it? To what music-making ideal did it aspire? The answer is: rhythm 'n' blues. Belfast was an industrialized British city that had experienced an influx of American military personnel and their music during the war. African-American music was more than a hobby in

Belfast; for many, such as those who donned black arm bands after the death of Otis Redding in 1968, it was a passion.[33] Morrison had grown up listening to his father's extensive collection of blues- and jazz-derived music, and it was this fundamental tradition – underpinning the boogie, soul and urban blues of Bobby Bland, Ray Charles, and John Lee Hooker, as well as the country blues of Brownie McGhee, Sonny Terry and Leadbelly – to which the young man was drawn. He was not alone, of course; many musicians from different parts of the archipelago (but especially London) had become fascinated with African-American blues and had begun the process of converting that fascination into a cultural phenomenon, the British rhythm 'n' blues movement, that in its turn would contribute to the emergence of rock music. The question of what should have led a generation of young, middle-class British boys to be so taken with a music so removed in space and experience is not easily answerable, although many have speculated. What is clear, however, is that Them disdained not only the commercialism of the showbands but also what it regarded as the attenuated 'pop' values of The Beatles, values to which many in the Irish beat scene assiduously subscribed.[34]

Perhaps the principal criterion concerning Them in its penchant for rhythm 'n' blues and its concomitant antipathy towards other popular styles was that of 'authenticity'. Indeed, this was a criterion which concerned most of the names associated with the so-called 'British Invasion', including The Animals, The Rolling Stones, The Pretty Things, The Yardbirds, Fleetwood Mac and Blues Incorporated, to mention but a few. Given the variegation of the African-American blues tradition, however, 'authenticity' was bound to provide an invidious basis upon which to formulate an aesthetic, for when you got down to it, it turned out that even the 'originals' were not so original. A typical Muddy Waters record, the influential 'Mannish Boy', for example, constituted an uneven and ultimately untraceable mixture of borrowings, extemporized interpolations and allusions to different musical traditions. Before the electric Chicago blues so lauded in Britain in the early 1960s, there was the acoustic Mississippi Delta blues; before that there was a bewilderingly diverse array of European and African folk traditions and genres. How far back did you have to go before you got to 'the real thing'? Moreover, the fact that commercial success was built in to the African-American blues tradition, in all its forms, meant as a fundamental principle that its more purist British disciples were in constant danger of being stranded in both artistic and commercial terms.

Nevertheless, both the deference to 'authenticity' and the assurance as to its access meant that British rhythm 'n' blues was infused with an arrogance often bordering on intolerance, especially with regard to other contemporary popular music styles. Of no band was this more the case than Them, the commercial image of which was, paradoxically, virulently *anti*-commercial, and which (much like its Decca label-mates The Rolling Stones) actively sought to reproduce in its music the aggressive, adult male sexuality characteristic of the African-American blues tradition. These qualities may be perceived in the band's breakthrough single from December 1964, a record which remains as one of the most incendiary, most influential moments in popular musical history.

The B-side 'Gloria' would represent an important recording if for no other reason than that it was Morrison's first significant compositional achievement. In its own context, however, it attempted to reproduce, both musically and lyrically, the qualities of the African-American traditions so valued by Morrison and his band-mates. With its energetic 'stomping' rhythm and its insistent, repetitive chord structure, the song connoted a youthful virility that made a powerful contemporary impression. It was this impression that cover versions sought either to reproduce or, as with the versions by The Doors and Patti Smith, to quote ironically. Whereas that particular track has attracted much attention in rock music history as one of the most significant and influential achievements of the British rhythm 'n' blues movement, the A-side has also been widely discussed, although not necessarily for the same reasons.

'Baby, Please Don't Go' was a typical product of the genre. As a song, it came with impeccable credentials, as David Hatch and Stephen Millward explain:

> 'Baby, Please Don't Go' began its recording career under the title of 'Don't You Leave Me Here' when it was recorded by Papa Harvey Hull and Long Cleve Reed in 1927. As 'Baby, Please Don't Go', the song was later recorded by Big Joe Williams (in 1941) and by Muddy Waters (1953) before Them helped to make the song almost a compulsory part of any aspiring 'British rhythm 'n' blues' band's repertoire during the sixties (1987: 23).

The track also came with one of the most instantly recognizable guitar figures from the entire popular musical canon. And herein, of course, lies a conundrum: who played the guitar? It's well known that producer Bert Berns recruited leading session men, including future Led Zeppelin guitarist Jimmy Page, to play on many of Them's early recordings. Page himself is sure that the celebrated recorded version represents his work, and most commentators tend to agree. Others, such as band members Eric Wricksen and guitarist Billy Harrison, dispute Page's account, maintaining that the signature riff was written and recorded by Harrison.

I've no desire to wade into this argument in search of the 'correct' answer. Consider, rather, the nature of the debate and the issues that are stake. As a group, Them had invested heavily in discourses of authenticity, deploying such discourses to identify both itself and the others from whom it wished to be dissociated. The blues ideal connoted a musician who *felt* certain emotions, *transposed* those emotions into appropriate musical forms, and then *performed* the resulting music in appropriate contexts. This ideal carried over into the various offshoots of the blues, including boogie, urban blues and the rhythm 'n' blues that proved so attractive to the likes of Mick Jagger, Eric Burdon, Eric Clapton and Morrison himself. In other words, rhythm 'n' blues musicians desired *to own, to occupy*, the music in a way that other contemporary 'pop' musicians did not. In this regard, of course, the studio has always been a problematic context for the performance of blues-based music, inasmuch as it places an array of artificial technologies between the musician and the listener. Nevertheless, blues-affiliated artists still wished to be identified with the music, because the emotion in it belonged to – was a direct expression of the personality of – the musician.

In many ways, Them *was* the guitar part from 'Baby, Please Don't Go' – the reck-lessness, the abandon, the energy, the depths to which it descended and the heights to which it soared were all expressions of the *meaning* of this band. Claims that that meaning was produced by a jobbing session player (as Page was at the time) who added both the riff and the improvizations during the course of an afternoon's 'work' represented an assault upon not only the band's musicianship but upon the ideal to which the musicians subscribed. Such a practice smacked of the factory, of management, of Tin Pan Alley, of the Brill Building, of the showbands, of everything from which Morrison and Them wished to distance themselves. It laid the stigma of inauthenticity across the work of a band which had come to fetishize the concept of authenticity, hence its recurrence as a theme amongst the musicians themselves, the fans who continue to invest so much in the band's music, and the commentators who attempt to make critical capital out of discursive contradictions such as this.

Versions of Them continued to tour and record until late in the decade, although it seems clear that the impetus was lost with the departure of an increasingly disillusioned Morrison. His subsequent work is probably better described as 'soul' than as rhythm 'n' blues, although neither term does justice to his restive musical imagination. The body of work that made Morrison one of the most celebrated popular performers of the last forty years is characterized by a profound sense of ambiguity towards his home place and the American culture to which he was drawn from such an early age. In Morrison's vision, both Ulster and the United States have their compensations and their drawbacks, their attractions and their lim-itations, and his music may be understood as an ongoing and evolving response to the paradoxical situation in which, as an Ulsterman with access to a particular African-American musical tradition, he found himself.[35] In this vision, early Them represents some kind of Edenic balance between the innocence of Belfast and the excitement of America, a time and place when these imagined places could be ex-perienced and appreciated as a function of their relationship with each other. The later work with Them, however – after the Ulstermen had experienced the bright lights of London, New York and Los Angeles – represents a fall from innocence, a loss of connection with home and, in consequence, a loss of the delicate relationship between home and not-home that allowed the music to *mean* in the way it once had. It's as if Morrison's subsequent career has been a penance for the sins committed in the name of Them, a constant search to rediscover the balance (he believes) he possessed at the outset of his career. Of such fantasies is the rock dream made.

Morrison's career may be understood as an ongoing dialectic between compet-ing desires, as described by Noel McLaughlin and Martin McLoone: 'belonging and yet trying to get away; the competing pleasures of the spirit and the flesh; the relationship between the local and the foreign, between the inside world and the outside, between Ulster and America, between the private and the public persona' (2000: 185). If the tension created by this dialectic accounts in large measure for Morrison's musical and lyrical concerns over the course of a long career, it's also a factor (and for many of the same reasons) that weighed upon the music of another of Ireland's rock pioneers: Rory Gallagher. Even more than Morrison, however, Gallagher's early career offers an illustration of the changes overtaking popular music-making in Ireland during the 1960s.

By 1961, when Gallagher bought his first electric guitar, rock 'n' roll was already somewhat *passé*, and both the British beat and rhythm 'n' blues movements were competing for the hearts and minds of young people across the archipelago (Hatch and Millward 1987: 87ff). None of these musical trends could claim his full allegiance, however. Born in the small Donegal town of Ballyshannon in 1948, Gallagher was too young to identify completely with the first wave of rock 'n' roll which had come over from the US during the mid-1950s. Neither did he belong fully to the following generation of Morrison and his fellow rhythm 'n' blues acolytes. His moment, rather, is that of the mid to late 1960s, the moment in which British supergroup Cream began to emphasize two elements that were to be profoundly influential upon the subsequent development of rock music: hardcore Delta and Chicago blues, and instrumental virtuosity. Before we may begin to appreciate Gallagher's engagement with these two elements, however, we have to backtrack a little to consider the nature of his musical career in Ireland in the earlier part of the decade.

Gallagher grew up in Cork listening to a range of American artists – Tennessee Ernie Ford, Guy Mitchell, Bill Haley, Buddy Holly, Eddie Cochran and Chuck Berry. Another of his enduring heroes from this period was British skiffle king Lonnie Donegan, through whom Gallagher became familiar with the music of Leadbelly and Woody Guthrie. He joined The Fontana Showband in 1964, not long after he had purchased the famous 1961 sunburst Fender Stratocaster that was to become his trademark in later life (Coghe n.d.: 14). Like many Irish musicians during the early 1960s, Gallagher ploughed the showband furrow for a number of years, earning comparatively good money as he helped churn out the popular hits of the day (Power 1990: 368ff). And as with many of his contemporaries, the kind of music Gallagher was obliged to play on stage was some considerable way removed from the kind of music to which he had become emotionally and intellectually affiliated during his formative years around the turn of the decade. Under his pressure The Fontana became The Impact and began to pursue something like a rhythm 'n' blues aesthetic in their shows across Ireland, Britain and Europe. Internal tension of the kind described earlier caused the band to split, however, and Gallagher found himself playing a season in Hamburg as the front man of a three-piece outfit featuring guitar, bass and drums, a musical combination he was to favour throughout the remainder of his career.

Returning to Cork in 1966, he formed The Taste with local players Eric Kitteringham (bass) and Norman Damery (drums). That anomalous 'The' which sounds so strange to modern ears is an indication of the musical context from which the band emerged. All showbands were prefixed with a definite article so as to indicate their inalienable identity – The Royal was *The* Royal and no other band. Even the beat groups by and large adhered to this practice. As a description of a popular music enterprise, 'Taste' was odd enough for contemporary journalists to remark upon.[36] Prefixing it with 'The' at least pulled the group back towards recognized practices and was a clear signal that the showbands still constituted the norm against which aberrant practices could be measured.

This first version of Taste toured throughout Ireland, including a regular gig at Belfast's Maritime Hotel, spiritual home of Van Morrison and Them. Gallagher's prodigious guitar talent and his increasing academic interest in the blues led him down the road mapped by British supergroup Cream. Formed in Summer 1966, Cream represented a conscious effort on the part of three of Britain's leading contemporary musicians to forge a popular musical aesthetic based on the blues rather than its rock 'n' roll or rhythm 'n' blues variants. It was clear from the outset that, as well as being seriously good musicians, Eric 'God' Clapton, Ginger Baker and Jack Bruce were serious about the blues. Clapton had already turned his back on The Yardbirds because of what he believed to be their compromised attitude towards the music to which he was so strongly attached. Cream's influence on the young Irishman was compounded when the latter formed a new version of Taste in London in 1968 and began to play regularly in venues such as The Marquee. This band supported Cream at their Albert Hall farewell concerts that year, and from this time Gallagher began to associate on a regular basis with some of the stalwarts of the British blues fraternity, including Jeff Beck, Mick Taylor, Peter Green, Alvin Lee and Clapton himself (on the Blind Faith tour of North America).

Cream was responsible for the foundation of the popular musical subgenre with which Gallagher is most closely associated: blues-rock. As I've suggested above, this form was organized around two central elements: the traditional, three-chord blues song and an instrumental ability to improvize at length around this basic chordal structure. The electrification of instruments owed much to the advent of rock 'n' roll, and the idea of a long, semi-improvized solo was clearly borrowed from the jazz tradition, but the impetus was hardcore Delta and Chicago blues insofar as it was discoverable on old recordings or preserved in the work of transitional artists such as Muddy Waters. In retrospect, the form had limited appeal for even the most dedicated of blues enthusiasts; certainly the music recorded and released by Cream does not represent a pure version of blues-rock, no more than does that of The Grateful Dead or Canned Heat, or indeed of Rory Gallagher himself. As with so much of the popular music we've considered so far throughout this book, blues-rock represented an ideal, an imaginary landmark used by musicians to map their place in the contemporary musical landscape. It would be fair to say, however, that the idea of blues-rock made a deep impression upon Gallagher and remained the most powerful influence upon all the music he created after 1967.

Taste's career culminated in its appearance at the Isle of Wight Festival in 1970, by which time both the idea of blues-rock, and the accompanying image of the white blues-guitar hero, had already undergone serious modification. The most significant figure in this process was probably Them's old *bête noire*, Jimmy Page, who through his work with Led Zeppelin continued to explore a peculiarly British response to the blues. In terms of both music and image, however, Gallagher appeared to stall around 1970. Commercially, his most successful period was between 1972 (when he won *Melody Maker* 'Musician of the Year' award) and 1976, during which period he produced two memorable live collections as well as a number of highly regarded studio albums. It was a drying well, however, for the very qualities that made him appealing for a decreasing minority rendered him radically uncool to the ears of the increasing majority, those generations for whom the blues revolution of the 1960s meant little or nothing. Despite Gallagher's apparent willingness to grow – manifested in the introduction of saxophone and keyboards in some of his later recordings, for example, and in his exploration of various acoustic styles – he was obliged always to defer to the tastes of his dwindling blues-rock fan base.

It's clear that both Morrison and Gallagher were profoundly influenced by the blues and that each managed to develop distinctive elements that enabled listeners to identify their music amidst the cacophony of modern popular musical noise. Whereas the former used the blues (more specifically, its electric rhythm 'n' blues variant) as a means to explore a range of individual concerns, the latter identified much more closely with the blues aesthetic and was concerned to produce (and with his original compositions, to reproduce) its lyrical and musical associations as closely as possible. Morrison emerged as one of the great *auteurs* of rock, and if his vision was coloured by the likes of Muddy Waters and Jackie Wilson on the one hand, figures such as Bob Dylan and John Lennon also made significant contributions (whether they or Morrison himself would acknowledge it or not). Gallagher, on the other hand, was not so much an *auteur* as a conduit through which a number of musical impulses passed. We can talk about 'the meaning' of a Dylan song, a Lennon song, a Morrison song; Gallagher's 'meaning', such as it is, was not something that was conveyed *through* the music, rather, it *was* the music. Having discovered the blues at an early age, he was content to build a career on that tradition, to accept its limitations as well as its opportunities. If the commercial wisdom of such a project may be questioned, the skill, dedication and love Gallagher brought to his life's work should not.

'Love' is an appropriate concept with which to approach the music of Philip Lynott and Thin Lizzy, as they are probably the best-loved single artist and band in the Irish rock tradition. The high regard with which Thin Lizzy is held must be put down in some measure to the fact that, the success of Them notwithstanding, they were the first 'Irish' band to achieve a significant degree of success within the world of mainstream Anglo-American rock and pop. Lizzy blazed a trail which every subsequent Irish rock act has, to some degree or other, followed. At the same time, the band's reputation has benefited from its synonymy with Lynott and the cult that has emerged around him since his untimely death in 1986. This cult must be put down in some measure to a national penchant for dead heroes; the late rock star tends to attract the same combination of nostalgia and adoration as Brendan Behan, another Dubliner who lived on the edge, and whose funeral (in 1964) was one of the biggest ever seen in Ireland. Over the years, Lynott's cult has been fed in some measure by the strong resonances that people perceive between the fact – and indeed the nature – of his death and the music that he created during his lifetime.

Besides all its other attributes, Thin Lizzy demands attention here because it is the first Irish rock band we encounter whose career was long enough to warrant a number of different musical emphases over a period of time. Musically speaking, the showbands didn't 'grow'; the success of such bands depended upon their ability to reproduce more or less the same values (sound, atmosphere and so on) time after time. Most of the beat groups didn't last long enough to have to confront the possibility of change; with these groups, the pattern was for a number of similarly motivated musicians to cluster together for a period of time, until lack of success, change of emphasis or some other combination of (musical or non-musical) factors precipitated change. Although Rory Gallagher had a relatively long career, in musical terms, he grew slowly, if at all; such was his identification with blues-derived music that any attempt to tamper with sound or image (even had he desired it) would have risked alienating his small core audience. On the other hand, longevity can enable some artists to grow and change as they explore different aspects of their identities. The career of Van Morrison, for example, may be considered as a narrative in which the artist pursues variations upon a number of key lyrical, musical and conceptual discourses. Such indeed is the 'meaning' of Morrison; like Dylan, he is an artist who explores his evolving responses to the world in intimate detail and reports his findings back to his fans in musical form.

Success (slow and limited though it was) meant that Thin Lizzy survived longer than many of its contemporaries. The band's growth during the 1970s and early 1980s mirrored the different impulses that informed Irish popular music-making practices during this period. As teenagers during the late 1960s, Lynott and drummer Brian Downey had played in a number of local groups (including The Black Eagles, Lynott's first group) before coming together with Eric Wricksen (formerly of Them) and Belfast guitar ace Eric Bell to form the first version of Thin Lizzy.[37] Although open to many influences (including, surprisingly in retrospect, the whimsical psychedelic folk music made by their friends in the trio Dr Strangely Strange), perhaps the most enduring of these pre-Lizzy associations was with Skid Row, a Dublin-based rock group whose influences included British blues-rock and American roots music, and whose personnel, Brendan 'Brush' Shiels, Gary Moore, Noel Bridgeman, constituted the leading edge of Ireland's response to the developing phenomenon of rock music.

Thin Lizzy's early recordings (after it had pared down to the three-piece of Lynott, Downey and Bell) reflect all these influences. It was this spirit of eclecticism that encouraged the band to release 'Whiskey in the Jar' as its first single, a record that gave it a surprise British hit in 1973, and that hung around its neck for a number of years. That particular track became Thin Lizzy's signature tune for a number of years, and has been widely interpreted ever since as an attempt – self-conscious or not – to marry the values and practices of two very different traditions: one (the ballad) old and established, the other (rock) new and evolving. If there *is* such a thing as 'Irish rock music', the argument went, surely it would sound something like this? Lynott and his fellow band members were dismayed that what had emerged as something of a studio joke came to dominate their early image, but in

retrospect it's not as invidious an interpretation as it seems. Whatever the derivation of Thin Lizzy's version of 'Whiskey in the Jar', the song itself – with its anonymous narrator, its story of violence and crime, its celebration of masculinity and
concomitant mistrust of women – is certainly related to many subsequent Lynott
compositions.

'Whiskey in the Jar' is an Irish rock song, then, insofar as it drew on the values
of those disparate traditions and practices. The identity of Lynott himself was
similarly dispersed, and the results of his unique life experiences may be traced
through the music that he made and the persona that he developed. Approached in
a particular way, Lynott's life story is infused with all the romanticism that informed
the musical values he pursued throughout his career. He was raised, educated and
socialized in a working-class community on Dublin's south side during the 1950s
and 60s, and could therefore be expected to conform to many of the values that
characterized such a community at that time, in that place. Those values included,
for example, the acute sense of both national and gender identity that had emerged
during the traumatic revolutionary period earlier in the century, and which continued to inform Irish culture well into the modern era. At the same time, he was an
illegitimate black man raised in a country which stigmatized illegitimacy, and in a
community in which whiteness was more or less universal.[38] In other words, Lynott
was a contradiction, an insider who was also an outsider, someone in whom the
most basic of human experiences (such as belonging and exclusion) and emotions
(such as identification and alienation) were in conflict.

As the 1960s progressed, Lynott discovered a medium through which he could
express the contradictions in his own life: rock music. As a hybrid of various popular musical styles, it was natural that rock music would come to connote different
values for, and indeed within, different individuals dispersed over time and space.
The story told by rock music is both a comedy and a tragedy; as a form it accom-
modates competing tendencies towards celebration and eulogy, pleasure and pain,
Dionysus and Thanatos. As he began to move towards artistic consciousness in the
late 1960s, the young Lynott found himself heir to a set of lyrical and musical
traditions in which the core contradictions of his own life could be articulated and
explored. Of course, this is not to imply any kind of direct allegorical correspondence between Lynott's experiences growing up in Dublin and the songs he
composed later in his life; it *is*, however, to suggest a close identification between
medium (rock music) and message (Lynott's life experience), and the emergence of
the latter in a range of lyrical, narrative and musical discourses made available by
the former.

Lynott's mature work with Thin Lizzy is dispersed between the two competing
impulses that characterized his responses to the context (specifically, the working-
class Dublin community) in which he was raised and the culture (specifically, the
popular music) to which he was exposed from an early age. How did these competing impulses manifest themselves? Well, for one thing Thin Lizzy was widely
classified during the latter part of its career as a 'hard rock' band, and displayed
many of the attributes of that subgenre: driving bass, pounding drums, muscular

vocals, guitars that alternated between screaming solos and power chords, all brought together to produce a sound characterized by aggression, energy and, above all, loudness. As part of this 'hard rock' image, Lynott was responsible for developing the mythology of the rock band as a specifically patriarchal family unit in contradistinction to alternative models in which the family is possessed of strong feminine associations. In songs such as 'The Rocker' (1973), 'Jailbreak', 'The Boys Are Back in Town' (both 1976) and 'Renegade' (1981), Lynott depicts men in groups of various size who are involved in a variety of 'manly' activities, often illicit, always violent.

Now, in some respects these men are obviously related to the well-established icons of outlawed masculinity who figure so strongly in American culture. As characters, 'the rocker' and 'the renegade' are linked intertextually to figures such as Billy the Kid, Marlon Brando and Jack Kerouac, while the 'gangs' which feature in 'The Boys Are Back in Town' and 'Jailbreak' are of a piece with the outlaw bands which have permeated American culture since the nineteenth century. It was Lynott's status as an 'outsider' within his own community that facilitated his close identification with such anti-heroes. The 'boys' whom he mythologized time and again in his songs are far removed from the 'boy next door' image purveyed by the showbands. At the same time, and without getting into the muddy waters of psychoanalytical discourse, we could speculate that the combination of a matriarchal familial culture and the absence of a strong central male figure in Lynott's domestic life left him deeply ambivalent towards received gender roles. His response was to fetishize masculinity in some of its most extreme forms, and the results of this may be heard in both the songs he wrote and the sounds he, and the band he led, produced.

Given its close association with maverick masculinity, rock music could easily accommodate the young Irishman's imagination in this regard. But these impulses towards violence, misogyny and abandonment of the hearth expressed only one dimension of Lynott's bifurcated imagination. If, as the lyric of 'Warriors' (1976) has it, his head was ruled by Mars, then his heart was ruled by Venus. In simple terms, the hard man also possessed a 'tender' side that embraced the discourses of domestic love and poetic romanticism so disdained by his 'tough' alter ego. This tender persona owed something to Lynott's time as a 'folkie' in the late 1960s and also to his response to a version of Irish (or more specifically 'Celtic') history made popular in Ireland by the cultural nationalist revival of the nineteenth century. Thin Lizzy's early material – up until *Vagabonds of the Western World* (1973) – has a variety of progressive folk, hippy and romantic elements that may come as a surprise to those who are familiar only with the later electric guitar-dominated material. The wistful, weeping narrator of the predominantly acoustic 'Dublin' (from 1971), for example, is half a world away from the aggressive, swaggering narrator who appears in the barely controlled freak-out that is 'The Rocker'. Then again, whereas another early song, 'Eire' (1971), is also about fighting men but is overlain with a note of Celtic mysticism that makes it difficult to categorize, another song about Irish history, 'Emerald' (1976), gives full lyrical and musical rein to Lynott's warrior imagination.

All in all, the 'tough' and 'tender' represent the tendencies around which Lynott organized his musical imagination, and it was his ability to express these tendencies in a variety of forms and combinations that made him such a compelling figure on the contemporary popular musical landscape. It's probably fair to say that Thin Lizzy became the principal conduit for his more aggressive side, whereas the more romantic aspects of his identity were expressed in his poetry and eventually in his solo work. For many people, Lynott simply *was*, indeed, *still is* Irish rock, the personification in life and in death of the rock ideal. His tragic death from a drugs-related illness has seen him elevated to the pantheon of those artists who have seemingly sacrificed themselves to the rock 'n' roll lifestyle. This dangerous and manipulative stereotype – 'better to burn up than fade away' – fails to do justice to Lynott's work, or indeed his life. In reality it was his status as both insider and outsider, and his ability to formulate a local response to a global cultural phenomenon, that makes him such a seminal character within the history of Irish popular music.

Another pioneering Irish band who explored the interface between the local and the global was Horslips. Whereas the national identity of both Lynott and Lizzy was more to do with deeply embedded cultural and temperamental attitudes, Horslips wore its Irishness on its sleeve, functioning from the outset with a self-conscious intent to fuse the different musical traditions of Irish traditional music and rock music. The band's musical adventures throughout the 1970s offer an instructive example of both the benefits and the limits of hybridity as a deliberate cultural strategy.

Horslips formed in Dublin in 1972 when Barry Devlin, Eamon Carr and Charles O'Connor met while working on a beer commercial for an advertising agency. This professional marketing context is indicative of the educated and / or artistic background shared by all band members, including flautist / keyboardist Jim Lockhart and guitarist Johnny Fean who joined soon after; indeed, a common class and educational background was one of the things that brought the band together and sustained it over a decade-long career.[40] While it would be invidious to claim a direct or natural link (in terms of ability or ambition) between education, class and artistry, it certainly seems to be the case that all five members of Horslips were highly amenable to the idea of musical hybridity, and that this idea was formulated as a deliberate response to the politico-cultural situation of Ireland in the early 1970s.

Before going on to consider the music itself, it's important to acknowledge that Horslips broke new ground in Irish rock music in at least two other ways. With its background in professional media, the band realized from the outset that popular music-making was a business as well as an art form, and that the matters pertaining to the former shouldn't be left to luck or wishful thinking. With this in mind (and without, it must be said, interest from any established label), Horslips was the first Irish rock band to form its own record label (called OATS) and to follow this up with the negotiation of licensing and distribution deals with major international record companies. It did this, moreover, at a time when the process of record-making was regarded by many, including musicians and others within the industry itself, as an impossibly arcane mystery. Forming your own label was one way to maintain the greater financial and artistic control that so many artists, then and since, craved. Not only did Horslips prefigure punk's 'do-it-yourself' ethic (albeit for different reasons) by a number of years; it also anticipated the concept of the label-owning artist at least two decades before digital technology and home recording made it commonplace.

The other point worth noting is that, although formed in Dublin, Horslips was in fact never a Dublin band, either in terms of membership or fan constituency. When it began the first of its many tours of the island in the early 1970s, the venues in which it performed were by and large the ballrooms that had been the mainstay of the showband scene. The adaptation in this way of the forms of one dispensation to those of another bears out classic cultural theory.[41] Put in more practical terms, however, Horslips provided a first experience of rock music for many Irish people at a time when the form was dominated by the main conurbations and a few minor scenes in the other population centres. Certainly, Horslips did play in Dublin and Belfast, Cork and Limerick; but it also brought chart music and a glam-rock image to unfashionable venues the length and breadth of the island (including rural parts of Northern Ireland at a time when the band members were readily identifiable as 'Fenians'). It did this, moreover, at a time when contemporary wisdom maintained that any Irish rock band with aspirations beyond local heroism must relocate to England (which in effect meant London). One of Horslips' greatest legacies to subsequent generations, then, was to mitigate rock's urban inheritance and to make the music available to people – fans and musicians – previously marginalized on account of their provincial location. In this context, every Irish band with rural roots owes something to Horslips' pioneering example from the 1970s.

But what about the music? As we've seen earlier in this chapter, Anglo-American rock music and Irish traditional music had been developing alongside each other in Ireland throughout the 1960s. Although they occasionally met and overlapped (in the neutral space of the folk boom, for example), these musics were on the whole considered by the majority of practitioners and adherents to be antithetical in terms of their sonic and attitudinal qualities. Whereas the former was new, electric and loud, the latter was old, acoustic and quiet (or at least quieter); whereas rock was an impure, bastardized fusion of many different traditions and genres, trad. was the inalienable expression – continually renewed yet forever young – of Irishness. The emergence of institutionalized forms of traditional music during the 1950s and 1960s consolidated the notion (itself based in the cultural nationalist discourse of the nineteenth century) that this particular form of music was 'essentially' Irish in a way that others, classical, jazz, rock or whatever, could never be.

This was the situation confronted at the outset of a new decade by the five young men who would go on to form Horslips. Rock and traditional music had distinctive sonic qualities and ideological resonances in contemporary Irish culture, to each of which Horslips was sentimentally and politically drawn. Collectively, it maintained a deep interest in Irish cultural history – its legends, its heroes, as well as its music. Yet the five men were also children of the rock 'n' roll revolution, as familiar with Ray Charles and Captain Beefheart as they were with Carolan and Cú Chulainn.

Coming together in the way they did, in the time and place that they did, the members of Horslips had both motivation and opportunity to experiment with the discrete musical discourses that constituted their collective cultural inheritance. The band's desire, as drummer Eamon Carr put it,

> was to provide an essentially Irish rock music, something distinctly our own, to galvanise each style with the other. We felt it was very important to convey our Irishness – a sense of our own identity and heritage . . . People could pick up on aspects of our music and look again at Ireland. Since our work had the rock context, most young people could relate to it immediately and learn a lot about Irish folklore as well (quoted in Prendergast 1987: 81).

The results of this experiment were to prove highly influential on the future tenor and direction of Irish rock music.

'Folk-rock' was very much in the air during the early 1970s, especially in England where groups such as Steeleye Span (with whom Horslips toured Britain in 1973) and Fairport Convention experimented with a mixture of electric instrumentation and 'traditional' material, and where even more identifiable 'rock' bands such as Yes, Genesis, Jethro Tull and Led Zeppelin dabbled with folk idioms. Many of the criticisms directed at these artists by a folk-trad. rump would in time attach themselves also to Horslips. In Ireland, meanwhile, Sweeney's Men had indicated some of the paths which an Irish folk-trad.-rock fusion might explore, and it was these paths that Horslips would follow throughout the 1970s with a high degree of intelligence, imagination and talent. The band broke onto the Irish scene with the single 'Johnny's Wedding' in 1972, as clear a statement of intent and direction as possible. The following year it released *The Táin*, a concept album based on an ancient Irish legend, and the first of two great experiments in transposing its own local culture into an international rock idiom.

The highlight of this album was the track *'An Dearg Doom'*, containing in its signature electric guitar figure perhaps *the* most recognizable sound within the canon of modern Irish popular music. The figure itself was based on an ancient Irish melody entitled *'Marcshlua Uí Néill* (O'Neill's March)' which, although well known amongst traditional musicians, had come to public prominence just a few years earlier when it was released by the traditional music label Gael Linn on the album *Ó Riada sa Gaiety* (1969). This was a recording of a controversial concert performed in the Gaiety Theatre in Dublin by Seán Ó Riada and Ceoltóirí Cualann. Although applauded in some circles for raising the profile of the ethnic tradition, to some it seemed clear that Ó Riada's approach to the material – formal attire, scoring, concert context, and programme format – were bringing the values of European art music (in which Ó Riada had been trained) to bear upon traditional Irish music.

If Ó Riada's version was widely considered to be an 'alienation' of ethnic values and practices, however, the incorporation of *'Marcshlua Uí Néill'* upon electric guitar as part of an Anglophone rock song was regarded by many hardcore traditionalists as little short of blasphemy. The riff is played by Johnny Fean in such a way that the underlying 4/4 pulse of the marching tune is adapted fairly unproblematically to the driving 4/4 pulse of rock music, whilst during the verses Barry Devlin and Eamon Carr deploy bass and drums to create a subtle rhythmic counterpoint to the main guitar theme. The track must have sounded uncanny to contemporary ears: simultaneously known and unknown, odd yet familiar, especially during the end section beginning at 2.34 which, with its introduction of 'real' traditional instruments played by O'Connor and Lockhart, sounded unmistakably like the Ó Riada version.

Not only did Horslips *sound* 'strange'; with their long hair and 'hippy' gear its members presented a direct *visual* challenge to the music's associated iconography. Throughout the decade, in fact, the band maintained an uneasy relationship with the ethnic tradition that constituted one of the two primary colours upon their musical palette. In terms of music, lyrics and concepts, each of the next four albums, culminating in *The Book of Invasions: A Celtic Symphony* (1975) (widely regarded as the band's crowning achievement), was profoundly influenced by that colour. Thereafter, Horslips turned to a more radio-friendly sound in pursuit of different effects and different audiences. While much of the music produced on the later albums shows a clear development from earlier concerns, generally it's that earlier music that has tended to dominate the band's image and reputation.

If the traditional music fraternity found it difficult to come to terms with Horslips' take on 'their' music, so too did the Anglo-American rock establishment, which at this stage was formalizing the process whereby the band's other domain, rock music, would be organized and policed. Here, after all, was a complex 'rock' music which had seemingly very little to do with rock 'n' roll or its blues-based precursors. One of the dangers faced by 'fusion' artists is that they will offend adherents of each of the genres they're trying to fuse, and so it was with Horslips: while disdained by many within the trad. community, it (like many of its 'progressive' brethren) also attracted the derision of those sentimentally affiliated with 'real' rock music. 'Celtic Rock' was the subgeneric category invented to 'contain' Horslips, one which has trailed the band (and its heirs) ever since. Even when used with the most benign or sympathetic of intentions, however, the term 'Celtic' connotes a number of associations from earlier points in Irish cultural history that render it deeply problematical when applied to modern cultural initiatives. Horslips' music was 'Celtic' in one way, insofar as (some of) it engaged at a lyrical level with various narratives and characters from ancient Irish history. It was 'Celtic' in a different way, insofar as it came to represent the same old combination of Irish whimsy and magic for British, European and North American audiences steeped in two hundred years of such debilitating racial stereotypes.[42]

The fact is that Horslips – with its ethnic instruments, concept albums and 'hippy' connotations – belong quite clearly to that great wave of experimentalism that overtook Anglo-American popular music-making towards the end of the 1960s. Whereas in Britain and the US such experimentalism was animated by an internationalist counterculture ranged more or less self-consciously against the social, cultural and political systems of the Cold War establishment, in Ireland the situation was somewhat different. The island had been shaken during the 1960s by reformers of various kinds, but recession in the south and war in the north served to excite forces of reaction and retrenchment. Each side tended to misrepresent traditional music: whereas for conservatives it had to be heroically defended as the sonic embodiment of Irishness, reformers tended to regard it with suspicion as yet another sign of the cultural (and indeed political) backwardness from which they were heroically attempting to free the island.

Horslips' achievement was to bring the legacy of rock experimentalism to bear upon Irish traditional music, releasing it from those who attempted to recruit it for one or another socio-political agenda. Despite what modernizing urban intellectuals might say, traditional music *did* articulate some key aspect of national identity; it did so, however, in a way that was not *reducible* to national identity, despite what conservative agents might argue. Out of such a cultural conundrum, Horslips managed to produce a body of brilliant music.

As suggested above, *The Book of Invasions* from 1976 marked the culmination of Horslips' achievement and impact. The band's subsequent influence, such as it is, on the story of Irish rock music derives in the main from this album, on which it brought the fusion of traditional and rock music that had animated its early career to something like perfection. Towards the end of that same year, however, a little-known band from London released a record that was to have profound implications for the entire future course of rock music, in Ireland as elsewhere: the track was 'Anarchy in the U.K.' and the band was The Sex Pistols.

2

'I Don't Wanna be Like You'
Punk and its Legacies

INTRODUCTION

The upturn in Irish economic fortunes that had characterized the 1960s was followed by two decades of uncertainty and underachievement (Brown 1985: 326–55; Lee 1989: 511ff). Despite accession to the European Economic Community in 1973 and a clear overall improvement in general standards of living, the island suffered badly in the aftermath of the international oil crisis of 1974/75, and its poor performance was reflected over the coming years in rises in both emigration and unemployment. Northern Ireland was part of an ailing UK, ever so slowly coming to terms with its diminished global status and the urgent need to re-orient its economy. In the south, meanwhile, Éamon de Valera – the self-appointed conscience of traditional Ireland – died in 1975, and with his passing the Republic finally had to face up to the reality of what it was: a small state with limited natural resources, whose economic fortunes were increasingly dependent upon offshore bureaucracies and businesses not necessarily sympathetic to its fate.

It was during this same period that Ireland became synonymous with the Troubles. The events of January 1972, which came to be known as Bloody Sunday, led to direct rule from Westminster (March 1972) and an extended, high-profile army presence throughout the province. Government-sponsored initiatives such as the Sunningdale Agreement (December 1973) and the later Anglo-Irish Agreement (November 1985) were (at best) misjudged or (at worst) evasive, and in any case consistently failed to win the grass-roots support of the communities at which they were aimed. Images of death and destruction were frequently beamed around the planet, confirming a widely held impression of the Irish as a benighted people possessed of neither the imagination nor the will to find a perspective on their little

46

local problem; and whereas many people in the south had been initially sympathetic to the Catholic / Republican cause, the vast majority – the same majority that had declared its modernizing, liberalizing aspirations in the EEC referendum of May 1972 – soon became embarrassed to be associated with what it considered to be the obsolete ideologies fuelling the conflict. The same is, by and large true in respect of the British response to the Protestant / Loyalist community. Thus shunned by the communities to which they ostensibly 'belonged', both sides settled down for a long attritional war, while the British army and the 'security forces' adopted the ambivalent policing role that was to occupy them for the duration of the conflict.

The early 1970s are the lost years of Irish rock, a period in which, in Ireland as elsewhere, there was a long, slow comedown after the heady days of the 1960s. The 'pioneers' discussed towards the end of the previous chapter – Van Morrison, Rory Gallagher, Horslips and Thin Lizzy – were all active during this period, and producing some of their most compelling popular music. Apart from them, however, it's generally accepted that there was little to get excited about on the Irish music scene. Expatriate Gilbert O'Sullivan emerged as a fully fledged pop idol over in England in the early part of the decade, while, a little later, the quasi-Irishman Chris de Burgh began to carve out the particular niche that he has occupied ever since. The contemporary British vogue for the kinds of glam and art rock practised by artists such David Bowie and Roxy Music failed to make much of an impression in Ireland.[1] Instead, a variety of 'heavy', experimental, jazz-oriented, vaguely 'progressive' bands – the likes of Andwella's Dream, Elmer Fudd (home for a time to the 'Clontarf Cowboy', guitarist and composer Philip Donnelly), Fruupp, Mushroom, Naïma, Stud, Supply Demand and Curve, and so on – tended to dominate. The diversity of music created by these bands bears out Allan F. Moore's point that 'at no time was progressive rock a unitary style: it extended from "art" rock on the one hand through "hard" rock to styles of "folk" rock' (1993: 61). The one thing these bands shared, however, was a desire to express themselves above and beyond the requirements of mere 'entertainment'. And herein, of course, lay the difficulty: when 'entertainment' becomes a problem, disdained because of its association with business and popularity, why bother making music at all? Just as elsewhere, the ideas and practices that had overtaken rock music in the latter part of the 1960s were now threatening to alienate the very people who had formed rock's constituency since its inception as a dance-oriented, entertainment-led genre in the 1950s. Growth and evolution there must be, but it may be understood in retrospect how an uncritical faith in rock as a sophisticated, upwardly mobile art form led many Irish artists down a variety of blind alleys during the early 1970s.

Everyone knows what happened next, and it is indeed the Irish response to the punk revolution in rock music with which this chapter is in the main concerned. Before moving on to that, however, I want to mention briefly a number of developments – some global, some more local in aspect – which had a significant bearing on the evolution of Irish rock during the 1970s and 80s. First of all, it's clear that the Republic was continuing along the liberalizing and modernizing path that had been mapped out in the previous decade, and that Irish society was as a result becoming more open during the 1970s. It was during this period that foreign artists, including many British writers and musicians, first began to make use of Ireland as a convenient tax haven. Section 2 of the Irish Finance Act of 1969 introduced legislation which exempted 'artists' (subject to certain criteria) from paying income tax.[2] At the same time, high-earning British citizens (such as rock stars) could avoid their own country's tax laws (which, under the Labour administrations of Harold Wilson and James Callaghan, became draconian after income rose above a certain amount) if they lived outside the country for a proportion of each year. Ireland, and especially Dublin, became one such convenient location, and the presence of these once-exotic figures in familiar locations was a fillip to a local music scene which, like much else in the culture, had distinct tendencies towards both dependency and inferiority.

Another high-profile foreigner who dropped in for a visit in September 1979 was the late Pope John Paul II. For twenty years, as we've seen, the south had been steadily becoming more secular, to the dismay of those with an investment in old-school conservative Catholicism. Some people regarded the Pontiff's visit as an opportunity to stem the filthy modern tide. Certainly, the levels of near-hysteria that accompanied his visit, and the one million people he pulled to his Phoenix Park gig, seemed to indicate that the Republic was, for all the talk, still a deeply Catholic country. This, of course, did nothing to placate Loyalist fears in the North. At the same time, for many of the denizens of what would shortly come to known as 'Dublin 4', the response to the Pope's visit was both a confirmation of their suspicions regarding 'traditional' Ireland as a land of police and priests, and a spur to press on with the work of freeing Ireland from the grip of an invidious dogma (or at least an invidious interpretation of Catholic tenets) that had plagued the country for far too long.[3]

On one level, the Pope's visit was obviously intended to function as a triumphalist rallying cry to the country's youth, but for some young people it may have had the opposite effect. Irish artists had been suffering at the hands of paranoid and vindictive religious types since the foundation of the state (Smyth 1998: 145–9). So it's not surprising that, given their aesthetic (and indeed material) investment in notions of freedom and communication, the Republic's artistic community (including its rock musicians) on the whole gravitated towards the secularizing agenda that became associated with 'Dublin 4'. One observable effect of this affiliation was the belief, prevalent amongst young Irish rock musicians since the 1960s, that success was categorically unobtainable in Ireland – in the parlance, that you couldn't break a band from Ireland. This axiom was being challenged at the time by Horslips, which had founded its own label out of a mixture of frustration and enterprise; it would in time be disproved by a band whose first release, 'U2: Three', was hitting the shelves at more or less the same time as John Paul II was telling the young people of Ireland that he loved them. But U2's challenge to Irish rock orthodoxy would only emerge later; in the meantime it – like all the other big fish – found the Dublin pond far too small and set off for new waters as soon as it could. Likewise with the rest of the country's more ambitious musicians, for whom the search for success led away from 'holy Ireland' to London via Holyhead.

Another event that impacted significantly upon Irish popular music during this period occurred in the early hours of 31 July 1975, when five members of The Miami Showband who were driving towards Dublin after a gig in Banbridge, Co. Down were forced to stop by a number of armed men posing as members of the security forces; they were in fact a Loyalist paramilitary unit. The latter's precise intentions were still unclear when a bomb they had been planting on The Miami's bus exploded prematurely, killing two of the hi-jackers; in the ensuing panic the gunmen shot and killed three members of the band and injured one more (another escaped). The death of these three young musicians, including multi-talented singer-songwriter Fran O'Toole, shocked people across the island, especially amongst the showband community (Power 2000: 269–71). Although it's impossible to calculate its precise ramifications, this execrable act did have at least two observable effects.

Firstly, music could no longer be regarded as immune to the sectarian strife that was tearing apart the north-eastern part of the island. Showband musicians had traditionally worked an all-Ireland circuit, travelling freely and frequently across the official border between the island's two states. In Northern Ireland, popular bands such as The Miami – which, although including four members from Ulster, two of whom were Protestant, was considered to be 'from' the Republic – had always had a 'mixed' audience of Catholics and Protestants. After the deaths, however, the myth of a sectarian-free popular music was shattered. It was clear that musicians were as likely as anyone else to be identified in the restrictive religious and / or political terms that defined the Troubles, and in such a climate it's understandable why the cross-border showband scene was immediately suspended. Thus deprived of significant markets, showbands on either side of the border became more insular and introspective than ever; while the scene itself, already under pressure from alternative forms of popular entertainment such as cabaret and disco, never recovered.

The second consequence of the Miami Massacre was to stigmatize Ireland as a problem destination for international rock acts, a stigma that was not really removed until the turn of the decade. While it's possible to put a negative slant on this – Ireland's backwater status confirmed and extended – Tony Clayton-Lea and Rogan Taylor speculate that lack of exposure to British and American rock may have had positive effects on the domestic scene. For one thing, 'promoters couldn't put on any concerts unless Irish acts were on the bill' (1992: 55–6), and while this gained useful exposure and experience for Irish bands, it also encouraged audiences, who may previously have been otherwise disposed, to begin to take such bands seriously. At the same time Irish rock, forced back on its own resources, became less *provincial* and more *parochial*; which is to say, less concerned to ape imported sounds and more confident in its own ability to articulate valid musical responses to the world.[4]

It's also worth bearing in mind that punk was the last great movement before the advent of two technological developments that were to have a profound impact upon the ways in which popular music would be produced and consumed: the introduction of the commercial compact disc and the inauguration of Music Television (MTV). Before noting the impact of these two developments, it's important to acknowledge that the study of popular music has tended to be dominated by a romantic aesthetic paradigm in which the individual subject and the text he / she produces are the focus of analysis. Lots of people can speculate on the meaning of 'God Save the Queen' by The Sex Pistols, but few know (or care) how the song was recorded, distributed, consumed or transferred between different playback formats. As Paul Théberge writes, however, 'virtually all music-making is based on some form of technology' (1999: 210); and elsewhere: 'recent innovations in musical technology . . . alter the structure of musical practice and concepts of what music is and can be . . . [They] place musicians and musical practice in a new relationship with consumer practices and with consumer society as a whole' (1997: 3). In other words, rather than being an incidental or innocent medium for the transmission of meanings carried by the musical text, technology serves to shape and delimit such meanings. In short: no meaning without form, no form without technology.

The advent of digitalization during the 1970s and the gradual replacement of analogue technology has indelibly shaped the sound, and thus the potential kind and range of meanings, of popular music in the last thirty years (Goodwin 1990). The idea of a mechanical device for storing large amounts of information actually goes back to the 1840s (an idea, incidentally, to which the Irish mathematician George Boole made a decisive contribution in his book *An Investigation into the Laws of Thought*, published in 1854). But it was only during the 1960s and 70s that technology and science had developed to the point where such a device became a real possibility. After much frenzied activity by collaborating multinational giants Sony and Phillips around the turn of the decade concerning the precise specifications for the new device (size, storage capacity and so on), the commercial music CD was launched as a new music reproduction format in the UK in 1983; just over twenty years later it has become the dominant medium for the production, transmission and sale of popular music, and all those involved in the field, including musicians, producers, engineers, retailers and fans, are still coming to terms with the revolution that it has engendered (Pohlmann 1989).

Part of that revolution has been a massive increase in home recording, something to which we shall come in Chapter Three. But in retrospect it's possible to see that vinyl was the natural format for punk, and that the CD ideal of a sharp, crisp, hiss-free sound was at odds with punk's sentimental and ideological bases. 'God Save the Queen' and *Never Mind the Bollocks* could only have been made – and, more importantly, could only have created the range of meanings that they did – in a context in which the seven-inch, 45rpm, single and the twelve-inch, 33rpm long-player were the accepted units of currency. Faced with the growing popularity of the CD as a playback format, meanwhile, Irish artists were obliged to negotiate special local circumstances, such as their skewed take on mainstream definitions of punk and New Wave, and the popularity of other genres such as traditional and folk. But it's fair to say that Irish popular music adapted rapidly and on the whole fairly unproblematically to the advent of the CD, and, with the exception of some dance-oriented genres (something else we shall be examining in the next chapter), is now more or less fully 'converted' to the CD as the accepted currency of popular music-making.

The same is, by and large, true of the Irish response to the re-orientation of the promotional pop video. In 1981 MTV started broadcasting non-stop videos on cable television in the USA, growing into a worldwide network in the following decade. In the years since, the systematic use of video has became an integral part of the way in which popular music is manufactured and marketed. Suddenly, how musicians *looked* became as significant as how they *sounded;* suddenly, the multinational music industries had a highly accessible medium for the dissemination of their favoured trends and artists.

It's not the case that MTV (or indeed the CD) represented the latest victory of large cultural formations such as the US or Japan or Europe over small ones such as Ireland, or that these technologies merely served to expedite the latter's eventual disappearance into the former. Technology does encode specific preferred meanings – meanings that much of the time answer the needs of the institutions (such as Sony and Viacom) responsible for their development; but technology is also capable of being decoded and deployed in ways and in contexts that enable alternative meanings to be activated. The paradox underpinning the CD and MTV (and this is true of all technological innovations) is that they simultaneously *limited* and *extended* the range of Irish popular music; as Théberge points out, 'each of these new technologies incorporates the same ambiguities of empowerment and dependency, creative potential and formal constraints, that lead to renewed levels of consumption' (1997: 254).

Other issues and influences will emerge in the following pages. We begin by looking at a movement which was ostensibly opposed to technology (as well as a great many other things), although it's typical of punk's contradictory status that its adherents relied at every stage on different forms of technology to develop and disseminate the movement's identity.

Punk and New Wave

In terms of money, popularity and just about every other aspect of the popular music industry worth mentioning, there's little doubt that Led Zeppelin was the 'biggest' band in the world in 1977 – every aspect, that is, except the one that dictates the ultimately inscrutable process whereby minor subcultures periodically emerge from the underground to become worldwide, era-defining phenomena. Punk may have been *the* great (or simply the greatest) rock 'n' roll swindle, but it was also a great watershed in popular music history – a movement, an attitude, an *idea* that made a profound impact on all subsequent practices in the field. Although 'mainstream' punk was a deliberately unformulated, or (according to its own rhetoric) anarchic, aesthetic, nevertheless it did quickly come to connote a number of recognizable challenges to established popular musical practices in areas such as song composition and performance, group format, record production and distribution, audience response and so on. A largely new musical vocabulary was introduced in a relatively short period of time, in other words, and began to compete with the languages that had been established over the previous twenty years.[5] And as the continuing vogue for 'punk' bands demonstrates, that language has proved to be both extremely resilient and endlessly adaptable.

In Ireland, punk's new vocabulary (which was derived for the most part from the aggressive cultural formations of Britain and the US) was not simply learned and reproduced verbatim. Rather, the challenge presented by punk to established practices was overdetermined, and as a result modified, by a range of local influences and concerns. In 1979, for example, a compilation entitled *Just for Kicks* was released, featuring songs by a number of new Irish bands. Although Dublin had developed a nascent punk scene throughout 1977 and 1978 centred on bands such as DC Nein and The Vipers, it's interesting to note that this album contains few, if any, tracks in the mould of any of the leading British punk bands such as The Sex Pistols or The Clash. The diversity and originality of its twelve tracks is in fact an indication of how swiftly punk had been adopted and then adapted in Irish popular music-making practices. With one major exception (of which more later), the bands featured on this album made little or no impact outside the Irish scene; yet they were for the most part involved in creating original, local responses to both the musical and the ideological ideals instigated by punk rock just a few years earlier.

A band not included on *Just for Kicks* is the one with which Irish (or at least southern Irish) punk has become synonymous: The Boomtown Rats. It's generally acknowledged that the Rats' engagement with punk was somewhat opportunistic; as a consequence, their subsequent close identification with the form is often regarded as offensive or erroneous by historians of the movement.[6] The band formed by Bob Geldof on his return to Dublin from Canada in 1975 predated the punk explosion of 1976 / 77, and was essentially a pub-rock outfit with little ambition beyond a London record deal for their traditional rhythm 'n' blues-based music.[7] The speed and relative ease with which Geldof and Rats' manager Fachtna O'Kelly (both former music journalists) affiliated to the burgeoning punk revolution in England is an indication of *their* insight into popular cultural trends, and of punk's basis in media-driven discourse. By the time the Rats signed with Ensign (owned by the major label Phonogram) in February 1977, they were already closely associated with the form, while Geldof himself had become one of punk's most recognizable figures.

The first single, 'Lookin' After No. 1', from August of the same year, had obvious affinities with the punk ethos and was one of the earliest records so designated to make a significant impression on the British charts. Musically, it was energetic, loud and guitar-driven, while its lyric spoke of alienation and disaffection. Geldof performed the vocal in that defiant, threatening persona (adopted also by contemporaries such as Johnny Rotten and Joe Strummer) that was one of the defining characteristics of early punk. At the same time, the song was more complex than the 'average' punk record, while it was clear from the outset that as a band the Rats possessed ambitions beyond the three-minute, three-chord, do-it-yourself values that had been part of punk's rallying cry since late 1976.

This is not to deny that the music of The Boomtown Rats, and in particular of Geldof as spokesman and chief writer, was fuelled by ideas and emotions similar to those that animated British punk, nor that punk rock provided an appropriate form through which those ideas and emotions could be expressed. 'No future' was a slogan that resonated as strongly in Dublin in 1977 as in London, although for different reasons. As an intelligent young Irishman, Geldof was bitter about what he considered to be his restricted cultural inheritance and about the society that had conspired to deny his generation the freedoms and the experiences enjoyed elsewhere. This bitterness was augmented by the 'boredom' (again, a key punk touchstone) he felt with the Irish music scene of the 1970s, an amalgam (as remarked above) of progressive, blues-based and folk-trad. music that had little to say to or about the society in which it was made. Whereas British punk (in line with Malcolm McLaren's selective take on situationism and other radical cultural theories) supposedly articulated an angry response to the fading power of a once-great empire, the anger of Geldof and The Boomtown Rats derived in the first instance from the conservative forces that, even after the modernization of the 1960s, still appeared to be dominating Irish life.

'Lookin' After No. 1' was followed by a number of punky singles, before the Rats scored a massive hit with 'Rat Trap', the song with which they became (in October 1978) the first Irish band to make the No. 1 position in the British charts. In narrative and lyrical terms this recording may still have nodded towards the anger and disillusion of punk, but sonically it had already left punk far behind, being, as it was, a complex, multi-layered piece of music with pretensions to work on a number of different levels. This is also true of *A Tonic for the Troops* (1978), the album from which 'Rat Trap' came, which is a sort of punk concept album, detailing the lives of various misfits and social outcasts. This was followed up by their second number one single – and what for many remains the band's greatest achievement – 'I Don't Like Mondays' (July 1979) which would also feature on that autumn's *The Fine Art of Surfacing*. The story of the young girl who shot several of her school mates on an apparent whim broke while the Rats were on tour in North America. It seemed redolent of the anarchy and violence informing the punk movement with which the band had been associating. With its delineation of a true case of random, death-dealing violence, however, 'I Don't Like Mondays' represents the sound of punk coming of age, for despite its apparent non-judgemental stance, at bottom the song is a plea for reconciliation between the institutional forces that have called forth violence and the young murderess who has turned a violent society's logic back on itself.

This was in some ways a reflection of what was happening to punk rock itself. By 1979 (indeed, by December 1976 in some accounts), the popular music industry had recovered from the shock of the punk challenge, and had begun the process of co-opting the next generation of bands, those who identified to some extent with the punk ethos, but not with the self-defeating logic by which commercial 'success' meant artistic 'failure', and vice versa. What two years of punk had revealed was that rock music could engage with anarchy, violence and nihilism as *energies* but not as *ends*. Like many of their fellow 'New Wave' bands, The Boomtown Rats were concerned to take advantage of the changes to popular musical discourse that punk had instigated, although they did so with the relative comfort of a record deal with an established company.

Despite its derivation in the particular social and cultural milieus of New York and London, the idea of punk circulated freely and took root in different ways in different formations. Of nowhere is this more true than Ireland where punk laid down roots that were both strong and multifarious. One of the island's first 'real' punk bands was The Radiators from Space (also absent from *Just for Kicks*), whose debut single 'Television Screen' (released on London's independent Chiswick label in April 1977) predated 'Lookin' After No. 1' by some four months and signalled, perhaps even more than the Rats' charting debut, a paradigm shift in modern Irish popular culture. With its memorable opening riff, sub-three-minute duration, thrashed-up blues structure and aggressive, unmelodic vocal, 'Television Screen' was severely at odds with prevailing 'rock' values. Horslips and Thin Lizzy may have been writing and performing songs about violence at this time, for example, but they did so in a variety of heroic and / or hyper-real contexts far removed from the one in which an obviously modern, obviously 'real' persona describes his desire to shove a Telecaster guitar through the eponymous television screen, which itself has become a medium of unwanted and offensive opinions.[8]

Like many Irish artists before and since, The Radiators from Space relocated to London at an early stage in a bid to further their career. Their second album, *Ghostown* (1979) (issued, after label problems, under the revised name of The Radiators) was a critical success but a commercial failure, and the band broke up shortly after. In any event, their take on punk rock was always different from that of their British counterparts. Songwriter and singer Philip Chevron explained:

> While we shared many of the characteristics of the UK punk bands – the energy and the attitudes – we had nothing to say about tower-blocks or anarchy. Our best songs came from our experience of growing up in an Ireland still paralysed by political and religious hypocrisies but which, we believed, was in its heart youthful and forward-thinking (quoted on *www.punk77*).

The same is true of the majority of bands from Ireland's first punk wave. Violence there was (including the death of a student at a punk festival in June 1977, after which The Radiators from Space, who had organized the event, found it difficult to get bookings); alienation and anger there were also, but these qualities were expressed in a variety of ways that, although related to the British and American parent movements, displayed many signs of their local Irish cultural inheritance. Chevron himself, for example, had sincere theatrical aspirations (something which he was able to indulge after the break-up of The Radiators in 1980).[9] Indeed, a penchant for the dramatic was something that was shared by a number of contemporary bands, including The Atrix (later produced by Chevron) and U2 (both of whom featured on *Just for Kicks*). Without doubt, however, the most daring of the punk-inspired Irish groups of the period was The Virgin Prunes. The fusion of noise, drama and shock tactics that characterized the typical Prunes' 'event' derived in some measure from the same matrix of avant-garde art and cultural theory that had inspired McLaren and Vivienne Westwood in London. Its true revolutionary potential could only emerge, however, in the context of a small, semi-modernized country such as Ireland was in the 1970s; a country in which art was simultaneously revered and suspected, and in which a predominantly youthful population was ready and only too willing to bring the fruits of its (hyper) education to bear upon the values of previous generations.]

On *Just for Kicks* we also find examples of punk's 1950s revivalist wing ('The Lady Loves to Rock 'n' Roll' by Rocky de Valera and the Gravediggers) and its close affiliation with reggae ('Silent Partners' by Zebra). All in all, however, the album is testament to the fact that punk was more important (at least in Ireland) for the energies that it released than for the forms that it instituted. These energies may be discerned coursing through much of the 'indie' music that has been produced in Ireland since the late 1970s, and that arguably still constitutes the norm against which every other kind of Irish popular music must be measured. And if intelligent, guitar-led, song-oriented bands are indeed the core of post-punk Irish rock music, then no band can be said to more representative than The Blades.

The Blades were really two bands linked by the immense talent of singer and writer Paul Cleary. The first was formed with his guitarist brother Lar and drummer Pat Larkin on Dublin's northside in 1977, which is to say, at the height of the punk revolution. This version of the band played short, punchy, guitar-driven songs that were ideal for live performance and for the singles market which the punk revolution had helped to revive. For many, the clutch of early releases (including 'The Bride Wore White', 'Hot For You' and the seminal 'Ghost of a Chance') represent the most attractive version of The Blades, when Cleary's pop leanings were still infused with the anger and energy of punk.

Despite this beginning, The Blades was never a punk band in any meaningful sense of that term. From the outset, Cleary's songwriting abilities – intelligent multi-level lyrics combined with interesting melodies and a respect for the classic song structures of The Beatles and Motown – set him and the band he led apart from the punk ideal. Early Blades' recordings do not sound like The Radiators from Space; although retaining a certain rawness, the material is altogether crisper and cleaner in terms of its texture, and Cleary's voice has more in common with soul than with punk. Neither, however, do The Blades sound like a traditional blues-based rock band. While they may have been similar in terms of instrumentation, the idea of a 'punk' trio (such as The Jam) was far removed from the power trios that had featured during rock's first spring a decade earlier. The fact is that The Blades – like The Jam in Britain – represented something new in Irish popular musical history: a pop-rock band that took many of its sonic, sartorial and semiotic references from punk. They were, in other words, one of the earliest and one of the best of the Irish New Wave bands.

The second version of The Blades lasted from 1982 until the band split up in 1986 and featured Brian Foley on bass guitar and Jake Reilly on drums. This was a more ambitious project, in which the songs were as a rule longer, while many of them also featured the brass instrumentation that was to become a feature of the later Blades' sound. Although it had never been entirely lost, the inclusion of brass was a relative rarity in the popular music of the late 1970s. It made a comeback in Britain in the early 1980s, however, with the likes of Dexy's Midnight Runners and Madness, and was indicative of the more sophisticated effects that such bands wished to broach after the mannered insouciance of the high punk era. While its revival during the immediate post-punk period demanded higher levels of musicianship from all band members, brass (also known as 'horns') also increased the scope and the texture of the music, especially in its recall of some of the rock, soul, and rhythm 'n' blues influences that punk had displaced.

As one of the distinguishing features of the showbands, brass had somewhat different connotations for the Irish rock group. The horn players who featured on the later Blades' output were, had they known it, only a decade or so removed from potentially lucrative, although artistically compromised, showband careers; indeed, the cabaret circuit which, by and large, succeeded the showband scene as the locus of entertainment-driven 'covered' music, still functioned as a lure for Irish musicians from every tradition. There was little chance, however, of the brass section in a Blades' song descending into the cheesiness which characterized its function on the showband and cabaret scenes. Incorporated as part of Cleary's arching pop melodies, and fused with the classic rock rhythm section of bass, guitar and drums, Blades' brass connotes a contemporary urban atmosphere reminiscent of classic Stax recordings. Far from the tawdry glamour connoted by the music of the showbands, The Blades' sound was characterized by excitement and a full commitment to the modern world.

All the classic Blades' characteristics come together on 'Downmarket,' a track from the band's only studio album, *The Last Man in Europe* (1986). 'Downmarket' encapsulates the social conscience that has always been an important dimension of Cleary's writing, and is one of a handful of rock songs which attempts to reflect Dublin in the early 1980s, a time of unemployment, emigration and recession. In the lyric, the aftermath of a 'successful' sexual encounter is offset against 'the problems of the nation' and the seediness of a city in which 'everything's black and white and grey'. Whereas the space of the typical pop or rock song was the domestic interior – where the protagonist and his or her love object could escape from an unsatisfactory world – punk had, by and large, relocated the protagonist outdoors, into the public sphere where she he could challenge established discourses; just so in 'Downmarket', in which an unsatisfactory domestic location (an unfamiliar bedroom) gives way to an equally unsatisfactory, yet much more visible (and potentially more dangerous) outdoor location (the street). Airports and stations have exotic and romantic associations that are far removed from those relating to the bus stop at which the protagonist finds himself waiting next morning. It was indeed for many 'a hopeless situation' in which release could be found only through meaningless sex, alcohol or the two epidemics that reflected Dublin's blighted state at the time: poker machines and heroin. Despite this, the music is surprisingly upbeat, with the horns providing drama during the chorus and the possibility of individual freedom during the solo. Overall, however, the mood is one of frustration bordering on desperation.

Despite everything that was in their favour, The Blades did not become a commercial success outside Ireland. Nevertheless, their music – as well as that of numerous other bands – was clear evidence of the extent to which the values introduced by punk had taken hold on Irish popular music-making practices, and furthermore of the ways in which these values were not uncritically adopted, but, rather were developed in the light of local traditions and concerns. Just as, say, The Jam comes into focus in terms of a peculiarly English pop genealogy that includes various 'mod' bands such as The Faces and The Who, so The Blades were, and remain, in terms of their popular musical 'meaning', the function of a peculiar local prehistory comprised of a wide array of musical, literary and other cultural influences.

ROCK OF THE NORTH

Punk rock made a particularly strong impression in Northern Ireland, and there are a number of reasons why this might have been the case (O'Neill and Trelford 2003). Northern Ireland has been, in one form or another, officially part of the United Kingdom for centuries; its popular musicians (indeed, all its artists) may have had more in common, in terms of its prevailing social and political structures, and also some of its cultural traditions, with their counterparts on the British mainland. (Recall Them's identification with the British blues movement of the 1960s, and the ease with which it was co-opted as part of the 'British Invasion'.) And yet, since the days of the first showbands and before, popular musicians from Northern Ireland had always performed throughout the whole island, and had been strongly influenced by trends from the southern hinterland. The issue of artistic influence is a tortured one in the context of Northern Ireland, therefore, and something which no one has adequately addressed at any point during the course of its existence as a political unit (although see Kirkland 1996). The fact is that, as with most other areas of culture (including, most centrally, literature), Northern Irish popular music occupies an ambivalent space between Irish and British traditions, and its prevailing aesthetic is one best described as 'fractured'. It may be that punk, with its focus on contradiction and conflict, flourished in Northern Ireland precisely because it enabled musicians to articulate this sense of fracture.

By the time of punk, Northern Ireland had been experiencing the Troubles for nearly a decade. Linked in the first instance with the counter-culture of the 1960s (the agenda of which was internationalist, radical and often class- and gender-based), the conflict had been rapidly re-articulated along sectarian lines by those on all sides with an interest in maintaining the status quo, and since 1968 had more or less settled into a series of binary stand-offs that tended to dominate Northern Ireland both in terms of its own day-to-day sense-making systems, and also its representation in the world at large: Catholic / Protestant, Nationalist / Loyalist, Republican / Unionist. During the 1970s the death toll mounted, positions became entrenched, the economy suffered and civil society was severely demoralized. Worse still, it seemed that young people were particularly vulnerable to this deadly binary logic. It was difficult for a youth-oriented popular music to flourish in such a society, as most of those who were so inclined tended to move away to centres such as London or Dublin, depending on the extent of their talent and ambition. The Miami Massacre was apparent evidence of the helplessness of music – any kind of music – in the face of ideologically-motivated violence. By the middle of the decade it was unclear if rock music could survive, let alone thrive, in a place in which politics (rather than taste, age, gender or any other cultural category) dominated questions of identity.

Northern Ireland was ripe for the onset of punk, and it was in this context that the Belfast music enthusiast Terri Hooley launched the region's first independent label, Good Vibrations (named after his city-centre record store).[10] The idea of the small independent label was one of the most positive aspects to emerge from a period characterized by cynicism and manipulation.[11] Hooley was determined to demystify the popular music industry and the idea of a pop record as some kind of arcane procedure that demanded more money and expertise than most people could manage. It's in the nature of any rock scene that the majority of acts are short-lived and anonymous; Hooley's role was to support some of the more focused bands of the period – such as Rudi, Protex, Ruefrex, The Moondogs and The Outcasts – bands which were happy to accept the first recording opportunity he offered, even as they continued to work towards a 'proper' London deal.

Hooley was responding to, and in turn encouraging, a vibrant punk scene that had been developing across Northern Ireland throughout 1977 and '78. In subsequent folklore, this scene offered a time and a place in which society's 'normal' sectarian divisions could be suspended and an alternative rhetoric, focused on 'the kids', could take over.[12] In reality, things were never so simple. As indicated above, the implicitly contradictory nature of English punk rock (obvious as early as December 1976 by the differing attitudes and sounds of The Sex Pistols, The Clash and The Damned) was overdetermined in the case of Northern Ireland by the society's fractured political status and by the context of politically motivated violence. In this context, any musical statement was always already a political statement. It's at this point that we're obliged to consider the two bands with whom Northern Irish punk rock is most closely associated: Stiff Little Fingers and The Undertones.

As Bill Rolston has shown, the tradition of political music is well established in Northern Ireland, so it was not as if punk was entering a cultural void in this regard.[13] Whereas traditional political music reflected the established political dispensation with reference to a range of traditional musical-lyrical forms '[the] dilemma facing punk groups [within Northern Ireland] was whether or not to sing about the "troubles"' (Rolston 2001: 59). Although fired by the same punk spirit to some extent, The Undertones and Stiff Little Fingers functioned differently from their brethren in both London and Dublin, and indeed from each other. It would be relatively easy to undertake a 'compare and contrast' exercise in relation to these well-regarded bands. The Undertones were from Derry, a city often regarded as the cradle of the Troubles, but also as the home of the Field Day theatre company, one that was in the vanguard of the attempt to think beyond the sectarian history that fed the conflict (Kirkland 1996: 131–46). Stiff Little Fingers were from Belfast, the

United Kingdom's own 'Beirut', a city in which geography, rather than biology, was destiny, and a place with a complex cultural resonance. The Undertones were 'the Irish Ramones', writing fast, short pop songs about 'real' life; Stiff Little Fingers were 'the Irish Clash', writing loud, abrasive rock songs about a different kind of 'real' life. Stiff Little Fingers (at the instigation of their English manager-cum-inspiration Gordon Ogilvie) turned resolutely to face the Troubles head on, writing about the minutiae of life in a society in which violence was always a possibility. The Undertones seemed (at least initially) to turn away from the Troubles, writing instead about the troubles of teenage life – (lack of) sex, overachieving relatives, chocolate bars and spots.[14]

Many of the differences between The Undertones and Stiff Little Fingers may be discerned on their signature records. 'Teenage Kicks' remains one of the most recognizable songs to have emerged in the Irish rock canon. Written by twenty-year-old guitarist John O'Neill in the latter part of 1977 (the rest of the band were still in their teens) and sung with a characteristic blend of humour and vulnerability by Feargal Sharkey, it describes a classic pop scenario in which the young protagonist's imagination is fired by the arrival of a new girl in the neighbourhood. Even in its title and locution, 'Teenage Kicks' harks back to a period (the 1950s) and a place (the United States) in which a number of new song genres emerged in response to the recently established socio-economic category of 'the teenager'. Once established, such popular song genres became available to subsequent generations for reiteration and re-interpretation; 'Teenage Kicks' *reiterates* the teenage love / lust scenario from early rock 'n' roll, and *re-interprets* it in the light of new technological and ideological developments. In the latter terms, if on the one hand the song represented a rejection of the dominant discourses of contemporary British punk (in which issues of domestic love tended to be downgraded in favour of public and political issues), on the other it also represented a rejection of the band's contemporary socio-political context, which was one of politically motivated violence.

Perhaps the most surprising thing about 'Teenage Kicks' is not that these five young men managed to create such a relatively pure expression of the teenage love / lust scenario in such inauspicious circumstances, but that people are surprised that they managed, or indeed wanted, to do so. As the band members themselves have averred from time to time, paramilitary recruitment was a constant option throughout their formative years, an option that claimed many of their contemporaries.[15] Although writing and playing popular music provided an alternative, it did not, as some critics and theorists have suggested, amount to a denial of the political context in which they found themselves. Rather, it was a strategy of survival in the face of an overwhelming assault upon a community's social freedoms; not a *collusion* with established power structures (and talk of collusion was very much in the air at the time, as the punk historian Jon Savage has documented) but a means of exposing, through the provision of alternative discourses, those same structures. Behind all the talk of pop versus punk, of the sixties versus the seventies, what songs such as 'Teenage Kicks' really said was: 'We will not be reduced to the discourse of violence you have introduced into our community; you may discipline our bodies, but you cannot discipline our imaginations.' In Northern Ireland in the late 1970s, this was a highly significant political statement.

Stiff Little Fingers, on the other hand, belonged to what Savage (2001: *passim*) calls the 'social realist' wing of punk: self-consciously in and of the world, deliberately looking to confront the negative energy of political injustice with the positive energy of rock music. 'Alternative Ulster' (and, indeed, much of the *Inflammable Material* album on which it featured) blatantly used the violence of punk to confront the violence of sectarianism.[16] After an uncertain opening in which the main guitar riff is played in isolation, the whole band crashes in and the song rattles along at a barely controlled speed, as urgent and as dangerous as the political situation that inspired it. The snare snaps, the guitars buzz, and Jake Burns' barking voice is ideally suited to express the kind of emotions – outrage, bitterness, fear – broached in the lyric. And yet no one is named, no one is shamed; history is simultaneously confronted and avoided. The lyric turns on a classic 'us and them' scenario in which an undifferentiated 'they' conspire to deprive 'us' of basic freedoms, and in which the only 'alternative' is the supposedly 'radical' (but in fact classically liberal) one that goes back to basics to change the meaning of the key terms at stake: in this case, 'Ulster'.

'Alternative Ulster' was a definitive statement in the context of Northern Ireland on the ability of rock to represent reality, or (another way of saying the same thing) the ability of art to intervene in life. All Stiff Little Fingers' other 'political' songs (even 'Suspect Device', which predated it by some six months) were variations on the central themes that the state's youth had inherited a situation not of their making, that they were having invidious options thrust upon them (to politicize or not) and that for many people the security of entrenched violence was preferable to the diffi- culties of imagination and understanding required by peace. At the same time, as ostensible subscribers to a cultural trend – punk – that was itself fatally contradictory, Stiff Little Fingers found their own position ('the band who sang "Alternative Ulster"') to be increasingly untenable. The closest parallel is provided by The Clash which, despite its impeccable credentials (especially after the sordid demise of The Sex Pistols), was ever more strung out between the demands of its aesthetic (punk) and its medium (popular music), and which eventually had to jump one way or another. It was as if punk offered the possibility of social activism, of making a difference, only to snatch it away at the last minute, for the idea of *making* anything (a record or a difference) was ultimately a collusive, anti-punk gesture. Just so with Stiff Little Fingers, who were obliged to harness it in their efforts to combat violence, to consort with the types they indicted in their music, to invoke the hopelessly reified notion of 'the kids' as 'an enthusiastic but ultimately non-threatening' (Rolston 2001: 59) alternative to 'the men of violence', and ultimately to trade independence for success. Like many other bands, in other words, Stiff Little Fingers tapped the energy of punk during the late 1970s, but in doing so became fatally infected with the paradoxical self-destructiveness upon which punk was founded.

Considerable debate continues to rage regarding the various cultural strategies for representing (and in doing so, coping with) situations of violence; nowhere is this debate more keenly conducted than in the annals of Northern Irish punk where Stiff Little Fingers are regarded by many involved in the original scene as little more than charlatans (O'Neill and Trelford 2003: *passim*). At least so far as these representative songs are concerned, however, it would seem that in the context of the Troubles, The Undertones and Stiff Little Fingers embodied different impulses that were both equally valid and equally limited: 'Teenage Kicks' was 'valid' in the sense that the sexualized body has always constituted an 'other' to the politicized body, but 'limited' in the sense that focus on the individual tends to neglect the effects of larger historical processes; the 'teenager' inhabits the near past, the present and the near future, and as such doesn't possess the experiences or the imagination (or indeed the desire) to engage with the overarching temporalities that bear upon his her life. 'Alternative Ulster' was 'valid' in the sense that the politicized body has always constituted an 'other' to the sexualized body, but 'limited' in the sense that focus on larger historical processes tends to neglect the needs of the individual. Both were 'limited' in the sense (associated with Adorno) that modern popular music is invariably bound to the commercial, social and political structures within which it is obliged to operate, yet 'valid' in the sense (associated with Benjamin) that modern popular music also possesses the ability to 'mean' beyond and between those structures.

NO SLEEP 'TIL TUAM

If Dublin and Belfast have been considered 'peripheral' to the international popular music industry since its inception, what of those places considered to be 'peripheral' in national terms, places, that is, positioned as geographically marginal in indigenous cultural discourses? This question raises one of the most important theoretical-methodological issues attending the study of popular music in recent years: space. The interest in space occurred largely as a response to a so-called 'spatial turn' in the humanities, one early advocate of which was the American geographer / philosopher Edward Soja. In his celebrated 1989 study entitled *Postmodern Geographies: The Reassertion of Space in Critical Social Theory*, Soja claimed:

> Neo-conservative postmodernism is using deconstruction to draw even more obfuscating veils over the instrumentality of restructuring and spatialization, reducing both history and geography to meaningless whimsy and pastiche in an effort to celebrate the postmodern as the best of all possible worlds ... A new 'cognitive mapping' must be developed, a new way of seeing through the gratuitous veils of both reactionary postmodernism and late modern historicism to encourage the creation of a politicized spatial consciousness and a radical spatial praxis (74–5).

This assault upon the 'whimsy and pastiche' associated with 'reactionary postmodernism' had implications for both the making and the analysis of popular music. At the same time, Soja's idea was not to convert a generation of historically minded academics into geographically minded ones. His aim, rather, was to instigate an (inter)disciplinary revolution both within and without the academy, based on the dual premise that (a) both culture *and* criticism have always been thoroughly informed by both *temporal* and *spatial* dimensions and (b) critical discourses of all kinds have, since the advent of Romantic historicism during the nineteenth century, worked to fetishize the former whilst denying or downplaying the latter. Which is to say: Soja's aim (in his own words) was 'to spatialize the conventional narrative by recomposing the intellectual history of critical social theory around the evolving dialectics of space, time and social being: geography, history and society' (3).

As remarked above, the 'spatial turn' was not slow to make itself felt in popular music studies also. Following Attali (1985) and Lefebvre (1991), we see that music functions within a sonic economy in which different noises produce, and are in turn produced by, different spaces within society, such spaces being dialectically linked with that society's power structures. In short, space produces sound and vice versa, and the manner in which this is enabled (or not) to occur is a political process. This realization gives rise to a form of analysis 'that explores the promises and possibilities of a cartography of sound as a territory of power.'[17] Such an analysis would focus upon the complex array of interrelated spatialities that inform every aspect of the popular music text, including most centrally: (i) the social, political and economic contexts within which it is produced and circulates; (ii) its own peculiar formal structure (for example, the places to which it alludes and the textural spaces created by its sound); and (iii) the places within which it is consumed.

I don't want to spend too much time on this issue in a dedicated section, or to essay any particular analysis inspired by this methodology; by now it should be clear that a spatial awareness informs (to a greater or lesser degree) every cultural and critical concern broached in this book from beginning to end. However, one aspect – touched on time and again – *is* probably worth highlighting, and that's the extent to which the geography of Irish popular musical practices relates to the geography of other Irish cultural and political practices. I've already alluded, for example, to the way in which the showbands and the beat groups of the 1960s responded (in very general terms) to a traditional divide between rural and urban space in Ireland, and how both the musical and the underlying spatial practices were affected as a consequence. Likewise, we've remarked how musicological and attitudinal differences between bands such as Thin Lizzy (which based itself in Britain but occasionally returned to Ireland) and Horslips (which remained based in Ireland but occasionally left to tour and record) were manifested in terms of their different attitudes towards issues of space and place; also noted was the way in which the music of Van Morrison might be addressed in terms of its invocation of a series of locations imaginatively identified as *home* and *not-home*, the attractions of each and the ability to travel between these locations.

A somewhat crude division underpins these points, turning (on one level) on a traditional opposition between urban space – which in a country the size of Ireland usually means Dublin or Belfast – and non-urban space in Irish cultural history, and (on another level) on the identification of Ireland as a traditional, or pre-modern, place.[18] Such a division needs to be modified, however, when we come to consider the many non-metropolitan 'scenes' and musicians from around the country who may yet be quite clearly identified as operating in terms of a rock aesthetic. It's interesting, also, that despite the geographical fluidity of modern musical scenes, certain characteristics – musical and otherwise – tend to accumulate and become identified with certain places. Which is to say: as musical scenes are produced by the assembly of interest in certain kinds of music, so those scenes in turn contribute to the 'production' of certain places, their meanings and their imaginative limits. We've already noted, for example, punk's success in Belfast and throughout Northern Ireland generally. During the same period a tradition of 'mad' Cork bands began to emerge (although it was of course possible to be 'mad' in different ways and to different ends).[19] Nun Attax and its offshoots Five Go Down To The Sea? and Beethoven played densely structured yet 'noisy' music that took the anarchy of the punk parent movement to surreal levels; routinely dismissed as typical Cork eccentrics, the various bands fronted by Finbarr Donnelly (who was actually born in Belfast but relocated with his family to the southern city at an early age) in fact represent a road seldom travelled in Irish rock history. Although less threatening, the music of The Sultans of Ping F.C. and The Frank and Walters also operated at a tangent to the rock mainstream, incorporating as it did elements of humour, quirkiness and deliberate gaucheness. Microdisney – widely accepted as one of the most innovative bands in the Irish rock tradition – began as another 'noisy' Cork outfit, although later it modified its sound and made considerable (although not decisive) inroads into the British independent rock scene.[20]

Similar scenes tend to occur in many of the island's smaller towns and cities, each of them throwing up a number of bands who achieved greater or lesser degrees of national (and occasionally international) success. Thus, over the period in question here, we find bands from Carlow (Azure Daze), Galway (Toasted Heretic), Drogheda (The Dreads), Kilkenny (Engine Alley), Newry (The 4 of Us), Tuam (Blaze X) and Limerick (Tuesday Blue). No matter how active or interesting local scenes were, however, these bands inevitably gravitated towards the major population centres where were located the audiences, the venues and the rest of the rock paraphernalia that they needed.[21] This movement from hinterland to metropolis is typical of national popular-music scenes the world over, and – as in the case of Ireland – reflects a wider spatial dispensation that has developed over an extended period. As Irish rock headed towards its third decade, however, there was one band that challenged the form's accepted range of sound and meanings *and* the received spatial logic upon which it depended: The Saw Doctors.

Formed in Tuam, Co. Galway in 1988 around the core song-writing partnership of Leo Moran and Davy Carton, The Saw Doctors came to public prominence the following year when they were drafted as support for a British tour by The Waterboys (whose main man, Mike Scott, also produced some of their early material). Catapulted to fame by the success of the single 'I Useta Love Her' (1991), The Saw Doctors quickly divided opinion between those who saw them as the worst, and those who considered them the best, thing ever to happen to Irish rock music.

For the former, they were 'designer rednecks', 'bogmen' and 'culchies' with little conception of the meaning of the music. For the latter, here finally was a band with none of the pretensions of the Dublin scene, a band who managed to express the real concerns and experiences of real Irish people through the medium of rock 'n' roll, and whose unselfconscious articulation of 'the local' gave them that air of authenticity so valued in rock discourse (Jones 1995). Not since the days of the showbands and the beat groups had popular music polarized Irish opinion in such an emphatic way; the controversy persists to the present day.[22] Largely avoiding the supposed Irish rock music industry base in Dublin, over the past fifteen years The Saw Doctors have brought their brand of 'local music' around the world and back again to their home in Galway.

In the context of Irish rock history, The Saw Doctors were remarkable for a number of reasons from the outset. Most obviously, the band played songs about the real issues facing their contemporaries in the small-town west of Ireland, in all its boredom, banality, humour and romance – songs far removed in tone, vision and sound from the majority of material in the rock tradition. Form tied in with content insofar as this material was sung in the accent and idioms of the people it described, while their sounds and structures (although recognisably of the rock family) had many eccentricities. This gave The Saw Doctors an air of enthusiastic amateurishness that, while corresponding to some extent with punk's assault on mid-Atlantic professionalism, had little in common with any of the established sub-traditions of international rock music. In fact, the band appeared to engage at least as much with folk and country 'n' western traditions as with the world of rock music within which they ostensibly operated. And as with folk and country music, much of the power of The Saw Doctors came from a sense of depth, of an extensive cultural accretion beneath the apparent simplicity of the melodies, the lyrics and the emotions they expressed. During the 1990s, both the material and the image chimed very precisely with a great many Irish people at home and abroad, as well as a great many others throughout Britain, North America and Australia who, although perhaps unfamiliar with Clare Island or Joyce Country, identified with the experiences described in the typical Saw Doctors' song.

'The Saw Doctors', wrote Kieran Keohane in an essay from 1997, 'articulate one polarity of the economy of desire in the Irish spirit: the desire to be connected with the local and the familiar' (277). Keohane found this desire most fully articulated in one of the band's most representative songs. 'N17' (1989) is an emigration song, a genre with its roots in the eighteenth century but updated here to respond to the economic crisis of the 1980s and the great wave of departures to which it led. Like many of his contemporaries, the young narrator of 'N17' '[doesn't] see much future' when he leaves school, so he says goodbye to his hometown (in this case Tuam) and takes the road for the airport, which in its turn will set him on a longer journey to life on a 'foreign soil'. Emigration songs typically oscillate between emotions of nostalgia and regret towards the lost homeland, on the one hand, and bitterness and anger towards the circumstances that necessitate relocation, on the other. Although remarkably free of the latter, 'N17' is clearly animated by the former, what Keohane calls '[a] nostalgic yearning for an Irish lost Eden of Tuam' (279). Such a 'yearning', he warns, means that The Saw Doctors flirt with 'some of the elements of an Irish proto-fascist traditionalism: the uncritical value of all that is connoted by "blood, race and soil"' (278). And yet, he continues, the prevailing emotion of the band's music, exemplified by this song, is 'melancholia' – a realization that home is lost, masked by a determination to party hard in search of some kind of future.

This analysis is borne out to an extent by the imaginative geography of 'N17', which on one level establishes a clear opposition between a valued past – there, in the west of Ireland, the place that is absent – and an unsatisfactory present – here, on this 'foreign soil', the place in which 'I' find myself. It's interesting, however, that 'home' is symbolized not by a defined *place* – the house, the farm or the familiar local landscape, for example – but by an arterial *space*, the N17 road that runs between Galway City and Tuam, and by the 'stone walls' that line it. How can a road, especially a relatively major road such as the N17, become in itself a symbol of home? Why are 'walls', with all their connotations of enclosure and imprisonment, chosen to represent all that is left behind instead of potentially much more sympathetic architectural features such as the hearth or the room (kitchen, bedroom, etc.)? Why is the prevailing memory of Tuam not school prefabs or friends or family, but a road upon which the protagonist used to travel 'with just my thoughts and dreams'? Is 'home', in other words, the straightforwardly positive location the listener is encouraged to consider it to be? It's interesting also that the music displays none of the yearning plaintiveness or the strident anger of the emigration genre. Rather, it's a jaunty, mid-tempo work-out in the guitar-friendly key of G major, with a sing-along chorus and 'ethnic' instrumentation (accordion and tin whistle) added to the rock rhythm section for extra colour and drama, especially in the closing sections. The protagonist may be missing 'the girls of Tuam', but he seems to be having a reasonably good time all the same.

I think it would be a mistake to indict The Saw Doctors – as Keohane and many within the Irish rock music fraternity continue to do – for their emphasis upon the local and the familiar. In traditional sociology (which we might refer to as 'modernist' in this sense), the distinguishing characteristics of the community were widely understood to be 'locality and community sentiment' and its occupation of a specific, delimited 'territorial area' (MacIver and Page 1970: 297). Typically of the 'postmodernist' context within which they emerged, however, The Saw Doctors have managed to *recreate* this sense of local community amongst a fan base that is multinational, socially disaggregated and geographically dispersed. The band's music may appeal to conservative, not to say retrograde, elements among its fans, both Irish and otherwise. But its overall effect, I suggest, is to disrupt the co-ordinates upon which established Irish spatial discourse depends.

If the mutability of the (post)modern rock scene may be seen as a peculiar effect of multinational capitalism and its drive to reproduce 'the local' as depoliticized simulacra, it's also possible to argue (as Mark Olson does) that the 'alternative modalities of fandom can signal new forms of political community. An authentically migrant perspective would,' he continues, perhaps, be based on an intuition that the opposition between here and there is itself a cultural construction, a consequence of thinking in terms of fixed entities and defining them oppositionally. It might begin by regarding movement, not as an awkward interval between fixed point of departure and arrival, but as a mode of being in the world (1998: 270).

It is precisely this 'mode of being in the world' that 'N17' articulates, for what ultimately emerges from that song is a realization that 'home' is not, has never been, the unproblematic place described in the emigration song genre. It is, rather, a space that is overlain with contradictory emotions and impulses: the desire for community, certainly, which is in part a desire for complete immersion in a familiar landscape; but an equal and opposite desire to leave behind the limitations and frustrations of the everyday, to travel in search of new sites of authenticity. More than any other modern cultural form, this latter desire is most fully articulated by rock music. In an Irish historical context, the process of leaving demands to be articulated in certain discursive terms, determined in large part by the cultural, social and political history of the island, and by the emotional economy of bitterness and nostalgia to which this history has given rise. 'N17' apparently concurs with this history and this economy.[23] Read against itself, however, the song shows that 'the desire to be connected with the local and the familiar' exists in an existential bind with an antipathy towards 'the local and the familiar', and the individual's equal and opposite desire – however faint, however repressed or remote – to travel, to forsake the community in search of a fully realized self. The Saw Doctors may have become one of the world's favourite local bands; as they did so, however, they could not help re-articulating the relations between the local and the global, between the desire, on the one hand, to identify completely with a place, and a competing desire, on the other, to travel between places.

FOLK (CON)FUSION
In Chapter One, I likened Irish acoustic-based music during the 1960s to a broad river made up of many overlapping streams and currents. Such was the extent of overlapping at the time, in fact, that the established generic terms do little to describe the levels of sonic innovation sought, and occasionally achieved, by musicians working within the broad parameters of folk and traditional music. Nonetheless, the river metaphor extends and holds good for the 1970s and 80s, a period which threw up many diverse, and some extremely successful, practitioners of these particular forms of music. Indeed, such was the strength and resonance of Irish acoustic-based music, as well as the various hybrid forms to which it gave rise, that for many people and performers worldwide it became *the* predominant form of 'Irish music'. Moreover, as reality and representation became interchangeable, this situation led in time to the idea that folk-trad. music in itself represented *the* quintessential sound of Irishness. This idea (typical of the culturalist logic of the modernist / capitalist / liberal-humanist matrix) maintains that in any cultural formation, identity (in this case Irishness) and expression (in this case music) form

an organic whole that can only be undone by some kind of illegitimate tampering and / or discursive violence. The period under focus here reveals a number of confirmations of, and challenges to, that basic idea.

The acoustic music which had emerged during the 1960s continued to be developed in the following decades by musicians who referenced the generic and stylistic characteristics of both traditional music and progressive folk. As a function of its multi-generic basis, the sounds produced by these musicians could be both familiar and exotic, often within the same song. 'Mariner Blues' (1971) from the eponymous album by Tír na nÓg (formed in Dublin in 1969 by Sonny Condell and Leo O'Kelly), for example, is an extremely mellow song played predominantly on acoustic guitars; while sound and title function to locate this track in the world of late hippy pastoral, its setting and theme recall more established 'traditional' themes concerning nature, love and loss. The following year's *A Tear and a Smile* is generally regarded as a flawed attempt to latch on to the folk-rock vogue, while *Strong in the Sun* (1973) is rockier still. When Condell went on to co-form Scullion in 1975, he took with him the specialized guitar tunings that lent an unmistakable 'folk' dimension to the new band's acoustic-pop sound. On a somewhat different tack, the material collected on Mellow Candle's *Swaddling Songs* (1972) represents perhaps the most exquisite justification of folk-rock ever recorded; on tracks such as 'Silver Song', the Dublin outfit achieved levels of musical and lyrical beauty seldom equalled in the genre.

The band that made probably the most powerful impression upon the period (and indeed on subsequent Irish music-making), however, was Planxty. Its story is well known and does not need to be rehearsed at any great length here; suffice it to say that over the course of its stop-start existence Planxty provided a vehicle for some of the most influential musicians of the modern era: Christy Moore, Andy Irvine, Donal Lunny, Liam O'Flynn, Paul Brady, Johnny Moynihan, Matt Molloy; and with their particular fusion of traditional, folk and occasionally other kinds of music, these individuals set benchmarks in musicianship and vision that remain challenging to this day. The possibility of such a band had been broached by the Moore-driven *Prosperous* album (1972), which itself drew on the example of pioneering fusion experiments such as Emmet Spiceland, Sweeney's Men and The Johnstons. Utilizing the strengths of its individual players, Planxty referenced a variety of acoustic traditions – indigenous dance music, ballads and contemporary folk music – to produce music that was clearly 'Irish', although not in any straightforward or received sense of that term. On the so-called *Black Album* debut of 1973, O'Flynn's command of technique and Irvine's flair for melody are counterpointed by Lunny's instinctive grasp of harmony and Moore's (early) Dylanesque leanings. What this revealed was that 'Irish music', such as it was, didn't need to be protected or ring-fenced; in the hands of Planxty it was clearly robust enough and confident enough to take its chances in a noisy world. Or, to describe it in the terms introduced above, rather than expression (music) following reality (Irishness), expression was clearly leading 'reality' down paths it had avoided for decades, and thus anticipating the demise of protectionism and the rise of hybridity as a significant force within modern Irish cultural discourse.[24]

Typically of the small scene with which they were involved, the different musicians who were involved with Planxty during the 1970s went on to play and record in many different line-ups and combinations. Donal Lunny co-formed The Bothy Band in 1974, a group almost as influential and well-regarded as Planxty and whose various contributors – Tríona Ní Dhómhnaill, Mícheál Ó Domhnaill, Paddy Keenan, Matt Molloy, Paddy Glackin, Tommy Peoples, Kevin Bourke – loom equally large in the story of modern Irish acoustic music. Irvine played for a short time in 1976 alongside the likes of Frankie Gavin and Alex Finn in another of the great 'supergroups' of the modern era, De Dannan (formed in Spiddal in 1974). Also in 1976 Irvine and Brady released possibly the most influential album of the decade, if not the entire modern tradition, before the latter went on to record the award-winning *Welcome Here Kind Stranger* (1978); having explored this kind of music as far as he wished for the present, Brady reverted soon afterwards to the rock idiom that was his first love.[25] De Dannan recorded a 'traditional' version of The Beatles' 'Hey Jude' (1980), while Stockton's Wing combined the singer-songwriter instincts of Mike Hanrahan with the virtuosity of various traditional musicians. Other memorable fusion initiatives from this period include the albums *Camouflage* (1976) by Sonny Condell and *Midnight Well* (1977), an intriguing combination of traditional, country and pop by the American Thom Moore and a collection of contemporary luminaries. Much of this material was released on the Mulligan label, founded by Donal Lunny primarily as an outlet for Irish musicians who wished to fuse roots music with other traditions and influences.

It's important to remember that all this activity was going on at more or less the same time that punk-inspired performers such as Philip Chevron, Bob Geldof and Paul Cleary were preparing to take Irish rock in radically different directions from those established by a previous generation of artists such as Rory Gallagher, Thin Lizzy and Horslips. Ireland in the late 1970s, in other words, was an extremely noisy place, awash with different sounds – overlapping, integrating, sometimes harmonizing, sometimes creating the wildest dissonance. Folk-trad. artists such as Irvine, Brady, Moore and Lunny had both musical inclinations and personal connections that tended back towards classic rock, but also forward towards punk's iconoclastic, pioneering spirit; indeed, in some ways, punk's relationship with classic rock mirrored the relationship between bands such as Planxty and the traditional music with which (according to some) they played so fast and loose.

Of course, bands such as Planxty, The Bothy Band, De Dannan and Stockton's Wing remained primarily acoustic in orientation, no matter how many overdubs or electric keyboards they employed in the studio. The same can't be said of Moving Hearts, the group formed by Lunny and Moore in 1981, and in many ways the culmination of the crossover spirit that had been animating Irish acoustic music since the late 1960s. Moving Hearts had what Lunny described as a 'rock 'n' roll chassis' (quoted in Heffernan 2000, episode 3) provided by the bass guitar of Eoghan O'Neill and the drums of Brian Calnan. On top of this chassis they stacked a range of virtuoso performers playing instruments that carried the expectations and connotations of different traditions: Lunny himself on keyboards and a specially adapted electric bouzouki, Declan Sinnott on lead guitar, Keith Donald on saxophones and Davy Spillane on pipes and whistle. On lead vocals and amplified acoustic guitar, Moore provided a focus that was more typical of rock than traditional or folk music; trad. singers, after all, tended either to be unaccompanied (as in *sean-nós*) or more integrated into the band (as in the ballad tradition), while the more vocally inclined folk music tended to favour ensemble performance or the genre of the solo singer-songwriter-interpreter (the genre with which Moore has in fact become most associated in the latter part of his career).

The band's eponymous album from 1981 reached No. 1 in Ireland and was at the time the most successful indigenous record ever released. In musical terms it was unlike anything that had appeared before, and was, as a consequence, difficult to categorize in conventional terms. The English folk-rock movement of the early 1970s had also attempted to bring modern sensibilities to bear upon traditional musical values, and it instituted a sound that has remained influential down to the present. The marriage of traditional and modern is not always felicitous, however, and whereas the music of Fairport Convention or Steeleye Span and their heirs can sound self-conscious or merely quirky, Moving Hearts aimed to achieve a much more integrated meshing of old and new. On tracks such as 'McBrides', 'Category' and 'Lake of Shadows' (the album's three instrumentals) the band, by and large, succeeded. Pipes, saxophone and electric guitar vie for dominance on these tracks, each bringing its peculiar textural and conventional expectations to the sound, frequently overlapping in unison or contrapuntal passages. While this is going on at the front of the mix, the underpinning chassis of bass guitar and drums adds extra dimensions to the music's harmonic and rhythmic identity. The overall effect is that the ear is constantly surprised as the music slips – sometimes seamlessly, sometimes jarringly – between a number of recognizable styles, including traditional, folk, rock and jazz. While some found this an irritating experience (music, like everything else, should be itself rather than always looking to be something else), others enjoyed the listening challenge of moving with the music and of tracing along with the musicians a track's individual narrative of connotations, expectations and meanings.

If Moving Hearts was a difficult band to categorize in musical terms, many commentators had no such difficulty with regard to their extra-musical profile, which was widely characterized as heavily politicized, if not outright republican. Band members resisted such a designation at the time, claiming that their music spoke to and for an unspecified political underclass, irrespective of time or place, a credible claim when one considers Moore's affinity with folk musicians such as Dylan and Woody Guthrie. Certainly, tracks such as 'Hiroshima Nagasaki Russian Roulette', 'Before the Deluge', and 'Landlord' chimed with folk music's traditional dissident stance towards establishment values and practices. Even the cover of Philip Chevron's bitter 'Faithful Departed' (from The Radiators' *Ghostown* album of 1979) was locatable within a venerable tradition of Irish dissent, while adding yet another dimension to the band's already eclectic compendium of styles.

However, Moving Hearts' career coincided with one of the most active and emotive periods in the Northern Irish conflict, culminating in the death of ten hunger strikers in 1981; as a self-elected 'politicized' initiative it was not unlikely that these events would register both in the band's music and upon its wider profile. Songs such as 'Irish Ways and Irish Laws' and 'No Time for Love' were criticized at the time as apologies for contemporary radical republicanism – as represented by the provisional IRA – the first with its fanciful racialist myth of unsullied Irish origins, the second with its attempt to make common cause with the political dissenters of other times and places. In this analysis, the band's worst crime was to associate its musical expertise with a crudely rendered portrait of Irish history. Above and beyond any vulgar proselytizing impulse, there was a perceived danger that the sophistication required to play (and listen to) these songs, with their challenging time signatures and complex structures, would lend an unwarranted seriousness to the political opinions they expressed. And while there's no evidence that anyone ever took up arms because of a Moving Hearts performance, the band's flirtation with the glamour of armed resistance was all the more potent because of the particularly obnoxious nature of the British and Unionist presence in Northern Ireland at the time.

On the other hand, there were few amongst the international rock intelligentsia who objected when punk attempted to politicize popular music in Britain towards the end of the 1970s, or when hip hop attempted to do the same in the United States a decade later; on the contrary, these movements were widely celebrated (at least during their early stages) as radical convergences between politics, culture and theory. Not so in Ireland; whereas class (and to an extent gender) might be allowed to perform its time-honoured 'folk' function of providing a highly visible (yet increasingly remote and *passé*) rallying point around which 'we' could mobilize, nationalism, both in terms of its means and its ends, has always seemed distasteful to Irish rock's critical community. Irish popular music, in fact, seemed subject to the same process of revisionism that was overtaking Irish historiography and literary criticism at this time; and just as critics and historians were routinely taken to task for disseminating, consciously or not, what amounted to vindications of IRA policy, so Moving Hearts was attacked for inculcating a simplistic model of Irish history, and, more culpably, for contributing to a mindset in which violence became generally more acceptable as a valid response to violence.

Ultimately, there's no way to resolve the issue of 'political music', as the two words belong to different orders of discourse; judgements in relation to the one will not necessarily hold in relation to the other, music is always already 'political'. It should be noted, however, that the level of purely *musical* fusion achieved by the band runs counter to some of the ideas expounded at a *lyrical* level, much of the time in the same songs. Certainly, in sonic terms, the music of Moving Hearts represents a significant development in the history of Irish rock music; certainly also, the band contributed to an idea of musical crossover that has remained an important aspect of Irish popular musical discourse. What the music 'means', above and beyond that, depends upon your own political persuasions.

Moving Hearts went through a number of personnel changes over the period of its existence. The band had always been both older and numerically larger than its average Irish competitors; the dynamics of touring, management, repertoire, recording and so on were different as a consequence, and this militated against any sustained domestic success, which in turn made an international breakthrough unlikely. In more ways than one, the Irish rock community was not ready for the challenge of Moving Hearts. Once the charismatic Moore departed after the second album, and despite the considerable talent of replacements Mick Hanly and Flo McSweeney, the writing was on the wall. A contract-fulfilling instrumental album entitled *The Storm* (1985) signalled the end of the adventure.

The somewhat edgy air that surrounded Moving Hearts throughout its career was in distinct contrast to the atmosphere of calm and control radiated by the band representing perhaps the most successful attempt to bring Irish traditional music before a modern international audience: Clannad. Although eventually superseded by fellow family- and one-time group-member Enya, Clannad it was who first introduced and disseminated the form of ambient 'Celtic' music that has enjoyed such a vogue in latter years. The jazzy-trad. fusions of their first decade had already marked Clannad as an 'important' band; but it was only after the Enya-aided *Fuaim* album of 1982 and 'Theme from *Harry's Game*' (a top ten hit in Britain in the same year) that this family group from Gweedore in rural Co. Donegal began to make a significant – and significantly different – impact upon popular musical practices in Ireland and elsewhere. Rather than trawling through its long and incredibly rich career, however, I just want to take a moment to consider the provenance and impact of the 'Celtic' music with which Clannad has become associated, the point being, again, that whether you think it's 'a good thing' or not depends upon both musical and wider politico-cultural persuasions.

So-called 'Celtic music' emerged in the latter decades of the twentieth century as probably the most successful branch of the 'world music' marketing phenomenon.[26] It represented an attempt on the part of various critical and economic institutions to posit a connection between diverse musical practices – not only Irish, but a whole range of supposedly 'Celtic' regions and nations, including Ireland, Scotland, Wales, Brittany and Gallicia. In some accounts 'Celtic music' encompasses everything from Alan Stivell to U2 and numerous high-profile points in between. The key to its ideological status is in fact encoded in the seemingly unproblematical use of the term 'Celtic', a word with a long and troubled career in Irish cultural history. Despite its undoubted novel status in commercial terms, much of the time 'Celtic music' was composed, performed and received in terms of long-established discourses which emphasize 'Celtic' difference from mainstream or normative experience. Especially in relation to Ireland, 'Celtic music' in fact served to reconfirm certain stereotypical notions regarding an essential national recalcitrance towards modernity, and an innate – indeed, often a biological – difference from other musical formations.

Such notions have their bases in the work of two nineteenth-century figures dislocated in time and space from the exciting, sexy, global world of contemporary Celtic music: the French cultural historian Ernest Renan, and the English poet and social critic Matthew Arnold. As the leading British organic intellectual of his day, Arnold's self-appointed task was to co-opt Britain's Celtic margins into a peaceful political arrangement with the archipelago's dominant power, England. In a series of essays and lectures beginning in the 1860s, Arnold attempted to flatter the Scots, Welsh and Irish into acquiescence – the basic message being that the Celts were lovely people possessed of qualities without which the British imperial project could not advance (Smyth 1996). In his 1867 study of Celtic literature, Arnold produced a critical model in which the Celt contributed a range of identifiable tendencies to the English poetic tradition. He deployed an array of pseudo-scientific and cultural discourses to characterize 'Celticness' as a wistful, melancholy, sentimental, passionate category; the Celt is 'keenly sensitive to joy and to sorrow'; at the same time, however, he is 'always ready to react against the despotism of fact' – qualities which have haunted Irish cultural production ever since (Arnold 1900: 82).

Arnold's understanding of the Celt was itself based on that of the French cultural historian Ernest Renan who, just a few years earlier, had described Celticness, rather suggestively for present purposes as it turns out, in this way:

> Its history is itself only one long lament . . . If at times it appears to be cheerful, a tear is not slow to glisten behind its smile; it does not know that strange forgetfulness of human conditions and destinies which is called gaiety. Its songs of joy end as elegies; there is nothing to equal the delicious sadness of its national melodies . . . Never have men feasted so long upon these solitary delights of the spirit, these poetic memories which simultaneously intercross all the sensations of life, so vague, so deep, so penetrative, that one might die from them, without being able to say whether it was from bitterness or sweetness.[27]

The Celtic qualities 'identified' by Renan and Arnold were ones that have since come to characterize 'Irishness' in a range of highly effective discourses. Ultimately, both Renan and Arnold characterize Celticism as a *spirit* that might be approached through close study of pan-Celtic culture but that, because of its nature, must remain ultimately impervious to rational analysis. When incorporated into the British racial mix, such qualities, Arnold averred, would help to humanize what he perceived to be the Anglo-Saxon's characteristic gifts for worldliness and pragmatism. Basically, in Arnold's vision, the Celts were ideally suited to entertain the English after a hard day at the empire.

A century or so later, it seemed that not much had changed, and the echo of Renan's encomium to Celtic culture might still be heard. Despite energetic resistance during the Irish revolutionary period, the discourse of Celticism survived and re-emerged in some rather odd places throughout the twentieth century – one of the most unexpected being the *fin de siècle* vogue for 'Celtic' music'. The process may be observed, for example, in the revealingly titled *Complete Guide to Celtic Music: From the Highland Bagpipe and Riverdance to U2 and Enya* by June Skinner Sawyers (2000).[28] Problems beset this book throughout, beginning with the opening chapter (1–20) in which the author attempts to define Celtic music in quasi-scholarly terms, quoting linguistic, geographical and historical authorities to establish a link between those parts of western Europe washed by the Atlantic. However, the 'meaning' of the music remains for Skinner Sawyers ultimately recondite, unknowable – not because of inadequate research but because that is its essence, its nature, its distinguishing characteristic. Thus, the opening pages of the book introduce a rhetoric that pervades the entire volume, and is indeed familiar from the wider discourse of 'Celtic' music:

> When all the techniques are checked off, the element that the music of the Celtic lands most commonly shares is *something* a lot more intangible and certainly less quantifiable – a feeling or quality that evokes emotions of sadness or joy, sorrow or delight . . . All share, for lack of a better word, a Celtic spirit, a unique bond with one another that transcends time, distance, and political units.[29]

This 'something' (wonderful mystificatory term) animates the culture not only of the disparate 'Celtic' nations of Europe, but also of the Celtic diaspora, whether it surfaces in Nova Scotia, Chicago or Sydney. This notion – that there's a transhistorical 'feeling', 'quality', 'spark' or 'spirit' infusing an arbitrarily defined body of music – wouldn't pass muster in Media Studies 101; here it underpins an entire world-view. We're back, in other words, in the patronizing world of Renan and Arnold, in which the Celt functions as light relief from the rigours of the 'real' world, endowed with qualities characterized as valuable yet at the same time categorically disempowered *vis-à-vis* the critical and economic discourses in which they're recruited. Just as Arnold conscripted the Celt to perform specific tasks as part of his project to expedite the consolidation of late Victorian British identity, so the modern phenomenon of Celtic music performs specific ideological tasks within a global popular music market. The phenomenon of 'Celtic music', in other words, represents a lucrative niche market, in which certain unique experiences are offered to those willing to invest, emotionally, certainly, but also financially, in the notion of some inherent Celtic spirituality supposedly recalcitrant to the modern world. To put it in advertising language: tests have shown that Clannad washes your soul whiter than all comparable products!

Of course, critics and commentators such as Skinner Sawyers are not entirely to blame for this recourse to 'something'. Many of the artists whom she evokes have at one time on another bought into the 'Celtic soul' thing, as evidenced in a *Time* article from 1996 on the Celtic craze, in which Enya refers to her music's 'melancholy', Mary Black discusses the 'passion' of Irish culture and Christy Moore accounts for the success of Irish artists by pointing to the 'very interesting and colorful way' in which they use the English language (Walsh 1996: 79–80). And perhaps we shouldn't be too hard: as Noel McLaughlin and Martin McLoone point out (2000: 182–3), there are specific reasons – both commercial and ideological – for the continuing attraction of so-called Celtic music for artists from Ireland and elsewhere. Groups such as Clannad need to identify themselves and the music they make in such a way as to distinguish it from all the other kinds of music with which they're competing. At the same time, although Celticism may be rooted in ideological imposition, this doesn't mean that it can't be used in ways that exceed, perhaps even subvert, any disabling agenda to which it's attached. People need to belong, to identify with a place called home and with cultural practices that mark that home out as singular, different, specific. This perhaps explains the continuing vogue for 'Celtic' music, especially amongst the Celtic diaspora around the world.

The worry persists, however. 'Essence' segues irresistibly into the other discursive touchstone which inevitably attends 'Celtic' music: authenticity – another concept with an extremely troubled fate in Irish history, and responsible, when harnessed to one or another ideological agenda, for all manner of outrageous prescriptions and dangerous proscriptions. Like much of the discourse about popular music, *The Complete Guide to Celtic Music* is in fact organized around a central opposition between the authentic and the inauthentic. The author, with her extensive knowledge of the archive, is self-elected to differentiate between these categories. Time and again, artists, performances and individual musical texts are celebrated or condemned in the name of an 'authenticity' which, like the 'spirit' that animates it, is ultimately unlocatable. Like style, you've either got or you haven't got it. Recourse to such rhetoric bespeaks an arrogance borne of the elitism which has come to inform the traditional music revival since the 1970s, a revival built on popular success but that, with its tendencies towards protocol and hierarchy, came in time to aspire to art status.

The so-called 'Celtic music' scene was not the first, nor would it be the last, to adopt such a tendentious aesthetic. 'Keep it real' has been the vainglorious war cry of jazz, rock, punk and hip hop in their day. All those genres had to learn the lesson, however, that popular music invariably emerges from a complex matrix of business interests, creative energy and audience engagement; over-investment in the latter two categories in the name of some putative 'real', 'true' or 'authentic' moment located outside the former invariably leads to hopeless attempts to sort out the worthy from the unworthy. These efforts always end in tears, and for two reasons: firstly, because in the realm of popular culture the *idea* of the authentic can only emerge, circulate and be consumed in strategic alliance with the inauthentic – which is to say, in alliance with the capitalist economic practices upon which modern popular music depends; and secondly, because the authentic *per se* has no existence in reality – it's the site of something that cannot be located, the name for something that never happened.

And then, of course, there was The Pogues, the band that (with the exception of U2) has attracted probably more column inches and more scholarly analysis than any other in this book. Again, in terms of the actual music there's not much to say that hasn't been said elsewhere: second-generation Irish Londoner Shane MacGowan led a rag-tag of English ex-punks and a few exiles from Irish music (Terry Woods and Philip Chevron) down a road that had never been travelled before by infusing (some aspects of) Irish traditional music with the spirit of 1977. The result was both anarchic and inspiring, wholly original whilst deferring openly to a set of cultural roots that was about as far removed from the contemporary British (and indeed Irish) popular musical imagination as possible. The band played a mixture of covers and originals; the former usually from the raucous ('Paddy Mad') rather than the sentimental ('Paddy Sad') end of the ballad spectrum, the latter predominantly composed by MacGowan, who in time became recognized as a writer of power and vision.

MacGowan's version of The Pogues explored the possibilities of punk-trad.-ballad fusion with great energy and enthusiasm for the best part of six years, achieving success with the albums *Red Roses for Me* (1984), *Rum, Sodomy and the Lash* (1985) and *If I Should Fall From Grace With God* (1988). This latter, the first to feature the experienced Terry Woods and the one on which MacGowan began to stretch himself as a writer, is generally regarded as the highpoint of the band's career. In between these albums they also produced a number of notable moments, including the 'Poguetry in Motion' (1986) extended player, which included perhaps the quintessential Pogues' song, 'A Rainy Night in Soho', and the brilliant 'Fairytale of New York' single from November of 1987, which featured Kirsty McColl on guest vocals and which gave The Pogues their highest chart rating. Also from this period (March 1987) came the collaboration with The Dubliners on the single 'The Irish Rover', a record that, apart from any of its other merits, focuses many of the issues that attend both the music and the wider cultural image of The Pogues.

For their many Irish critics, the problem with The Pogues had always been two-fold: firstly, they did not play 'Irish' music at all but travestied it in ways, and for reasons, that had more to do with expatriate fantasies than Irish realities, and that drew upon the least deserving features, sentimentality and violence, found in the music of ballad groups such as The Clancys and The Dubliners. 'Proper' Irish music was subtle, venerable, resonant with history, the deserving expression of a deserving people – far removed from the noise produced by this ill-favoured band (led by a particularly ill-favoured vocalist).[31] Secondly, and related to this, was the accusation that both the music and the image purveyed by The Pogues, and most especially by MacGowan, pandered to all the stereotypes regarding the Irish in Britain, the drunkenness, the aggression (as found in a track such as 'Sally MacLennane' or 'Boys from the County Hell', for example), and, beneath it all, the hint of Celtic wistfulness and poetry ('A Pair of Brown Eyes' or 'A Rainy Night in Soho'). As I suggested a number of years ago,

> it was the same old anarchic / mystical Celtic dialectic played out at another remove, leaving those who bought into this discourse in the same old temporarily attractive, but ultimately disabled, position. Some . . . could lose this identity next day as they would a hangover; for those who felt compelled to embrace it because of their nationality it could become a badge of permanent cultural disability (Smyth 1992: 5).

As a song, 'The Irish Rover' possesses levels of humour and gigantism that raise it above standard ballad fare; nevertheless, it's doubtful if many of the British record-buying public who made the record a hit managed to access those levels. The prevailing image, rather, was that of the conjoined bands cavorting together on the Top of the Pops stage, being 'Irish' in the usual ways that everyone could recognize.

And while it's clear that The Pogues admired The Dubliners, it's clear also that, infused with some aspects of the rock mythology that was also their inheritance, they (or at least MacGowan) took the ideal of the Irish ballad group for the reality in a way that the older band never did. Just as British post-punk is 'haunted' by the ghost of Sid Vicious, so 'The Irish Rover' is 'haunted' by the ghost of Luke Kelly (d. 1984), a figure who, possessed of talents similar to his own, was misrecognized by MacGowan as the ideal purveyor of Irish music (Scanlon 1988: 34).

If we compare 'The Irish Rover' with another famous collaboration from the following year, the album *Irish Heartbeat* by Van Morrison and the Chieftains, we find not only different musical, but different ideological, values at work. This album was celebrated at the time as a highly felicitous blend of styles, traditions and effects: traditional and rock, north and south, originality and canonicity, vocal and instrumental. Besides possessing an auto-critical element in the form of two songs, 'Irish Heartbeat' and 'Celtic Ray', that provide both musical and wider cultural contexts for the album itself, Morrison adapted the rich, expressive soul voice for which he'd become famous over the previous two decades to a number of traditional songs. The Chieftains demonstrate their flexibility throughout, functioning now as accompanying ballad band, now as a 'proper' traditional ensemble, and now as professional session musicians called in to lend an element of 'colour' to Morrison's musical musings.

As The Chieftains are to the Dubliners, so Morrison is to The Pogues; which is to say, not only do the former in both cases connote levels of musical authenticity, skill and subtlety not generally associated with the latter, they also connote forms of Irish identity generally more complex and more resonant. Rather than 'performing' the slow airs ('She Moved Through the Fair', 'Carrickfergus, and 'My Lagan Love', for example), Morrison tends to 'interpret' them as he would a jazz or rhythm 'n' blues standard. Likewise, his version of 'Raglan Road' is some way removed in terms of instrumentation and delivery from the supposedly 'definitive' version first recorded by Luke Kelly and The Dubliners in 1972. Kelly's famously powerful voice remains more or less 'constant' throughout the recording, seemingly relying on the lyric – rather than on his response to, or interpretation of it – to excite the required emotions of sadness and regret. Morrison, on the other hand, 'inhabits' the song in a much more organic sense, using his voice to wring every ounce of pathos and subtlety from Kavanagh's words and introducing repetition and seemingly improvised instructions to the band to give the recording the impression of a live performance. At the same time, the somewhat schmaltzy 'Irish' orchestral backing that gradually overtakes Kelly's version is at odds with his straightforward, barely inflected vocal performance; The Chieftains, on the other hand, provide a fully appropriate – both in terms of emotion and ethnicity – musical basis for Morrison's animated vocal. All in all, it's as if Kelly's performance remains subordinate to a meaning 'contained' *in* the lyric, whereas The Chieftains and Morrison attempt to liberate a range of meanings made possible *by* the lyric.

Even on 'rousing' ballads such as 'Star of the County Down', 'I'll Tell Me Ma' and 'Marie's Wedding', Irishness remains a 'quoted' category on *Irish Heartbeat*, mediated through levels of musicality and lyrical subtlety that render it a far from straightforward prospect; such, indeed, has always been to some extent the attraction of an artist like Morrison – the sense of elementary emotions and experiences churning away beneath what can seem like simplistic arrangements and lyrics. If Morrison has had to work long and hard to achieve such an impression, however, other artists have at various times adopted a much less self-conscious approach to the question of how identity is conveyed through music. Many people prefer what they (and presumably the concerned bands) consider to be the unmediated experience found in the music of The Dubliners or The Pogues; music that, if undeniably productive of certain stereotypical and regressive images in some contexts, nevertheless provides access to estimable discourses, such as honesty, loyalty, community and a generally affirmative attitude towards life, which the modern Irish (or aspirant-Irish, in the case of the diaspora) subject might wish to claim as his/her birthright. Identity, after all, is as much an effect of what you *do* as of what you *say you do*; in musical terms, authenticity is not merely a question of the right instruments played in the right way, but of attractive sounds produced in appropriate contexts. In that sense, The Pogues, as much as any of the musicians invoked throughout this book, were always 'authentic' inasmuch as they explored the interface between technology and ideology wherein Irish (musical) identity is under constant negotiation.

PUSHING THE ENVELOPE

When the CD was launched by Sony in Britain in March 1983, it was conceived as a principally adult-oriented medium. The artists who featured in the first round of releases – Linda Ronstadt, Chicago, Al Jarreau – were, in the main, safe, bankable and well-established (Cavanagh 2000: 78). Small regional labels had proliferated throughout Britain in the early 1980s, servicing a community of artists and fans who adhered to punk's 'go it alone' attitude, and whose musical universe was ordered not so much by the established pop and rock sensibilities of The Beatles and The Rolling Stones but with reference to the much darker, anti-establishment ethos of The Velvet Underground and Love. While there were many more opportunities for regional bands (including those from Ireland) to get a deal and to make a record, there was as a result much more noise competing to be heard. But now it was as if the major labels were calling the bluff of the indie rebels by completely turning their backs on its mid-to-late-teenage audience and the kind of left-field, guitar-oriented pop music that was the stock-in-trade of the indie movement. At the same time, by 1983 the indie ideal, exemplified in many ways by Rough Trade, had itself reached a related crisis point: how successful can you become before ceasing to be an indie? Can you do distribution and publishing deals with major labels and hang on to your independent status? What does it mean when your artists – for example, in Rough Trade's case, The Smiths and Scritti Politti – begin to achieve mainstream success?[32]

This was the industry context faced by young Irish rock musicians during the 1980s: on the one hand, reactionary major labels armed with their new toy, in pursuit of bankable artists possessed of cross-over appeal; on the other, sullen indies confused by the exigencies of the ideal to which they subscribed. The situation was exemplified in many ways by the act roster at Band Aid: the likes of The Style Council, Status Quo and U2 played, whereas the likes of The Smiths, The The and The Jesus and Mary Chain didn't. Discovering *why* this should have been so, in terms of business philosophy, band identity and of course *sound*, would tell us much of what we need to know about the popular music scene of the period.

The 1980s are often characterized as a fallow period for rock music, but at least in relation to Ireland this is unfair. Although punk's impact proved limited in an Irish context, it did succeed in opening a number of different paths that the island's musicians were keen to explore during the years that followed. Undoubtedly, the most productive (and most lucrative) of these paths was trodden by U2. Indeed, that band's success inspired a rush of activity in the early 1980s as many people within the industry looked to repeat the formula. That, allied to that fact that many new bands had their first recording experience on the 'Mother' label that was set up for that specific purpose by U2, meant that their influence, musical and otherwise, was pervasive. It's difficult to speculate counterfactually on how things might have been without U2, or what would have happened had its success been limited. In any event, and notwithstanding the influence of Bono and friends, it's clear that a wide range of musicians from around the country enthusiastically subscribed to the punk notion of a popular music reborn. While some of these musicians had their fifteen minutes or so of international fame, the vast majority failed to make any impression outside the national scene. However, this shouldn't detract from the recognition that Irish rock music was vibrant with invention and possibility during the 1980s.[33]

In this respect, it was in marked opposition to most other areas of contemporary island life. The Troubles had settled into a period of entrenchment and attrition after the hunger strike deaths of 1981; with none of the parties able to 'win' in conventional terms, shadowy forces constantly manoeuvred for position in a 'dirty war' that, while seldom making the front pages, sapped any progressive energies anyone within the Northern Irish state could muster.[34] In the south there was recession, unemployment and the highest rates of emigration since the 1950s. Such was the extent of the malaise, in fact, that pop offered to take a hand, with the controversial 'Self Aid' concert of May 1986. An obvious instance of the 'Aid'-mania sparked off by Band Aid, Self Aid was an attempt to focus attention on the dire economic straits into which the Republic had slid and to return some self-respect and hope to the working classes which suffered most as a consequence. Its critics, on the other hand, brought to bear upon the event many of the same criticisms that Band Aid and Live Aid had attracted; which is to say, they felt that it substituted effete, feel-good pop posturing for concentrated political action, and, as a consequence, let the ruling élite (those responsible for the mess) off the hook.

Whatever else it did, Self Aid provided a showcase for contemporary Irish musical talent (in fact, another standard criticism of such events is that musicians tend to be less interested in 'the cause' than in their own careers). However, the presence of Geldof and U2 was enough to give the event credibility in the eyes of its target audience, no matter what the more cynical members of the Irish journalist fraternity might write. But the issue of Self-Aid's 'real' status – radical critique or reactionary collusion – *vis-à-vis* contemporary Irish society remains, in the final analysis, beside the point: rock music is political *every day*, not just at special events such as Live Aid or Self Aid, in the noises it makes, the stories it tells, the situations it imagines engaging with, and, in the process, it modifies, officially sanctioned noises, stories and situations. As a socially salient form of popular music, rock both *reflects* the social order and *anticipates* its metamorphosis; Irish rock music of the 1980s is thus obviously a response to prevailing social and cultural trends, in Ireland and elsewhere, but more importantly it's the foremost contributor to the imagination of change. Therein lies its power and its importance.

The prevailing trend of the period was undoubtedly towards what might be called 'power pop' – a combination of New Wave attitudinizing, punk's emphasis on the song as the basic unit of popular musical currency, and a return to classic rock values in the areas of writing, performing and recording. Cactus World News was typical in this regard – purveyors of a big, 'sincere' guitar-driven sound that was fashionable for a short period in the middle of the decade. Similarly, bands such as Les Enfants, Light a Big Fire and Blue in Heaven played original, occasionally powerful pop music that drew on various post-punk traditions. Like Cactus World News, they all won good record deals with British labels which brought them to the brink of a breakthrough. However, evidence of the old show-business cliché regarding the inscrutability of success, all of them failed to make that breakthrough despite everything, including money, youth and talent, that was in their favour.

With its so-called 'Celtic' sound, In Tua Nua was also well fancied, but personnel problems and a 'difficult' band name intervened, things which may also have impacted upon the chances of Ton Ton Macoute and Auto da Fé. Fermanagh's Mama's Boys appeared to think punk never happened; all hair and attitude, their career's work eventually condensed into one memorable guitar riff (from 1985's 'Needle in the Groove'). The 1980s also saw the first stirrings of an Irish response to rock's traditional *bête noir* – dance music – with [The] Fountainhead (comprising Pat O'Donnell and Steve Belton) anticipating the two-bloke electronic pop-dance bands which became such a feature of the popular-music landscape during the 1990s.

Although typically eclectic in their sound and instrumentation, Na Fíréin wrote and sung through the medium of the Irish language. Rather than being acknowledged as purveyors of 'true' or 'real' Irish rock, however, its use of Irish exposed the band to a double prejudice: the more general one which maintains that effective rock music can only be sung in English (albeit American English much of the time), and the more specific one (just coming into force during the 1980s) that indicted the Irish language as the principal symbol of a culpable cultural nationalism. If you wanted a 'real' Irish rock 'n' roll band during the 1980s you had The Golden Horde; as much an idea as a band, Simon Carmody and crew remained keen to 'keep it real' throughout the latter part of the decade by providing yardsticks in terms of attitude and lifestyle (although not necessarily music) against which other bands could measure themselves.

Two of the most well regarded, and fondly remembered, bands from the 1980s were The Stars of Heaven and The Fat Lady Sings. After debuting on Eamon Carr's Hotwire label, the former signed to famous London indie label Rough Trade, for whom they made a small number of acclaimed records. Their music was 'roots' *avant la lettre*, steeped in Americana and the sweet, guitar-led sound of the Gram Parsons-era Byrds.[35] Artists such as Elvis Costello and Squeeze had flirted with country music in the earlier part of the decade, but there remained something parodic about songs such as 'Good Year for the Roses' and 'Labelled with Love'. In the meantime, 'Country and Irish' had become one of the mainstays of the domestic cabaret circuit (which itself had taken over from the livelier and more dynamic showband scene), and any gesture in the direction of the sounds and sentiments associated with that kind of music was risky for a young pop-oriented band. Nevertheless, The Stars of Heaven were determined to plough their own furrow, and their sessions for BBC radio DJs John Peel and Janice Long won them considerable support in the UK. Fronted by singing song-writing guitarists Stan Erraught and Stephen Ryan, and well supported by drummer Bernard Walsh and bassist Pete O'Sullivan, their music did not *retread* so much as *recover* the power hidden in the music, using its energies to articulate their own response to modern life, a classic example of sounds migrating and becoming meaningful in contexts different to the one in which they are first imagined. The Stars of Heaven were (and perhaps felt they were) a band out of time, too conscientious and too intelligent to attract a lumpen pop audience sated on mediocrity (O'Hagan 1987). Sadly, they split before their potential was realized, and for many people they remain one of the great lost voices of Irish rock.

Almost equally worthy (greater output always takes some of the gloss off cult bands), was The Fat Lady Sings, which ploughed the rock furrow between 1986 and 1994, at which time, disillusioned with the realities of the popular music industry, front man Nick Kelly pulled the plug. Having released four singles on minor labels (one of which was Belfast's Good Vibrations), the band had already established a reputation as a maker of thoughtful, melodic pop by the time it signed with East-West in 1989. Kelly showed every sign of becoming one of Irish rock's great *auteurs*, someone whose imagination and vision refused to be contained by the medium, and who stretched it accordingly – musically, at least, for it was his inability or unwillingness to come to terms with the non-musical aspects of the industry that did for The Fat Lady Sings. In 1997 Kelly released a solo album, *Between Trapezes*, that had been funded by internet subscription – an example of artists' ability to exploit technology that, along with other developments, may well eventually spell the demise of the established rock industry. The fact that his first band 'failed' in conventional terms is a reminder that rock music has traditionally been, and to a great extent still is, a process of negotiation between art and business, and that too much – or, indeed, not enough – reliance on either element is unlikely to bring either emotional or financial satisfaction.

Our brief trawl through the leading Irish rock voices of the 1980s brings us to Cork's Microdisney, regarded at the time, and since, as the producer of one of the most original sounds in the rock idiom to emerge from the island. Based around the core unit of vocalist Cathal Coughlan and guitarist Sean O'Hagan, Microdisney was in danger throughout its career of being dismissed as just another 'mad' crew from the southern city. If not 'mad', then eccentric they undoubtedly were, something due in large respect to their socialization in a milieu that was overlain with different, often contradictory, cultural impulses (McDermott, Hurley and O'Toole: no date). Although such eccentricity helped (after the band's move to London) to define its sound amidst the endless noise of contemporary popular music, it was not (unlike some such bands) an end in itself but a means to express, in words and music, a unique perspective upon the world. Formed in the late 1970s in punk's wake, Microdisney's recording career lasted from the single 'Hello Rascals' of 1982 to 1988's *39 Minutes* album. The band was feted in Britain where, alongside (although without the mainstream success of) their label mates The Smiths, they were in the vanguard of indie resistance to contemporary mid-Atlantic rock-pop. A felicitous connection with Rough Trade (the band's natural home, in many ways) faltered, leading to a frustrating period, and the band's eventual demise, under Virgin. Coughlan and O'Hagan went on to form two well-regarded bands, Fatima Mansions and The High Llamas, as vehicles for their independent pop visions.

The typical Microdisney song was melodic yet angular, fooling the listener into established 'song' modes before O'Hagan's guitar led sudden modulations to tangential, sometimes dissonant, keys. We might get home eventually, was the message, but we would have to go around the houses to get there. At the same time, Coughlan's unfashionable baritone (and his undisguised Cork accent) made the lyrics often difficult to discern – not that they yielded much conventional sense when they could be discerned. Songs such as 'Town to Town' or 'Loftholdingswood' do not really attempt to communicate a story or describe a situation with which the listener may, to a greater or lesser extent, relate; rather, they function to build up an impression or a mood, with images and phrases tumbling over each other in a seemingly random manner. In this way, the listener is encouraged to 'feel' what the song is about rather than to 'know' what it means. Moreover, if in some respects the 'ideas' of melodic and lyrical dissonance complemented each other, at the same time the distance between the clean, airy guitar sound and the deep vocal rumblings introduced levels of internal irony and contradiction that contributed to the need for an engaged, incremental response to the music. Unlike much rock and pop, in other words, which tends to lead the listener along more or less familiar lyrical and musical lines, the music of Microdisney demands a much more active listening experience, one in which 'meaning' is as much an effect of context and the listener's resources as it is of the musical 'text' itself.

To finish this section, I want to mention two bands which are closely associated with two remarkable subgenres that emerged during this period. The first is My Bloody Valentine and what has come to be known in rock discourse as 'shoegazing'. My Bloody Valentine was formed in Dublin in 1984 by American-born Kevin Shields and Dubliner Colm O'Ciosoig. Punk may have been one of the ingredients the band brought to the table, and indeed there are certain elements – most notably the ubiquitous thrashed guitars – of its sonic signature that are reminiscent of 1977. But the musical imagination of the two young men roamed further and wider than punk, which itself had been inspired (consciously or not) by another tradition almost as old as rock itself: an avant-garde, intellectualist tradition heavily influenced by media theory and aesthetics and found in the work of artists such Frank Zappa, Captain Beefheart, The Velvet Underground, The Stooges, Brian Eno and Television. Perhaps the most powerful confluence of punk aesthetics and art-noise, however, came from Patti Smith, whose influence upon successive post-punk generations was indeed seminal.

Finding little sympathy for, or understanding of, their musical vision in Ireland, Shields and O'Ciosoig quickly decamped for Germany, and soon after for London, which was to remain the band's base for the remainder of an enigmatic career. There they hooked up with various like-minded performers and began to develop the sounds – and the attitudes – that would be dubbed 'shoe-gazing' by the British musical press in the late part of the decade, a moniker that arose from the tendency of certain bands (My Bloody Valentine chief amongst them) to play with heads down during live performance, literally gazing at their shoes.[36] The band's earliest efforts culminated in the release of the album *Isn't Anything* (1988), introducing ideas and sounds that, alongside those produced by dance-oriented 'Madchester' bands such as The Happy Mondays and The Stone Roses, dominated the imagination of British indie-rock for at least half a decade.

Isn't Anything was an intriguing mixture of grace and power, or, to put it another way, of 'music' and 'noise'. Trying to decide where one ended and the other began represented the record's main challenge, and it was one enthusiastically taken up by the band's key demographic, which tended to be white and male (despite the presence of two women in the line-up: Bilinda Butcher and Debbie Goodge), and ranged in age terms from late teens through to late twenties. In this rock-that-isn't rock sound, electric guitars distort, voices 'sing' indecipherable words and melodies emerge only to disappear behind a wall of noise. Although studio-honed to a large extent[37], the music's true 'meaning' was only realized in live performance, the legendary loudness of which could bring tears to the eyes, and occasionally blood to the ears, of seasoned gig-goers (Cavanagh 2000: 360, 370). While some found it unlistenable, others hailed My Bloody Valentine as the latest in a long line of rock saviours, a band willing to reclaim rock's legacy of 'noise' in the face of overwhelming corporate pressure to turn it into 'music'.

All the musical and political issues attending the group came together on *Loveless* (1991), an album that was two years in the making and that nearly bank-rupted Alan McGee's Creation label (Cavanagh 2000: 353ff). Shields' fastidiousness (apparently he used nineteen studios to record and mix the album) seemed to be justified by a record that was hailed by critics as a vindication of My Bloody Valentine's reputation and a landmark in rock history; one of the few occasions in the history of the genre in which a band manages to express its response to the *Zeit-geist* in terms of its own sonic language. Translucent, airy and sensual on the one hand, the music was also droning, grinding and at times primeval. Because of its challenging sound and the band's radio-unfriendly reputation, however, *Loveless* failed to win the band many fans beyond their hardcore indie base. Dropped by Creation, Shields retired to his home studio (built with an advance from the band's new label Island) where, with various personnel, and without ever announcing the official demise of My Bloody Valentine, he failed to release a follow-up album.

The core members of this extremely influential band had been socialized in the peculiar musical culture of early 1980s Dublin, and the music they made may as a consequence be understood as in some ways a response to that culture (which itself, of course, represented an amalgam of local and international interests). At the same time, My Bloody Valentine's take on 'rock' music was so original that it seems somewhat beside the point to search for, or to insist upon, any contextual influence. The band's 'scene', such as it was, was the international sonic one that transcends conventional borders and boundaries. As such, it represents one of the points at which a nation-centred analysis of 'Irish' rock threatens to unravel, for the fact is that the music of My Bloody Valentine (and this is also true of Microdisney) is always capable of asking more questions of us than we are of it.

Some way removed from the sonic and attitudinal concerns of the 'shoe-gazers' was the loose affiliation of musicians who came to be described in the parlance of the period as 'raggle-taggle'. 'Raggle-taggle', writes the journalist Peter Murphy in an article on The Frames, 'was a rural idea that took root in the capital city, mainly centred around the busking community on Grafton Street' (2003a: 17). As Murphy describes it, the time was ripe for the emergence in Ireland during the late 1980s of a kind of music that combined elements of punk, hippie and a kind of rootsy rock associated with artists such as Neil Young and Bob Dylan.[38] Although international in impact, the catalyst for the Irish variation on raggle-taggle was the retirement of Mike Scott to Spiddal, Co. Galway in or around 1985, and his recruitment of Noel 'Nollaig' Bridgeman (a veteran of the Irish rock scene) and the accordion virtuoso Sharon Shannon (violinist Steve Wickham, formerly of In Tua Nua, had already joined in October 1984), for a new version of The Waterboys. Scott and friends spent the best part of three years soaking themselves in Irish traditional music and the accompanying lifestyle of western Ireland. They emerged in November 1988 with *Fisherman's Blues*, an album that combined folk, traditional and rock music in daring and exhilarating ways. The album was a commercial and a critical success, and suddenly, raggle-taggle had a sound – a combination of acoustic instruments and a rock rhythm section to perform 'authentic' rootsy (original and covered) material; a look – DMs and sandals, ripped jeans, long hair, beads, bandanas and all manner of gypsy accessories; and an attitude – somewhere between the stoned hippy who came before and the goofy slacker who came later.

One of the Grafton Street busking acts highlighted by Murphy was The Benzini Brothers, 'soon', as he writes, 'to morph into Hothouse Flowers'.[39] Although other musicians represented purer forms of raggle-taggle, this was in fact the band with whom the Irish variation is most closely associated, and that also represented its greatest artistic and commercial achievement. Hothouse Flowers emerged from the Dublin college / underground scene of the mid-1980s; and were subject to many comings and goings and much cross-pollination with other contemporary acts.[40] In 1985, core members Liam O'Maonlai (vocals / keyboards) and Fiachna Ó Braonain (guitar) won Street Entertainers of the Year, an accolade that led to some television work, interest from Bono and eventually the release of a single, 'Love Don't Work This Way' (1987) on U2's Mother Records. An intermission appearance performing 'Don't Go' on The Eurovision Song Contest in 1988 (Johnny Logan had won for Ireland in Brussels the previous year) brought the band to international prominence. The album *People* (1988), which was recorded in London on the London label, reached number two in the British charts in May 1988 and announced the arrival of what looked like being a true force in international rock music for some time to come.

Hothouse Flowers brought the idea, traceable to Morrison's *Astral Weeks* (1969), of Celtic soul fusion to another level. With Morrison the 'Celtic' element was mostly implied, reducible in most instances to an uncertain amalgam of mysticism and anti-materialism. As the products of a middle-class, Irish-speaking Dublin community, however, O'Maonlai and O'Braonain were fully familiar with traditional music and with the highly complex culture to which it made such a seminal contribution. At the same time, they – as much as any of their peers – were heirs to a vast and complex tradition of popular music (including, of course, Morrison himself), to parts of which they were strongly drawn in terms of sentiment, taste and experience. It was these two influences, perhaps irreproducible anywhere else in the world at this point, that came to constitute the Hothouse Flowers sound and that made them such an attractive proposition to so many, albeit for a relatively short period.

People was in fact a stunning debut that introduced many of the characteristic Flowers' sounds. The music was driven by the typical rock rhythm format of guitar, bass and drums, although the use of saxophone (played by Leo Barnes) added an extra colour to the band's palette. Its most distinctive attributes, however, were O'Maonlai's soulful vocal style and his energetic piano playing. Always more or less the focus of attention, he sang with conviction about the dynamics of interpersonal relationships in a style that recalled aspects of gospel and 1960s soul, but that also included recognizable *sean-nós* inflections. All in all, Hothouse Flowers possessed an aura of 'authenticity' (and herein lies the chief source of any raggle-taggle associations) that spoke to that section of the international popular music audience who felt alienated from the concomitant emergence of what, in retrospect, turned out to be the much more influential genres of house, techno and hip hop.

In this respect, 'People' was an entirely appropriate title for an album by a band that had honed its sensibilities amongst the crowds on Grafton Street and that retained a warm, folky feeling for the everyday emotions of everyday people. With some justification it may be claimed that this, and not the glorified showband values of The Commitments, was the real sound of 'Dublin soul'.[41] A second album, tellingly entitled *Home* (although recorded in various locations in Ireland, England and the US), reiterated the musical and lyrical values of *People* and repeated the success of that album to a large extent. Having become so closely associated with one particular form of musical 'authenticity', however, it became difficult to see how the band could grow beyond the values that had accounted for its initial attraction. Guest appearances and a greater concern for trad. forms ensued, but although remaining together in one form or another as a viable concern, Hothouse Flowers faded from view in the latter part of the 1990s.

Many other bands – Paranoid Visions, Dorian Mood, Tuesday Blue, Cry Before Dawn, The Gorehounds, An Emotional Fish – burned briefly in the public imagination, only to fade away when some combination of sound and circumstances deflected attention away from them. Others, such as Hallelujah Freedom, Scale The Heights, The Rocking Chairs, Missing Link, Flex And The Fastweather, Cypress Mine! and My Little Funhouse, warrant barely a footnote in the annals of Irish rock, testament only to the restless energy and impatient desire that characterized the period.

U2–1

Finally in this chapter we come to the band around which most of the issues discussed in this chapter come into sharp focus. Love it or hate it – and the rock music world is roughly equally divided on the point – U2 is unavoidable in the context of Irish rock history insofar as it is both extremely long-lived and extremely successful. The shadow of the U2 colossus lies over all the Irish popular music made after 1980, in terms of sound, attitude, packaging, management, success and so on. As we'll go on to see, expressions of pride and admiration of U2's achievement amongst Irish popular musical agents tend to be counterbalanced by expressions of resentment at their influence and / or scepticism with regard to its achievement. At the same time, U2's shadow extends backwards also, over the rock music that was made before it and that in many different ways contributed to its own possibility. Although the songs remain the same, the pre-1980 music of Van Morrison, Rory Gallagher, Thin Lizzy and The Boomtown Rats *means* something different when considered in light of the success and longevity of U2. All in all, U2 provides, as far as most people are concerned, *the sound of Irish rock* – the reality, as it were, with which alternative realities are obliged to contend.

Sometimes it's only by having a clear sense of what something is *not* that we can come to a clearer appreciation of what it *is*. In this sense, we see that U2 was clearly *not* part of that alternative strain of modern Irish music-making in which rock figures not as an unproblematic medium for the articulation of various responses to the world, but rather one highly contingent voice amongst many, a means to the end of questioning the world and its ways, rather than an end in itself.[42] In this respect, the irony whereby Ireland's most successful rock band developed alongside, and frequently overlapped with, Ireland's greatest *anti*-rock band, has often been remarked (Dunphy 1987: 85–107; Flanagan 1995: 348–9; Waters 1994: 57–65). The Virgin Prunes emerged from the same northside working-class milieu as (at least some members of) U2, and the two came together during the late 1970s to form the famous association that looms so large in the latter's legend. Lypton Village was 'a kind of unofficial opposition to contemporary Irish attitudes and mores' (Smyth 2001: 166), a form of conscious resistance to the perceived atmosphere of hostility and intolerance that hung over contemporary Dublin. The Villagers' flagrant violation of 'the rules' – in terms of behaviour, dress and eventually music – led to a variety of responses from their fellow young Dubliners, ranging from bemusement to violence.[43]

Although fledged, so to speak, in the same nest, U2 and The Virgin Prunes took flight in significantly different directions (although they would eventually meet up again around the time of the Zoo TV tour). The latter group became (after an infamous appearance on that barometer of Irish life, *The Late Late Show*, in October 1979) the island's best-known purveyors of a form of 'art' rock – combining noise and spectacle – which confirmed many people's fears and prejudices about 'the kids'. Indeed, this 'art' dimension (as remarked in an earlier section) – rock as avant-garde, self-conscious 'show' – represented a significant element within post-punk Irish popular music.[44] The Virgin Prunes continued to make this kind of music, upsetting and appalling as many people as they could, well into the 1980s; whether they desired, or indeed could have handled, the kind of mainstream success won by U2 remains a moot point; although at least two former Prunes, Gavin Friday and Guggi, have continued to pursue their independent muses in pursuit of some kind of recognition, the first as a kind of cabaret *artiste* (in the Berlin sense rather than the Ballymote), the second as a painter (again, in the more elevated, although perhaps less remunerative, sense of the term).

U2 was never an avant-garde 'art' band like their fellow Lypton Villagers, then, although it's fair to say that at least some sense of rock music as a kind of carnivalesque or highly sensitized response to prevailing definitions of 'reality' was always present as a factor in its music. It was this sense that was to come to the fore during the 1990s. Neither, however, was U2 solely or wholly identifiable as 'belonging to' any of the dominant post-punk subgenres, or indeed to the 'indie' umbrella under which many of those emerging subgenres tended to be gathered.[45] Despite its profile as a more or less straightforward New Wave band with guitar, bass, drums and vocalist, and despite the gradual revelation of the giants upon whose shoulders it *claimed* to stand, in retrospect it's clear that U2 – like all the most important contributors to the field – *made* its own sound and its own genre to a great extent.

At the same time, U2 (including the manager Paul McGuinness) was also truly original in that it famously bypassed the traditional route that took Irish rock artists through the often soul-destroying cacophony of the London pop world, where sounds, ideas and personalities routinely get lost in the relentless observance of 'business' systems and protocols. There can be no doubting that U2 has extended rock discourse in terms of sound and reach – *what* a song can sound like and *what* it can be about; in those terms alone its place in rock music history is assured. But the band's decision to 'crack' the United States, irrespective of its British profile, should be considered as equally significant as its musical and lyrical innovations, and certainly as one of the most important factors in the development of its own career.

Despite the fact that U2 was less fancied than some of its Irish contemporaries, and despite the perfect vision afforded by retrospect, it's clear from listening to any one of the eleven tracks included on *Boy* (1980) that something new was happening in Irish rock music (although the irony whereby that sound was facilitated by sympathetic non-Irish people, such as producer Steve Lillywhite and Island label owner Chris Blackwell, shouldn't be lost). Different critics and commentators have speculated on what that 'something' might have been, and what it might have meant, such interpretations in time forming part of the mystique surrounding the band. Certainly, there appeared to be a yearning for a new direction; new in musical terms, signalled by the incredibly spacious texture and the innovative approach to phrasing and structure apparent in songs such as 'I Will Follow' and 'A Day Without Me'[46], but new also in terms of the social, cultural and political meanings that were attached to Irish identity at that particular stage in history, and with which the young band members, through accidents of birth and domicile, found themselves having to deal.

Along with its relentless touring of North America, U2 continued to explore a number of musical and extra-musical issues on the albums which followed *Boy*. Aspects of the latter (an uncertain array of religious and lifestyle decisions) threatened to unravel the band around the time of the *October* album (1981); but with the reservations accommodated more or less to everyone's satisfaction, U2 went from strength to strength, with both *War* (1983) and *The Unforgettable Fire* (1984) reaching No. 12 in the US, and hitting the top spot in the UK charts.[47] The latter album inaugurated the band's long association with Brian Eno, a 'name' musician and producer responsible for some of the most significant innovations in modern popular musical discourse. His recruitment was as clear a signal as possible that the restless fire of the first five years was not about to be extinguished, and that U2 was a band determined to continue the search for answers to the questions that had first animated it: what does it mean to be a rock band, to be an Irish rock band, to be an Irish rock band here (wherever) and now (whenever).

In June 1985, four months after it had featured on the cover of *Rolling Stone* as 'Our Choice: Band of the '80s', U2 appeared with a number of other acts at the Band Aid concert in Wembley Stadium, London, organized by fellow Dubliner Bob Geldof. Initially chary of involvement in an event that had all the potential to misfire badly, U2 and its manager were eventually convinced by Geldof's relentless insistence that *something* had to be done immediately to expedite famine relief, in light of the fact that those 'in charge' could apparently no longer be relied upon to do *anything*. Still acutely aware of the dangers of self-aggrandizement, and of the irony of a situation that saw pop stars coming to the aid of famine victims, U2 took to the Wembley stage and delivered a performance that went a considerable way towards vindicating Rolling Stone's assessment, and to securing the Dublin band's identity as the 'best', 'biggest', 'most important' band on the planet for some years to come.

Neither the precise nature nor the long-term impact of U2's triumph at Band Aid are easy to pin down, but a number of causes and consequences suggest themselves. For one thing, despite the unprecedented size of the Live Aid audience, the years touring outside Ireland and the UK had enabled U2 to develop a highly effective stage presence. Since the band's earliest shows in Ireland, Bono had always been a highly mobile and interactive front man, his self-appointed job being to bridge the gap between stage and audience. His 'salvation' of a young female member of the audience during the extended version of 'Bad' at Live Aid may have seemed somewhat calculated to cynics and music industry veterans (whose knives had been out for the whole project since the previous Christmas's Band Aid single), but in fact it was typical of the kind of things he had being doing at U2 concerts for five years, part of the 'oneness' between band and fans that was to become such a significant element of U2's mystique. Added to this is the fact that, as Paul McGuinness subsequently acknowledged (in Heffernan 2000), Bono had intuitively assessed the event as primarily media-oriented and had recognized that such a gesture would have a much more powerful effect upon a television audience of around 1.5 billion than it would upon a live audience of around 75,000.

It would be difficult to calculate how Bono's gesture affected donations on the day, but certainly one of the longer-term effects was to offer a compelling image of rock music's ability to bring strangers temporarily together in pursuit of commonly acknowledged goals. For our purposes here, however, a more significant effect was the emergence of Irish rock – and indeed of Ireland itself – on what was literally a world stage. The Boomtown Rats were more than a little *passé* by 1985, but it was Geldof's anger that galvanized the whole event, and his energy that kept it on the rails when there were so many opportunities for (and so many people willing) it to crash spectacularly. One of the undoubted highpoints of the day occurred when he sang 'and the lesson today is: How to Die' (from 'I Don't Like Mondays'); although written at and for another time, its sudden appropriateness stunned the singer himself and the audience at Wembley and around the world. And if Geldof provided the event's energy and its conscience, U2, whose perceived ability to 'keep it real' contrasted so tellingly with the attitudinizing and bandwagoning of some of the other acts, provided its moral fulcrum. Add to this the fact that the Irish public's contribution to the relief fund was proportionately the highest in the world, and the significance of Live Aid as an event in modern Irish cultural history begins to come into focus.

Many people date the change in modern Irish fortunes to an influx of foreign investment that began around 1994; and we are all familiar by now with the impact that economic 'success' has had, for good and bad, upon life in the Republic in the years since. Nineteen ninety four was also the year in which the IRA ceasefire began, which in turn sparked ceasefires by Loyalist paramilitary organizations and thus inaugurated what came to be known (somewhat optimistically, as it turned out) as 'the peace process'. In line with the Attalian theory that underpins this book, however, it's worth speculating in passing on the degree to which the discourses of 'success' and 'peace', which play such important roles in the narrative of modern Ireland, were anticipated by the events of Live Aid. There could be no more striking image of 'success' than U2's performance on the day; the aura of confidence and conviction that underpinned its performance (despite private misgivings as to both its motivation and its execution) sent a message to Irish people worldwide: *your* response to life is valid and *your* articulation of that response can be both beautiful and compelling.

At the same time, the whole event was a testament to Geldof's ambivalent pride in the name of love; only *he* could have conceived of it, only *he* could have pushed it through despite the contradictions and the doubts. But if on one level Geldof's ability to convert compassion and empathy into positive energies represented some kind of victory over the values of his Irish youth during the 1960s and 1970s, on another level it represented, filtered through the mind and the body of this most prodigal of sons, the triumph of those same values and the realization of their implicit power. Band Aid was many things to many people; for a majority of Irish people at home and abroad it was, both through an identification with its main figure and through a willingness to donate substantial sums of money to strangers in need, an articulation of their desire for peace. It would be almost a decade before that desire found formal political articulation.

With its elevated position within the modern popular musical world firmly established after Band Aid, U2 retired into the studio to begin work on the album that would bring it superstar status. *The Joshua Tree* was released in March 1987, and both media and fan anticipation was answered by a collection immediately acknowledged as a cultural phenomenon and that has since become a landmark in international rock history. Produced to perfection by Daniel Lanois and Brian Eno, (parts of it) mixed with hit-making brio by Steve Lillywhite, and written and performed with stunning levels of skill and imagination by all four band members, *The Joshua Tree* completed U2's move from cult favourites to possible contenders to absolute victors. The record was motivated on the one hand by the band's established concerns with humanitarianism and the nature of 'truth' in the modern world, especially as that 'truth' was refracted through the modern world's dominant political and cultural power, the United States.[48] But it was also inspired by U2's growing fascination with its chosen form: rock 'n' roll music, its range, its limits, its potential.

The Joshua Tree remains the crowning achievement of the first phase of U2's extended career. Interpretations abound, for this great album (like all great art) is a mirror wherein different agents see different things. But of all the many things that *The Joshua Tree* might be, one is the culmination of twenty-five years of Irish rock music. If, on the one hand, the record engages with (and in fact significantly extends) the phenomenon of international rock music, at the same time – and without those involved in its production necessarily being aware of this – it's located on an intertextual network that links every Irish musician since the advent of rock 'n' roll. In this sense, we may claim that Bono's stage persona owes something – however remote, however improbable it may seem – to the charisma of Brendan Bowyer. The former doesn't have to like, or even to have witnessed, the latter to be influenced by, or relatable to, his work; it was there in the culture in which Bono was socialized, in the many and various noises that he was hearing in Ireland in the 1960s and '70s, contributing to his own understanding of stage performance in ways he wouldn't recognize or perhaps wish to acknowledge (and that we, therefore, can't recover). Similarly, the Edge's (anti-) guitar heroics relate to the guitar virtuosity of Rory Gallagher (a performer whom Edge did in fact witness at Ireland's first great modern rock festival at Macroom in the summer of 1977); U2's missionary identity is in dialogue with the gang imagery of Thin Lizzy, mitigating and in turn mitigated by Lynott's electrifying fusion of rock, romanticism and rebellion; and Paul McGuinness's appreciation of what it might mean to develop a successful 'Irish rock band' owes something to the achievements, and indeed the failures, of Horslips. It's one of the main theses of this book that this interconnectedness, this sense of noise echoing back and forth with greater and lesser levels of recognition, is one of the things that being 'an Irish rock band' must mean.

The Joshua Tree represents a moment in which the disparate musical and conceptual concerns that had inspired U2 since its inception are brilliantly reconciled. The accepted wisdom is that, on the following year's *Rattle and Hum*, things had become somewhat imbalanced. U2 was not, despite its best efforts, a kick-ass country-blues band, and it was clear that the search for 'authentic' musical roots and an interest in Americana had taken it in directions that neither its music nor its personalities could sustain. The accompanying film appeared occasionally *blasé* and self-righteous, and the band suffered from a degree of over-exposure which it hadn't had to negotiate up to that point. In retrospect, *Rattle and Hum* can be seen as a strong collection with many compelling moments; in some ways, it's the project that U2 *had* to undertake after the triumph of *The Joshua Tree* and the almost messianic aura that trailed the band in the aftermath of its release. But it was clear to the individual members of U2, at least, that this was the end of a road upon which they had set off from Mount Temple School on Dublin's northside just over a decade earlier. To survive in any self-respecting form, a new road, a new map, had to be discovered, and quickly. To switch the metaphor, U2 had to begin writing a new chapter in the story of themselves – a new chapter for them, and for us.

3

'First We Take Manhattan . . .'
Nineties into Noughties

INTRODUCTION

In the winter of 1986 the Republic of Ireland, according to the then Secretary of the Department of Finance, 'had the statistics of a Third World country' (Mac Sharry and White 2000: 356). The state was all but bankrupt, and neither the elected politicians nor the civil servants seemed capable of doing much about it. Tax and debt were high, living standards and morale were low; unemployment and emigration were spiralling towards record levels; doubt and cynicism were rampant throughout the media. The humiliation of an International Monetary Fund intervention seemed a possibility. In January 1987 the Labour / Fine Gael coalition government collapsed, to be succeeded after the ensuing general election by a minority Fianna Fáil administration. For many, however, it didn't really matter who was nominally 'in power'; like most small, unimportant states, Ireland was understood to be subject to the vicissitudes of international trends and to retain only limited control over its own economic fate.

Economists continue to debate whether the recovery that began to kick in soon afterwards was a return to the longer trajectory set in motion during the 1960s, or whether it represented an entirely new phase in the economic fortunes of the island. The precise reasons underpinning any turnaround are also uncertain. What does seem clear, however, is that the Republic began to experience unprecedented levels of economic growth in the early years of the 1990s, and that this growth very rapidly took on all the attributes of a boom: declining debt, high budget surpluses, low inflation and virtually full employment. In 1994 a London-based American economist came up with a name to describe Ireland's changed economic condition: the Celtic Tiger. And the expansion continued exponentially; more foreign capital led to more employment, especially in the services sector, while higher income and the so-called 'social partnership' system resulted in fewer trade disputes. Confidence bred confidence and by the onset of the new millennium Ireland could boast one of the best-performing economies in the world.

This recovery was complemented by developments in the cultural and political spheres. Mary Robinson, a feminist and civil rights lawyer, was elected President of the Republic in November 1990, and for many people this represented a great leap forward in the state's liberalizing, modernizing programme. Robinson claimed that her incumbency would be characterized by openness, tolerance and inclusiveness: 'The best we can contribute to a new integrated Europe of the 1990s', she said in her inaugural speech, 'is by having a confident sense of our Irishness' (Donovan, Jeffares and Kennelly 1994: 254). One of the clearest indications that this confidence was capable of redefining the meaning of Irishness in an international context was the *Riverdance* phenomenon. From its birth as a five-minute interval act during the 1994 Eurovision Song Contest, *Riverdance* went on to conquer the world, becoming a hugely successful stage show (it won a Grammy in 1997) and one of the best-selling videos ever (Brabazon and Stock 1999: 301–2). The beauty and charisma of the dancers Jean Butler and Michael Flatley, allied with the genius of the composer Bill Whelan, seemed to encapsulate the new Ireland that had emerged from the dark days of the 1980s into the light of a new era. What with a Booker Prize for Roddy Doyle and a Nobel Prize for Seamus Heaney, the 1990s were well on the way to becoming the decade in which Irish culture moved to the centre of the world stage.

The defining moment in the emergence of the new Ireland seemed to have arrived in August 1994 with the announcement of a ceasefire by the IRA. More than any cultural event or economic trend, this apparent commitment to peace signalled an acknowledgement of new times amongst the most ideologically intractable of the island's community, of the inevitability of change and of the desirability of participation in *the* world as opposed to the fetishistic identification of *our* world. The nineteenth-century values which animated the unionist / nationalist struggle have persisted in some forms into the twenty-first century; but at the time it seemed as if those political discourses could not resist the drive towards new definitions of Irishness that was manifest in the economic and cultural spheres.

For some, economic, cultural and political success were the rewards of a new attitude on the part of the Irish towards themselves and towards the rest of the world. Writing in 1988, the philosopher Richard Kearney welcomed the fact that 'our fate as a nation is increasingly influenced by international happenings and accords. "Ourselves Alone" is a catch-cry of the past' (7). 'There is much evidence', he went on to claim,

> that local culture can be enhanced rather than annihilated by contact with other cultures . . . [It] is often by journeying beyond the frontiers of Ireland – either physically or imaginatively – that we find a new desire to return and rediscover what is most valuable in it. Do our artists and musicians not show

us how we can proclaim Irish origins while transcending national barriers and communicating with the citizens of other European and world cultures? In the 1990s nothing should be allowed hinder our entitlement to a triple citizenship – of Ireland, Europe and the world (25).

It's interesting that Kearney should point to the arts, and in particular music, as a model for the renegotiation of Ireland's changing relationship with Europe and the rest of the world, for as we've seen throughout this book (and as we'll see in particular in this chapter) that process of musical renegotiation was neither straightforward nor innocent.

In the meantime, Kearney, like many others, was especially encouraged by the election of Mary Robinson. In an open letter shortly after her triumph, he wrote:

Your election to the highest office of this land was a good day . . . [The] story we are telling ourselves and others in electing you as President is that we are not just natives of an ancient land but citizens of a new society. We have come of age. We have performed a rite of passage from past to future (1991: 309).

Kearney regarded Robinson's victory as one for modernity over tradition, the defeat of 'the native', who is always guarding (sometimes to the point of hysteria and / or violence) the precious identity he received from the past, by 'the citizen', who bravely undertakes to make and remake identity in response to new circumstances. The native was not about to go quietly, however. In pieces such as 'Getting to know Dublin 4' (1993: 186–210), Desmond Fennell attacked what he termed the 'liberal agenda' and the revisionist (by which he understood, anti-Catholic and anti-nationalist) programme promoted by the likes of Kearney. Fennell regarded Robinson as a champion of the 'liberal agenda', with its smug cosmopolitanism and its arrogant dismissal of the beliefs held by the majority of the Irish people. The imagination of Ireland had been hi-jacked by a tiny group of middle-class intellectuals holed up in a south Dublin suburb, whose first allegiance lay with their fellow 'liberals' in Europe rather than with the benighted Irish majority. For anti-revisionists such as Fennell, the apparently benign and reasonable figure of 'the citizen' represents a capitulation to inimical forces (Unionism and European neo-colonialism) and a betrayal of the values which, insofar as it is at all possible, underpin a modern Irish identity.

Irish popular music during the 1990s was implicated in the increasingly malicious debates surrounding revisionism and anti-revisionism. If the former had a sound, for example, it might be something like the one produced by the artist known as Enya. Aided and abetted by the writing / production team of Nicky Ryan and Roma Ryan, the youngest Ó Braonain sibling and former Clannad member managed to catch the vogue for 'New Age' and 'World' music that began to make a significant impression upon the global market towards the end of the 1980s. Characterized by an ethereal vocal style (the result of hundreds of hours of painstaking studio work) and a general 'chilled out' ambience, the music of Enya held an enormous appeal for those many people around the world disposed to consider themselves as affiliated (either by ethnicity or by self-election) with a 'Celtic' perspective – something which, as I suggested in an earlier chapter, was linked with older, less benign ways of viewing Ireland and the Irish. This was not (nor should it necessarily have been) a consideration for Enya, however, who has become a global superstar since bursting onto the scene so spectacularly with *Watermark* (1988) and the international hit single 'Orinoco Flow'. Along with the millions of records, she has helped to sell an idea of Irishness as productive of a certain way of viewing the world and of a certain way of responding to the world in music. The fact of the matter is, however, that, in the era of the Celtic Tiger, Enya's most distinctive 'Irish' attribute is her commercial success.

A general upbeat mood informed the cultural, economic and political spheres throughout the island during the 1990s, and this in turn contributed to the development of a lively indigenous music scene. Music, as we've seen, had been a significant aspect of Irish popular culture throughout the modern era; but it was during the last decade of the old millennium that popular music-making came to the forefront of the Irish cultural consciousness, manifested in an exponential rise in the number of spaces, events and institutions connected with the practice – venues, showcase gigs and tours, recording studios, labels, festivals, publications, electronic media coverage, education, competitions and awards, societies and organizations and so on. 'Music', as Harry White put it, became 'the prepotent symbol of renascent [Irish] culture', the touchstone for national rejuvenation during a period of extended optimism and achievement (1998: 152). The island was awash with more popular artists than at any other time in its modern history, playing more different kinds of music to more discerning and more sophisticated consumers.

Amongst all this heightened activity, however, one central question remained, and in some respects it was the same question that had exercised the Irish popular musical imagination since the 1960s: how do you measure success? True, Ireland now had the economic and technological wherewithal to sustain a healthy domestic scene; true, removed from the spotlight of the UK and the US industries, Ireland could both develop and sustain innovative variations on the main popular musical genres. Many of the most celebrated and successful artists to emerge in Ireland during the 1990s remain virtually unknown outside the island. And therein, of course, lies the rub. No matter how 'successful' a band or an artist may be at home, no matter how challenging or inventive a musical vision they may possess, the fact is that an international recording deal remains the *sine qua non* of real success. Different artists may have different attitudes about the means of achieving such status; in some respects, after all, popular music may be regarded as a history of musicians resisting the attempts of various tiers of management to dictate the tone and trajectory of their careers. But it remains the case that there are few popular artists – in Ireland or elsewhere – who wouldn't swap all the domestic success they could handle for UK or US top ten record. Such is the nature of a discourse in which the drive towards dissemination and acceptance is always mitigating the drive towards articulating a personal musical response to the world.

Musically, the 1990s were dominated by a number of trends and developments, most of which we shall be encountering in the pages which follow. In the US, white-guy rock made a determined comeback in the face of various threats (most significantly rap and hip hop) to its historical hegemony. In the UK, Britpop (in particular the Oasis / Blur wars) and 'laddism' grabbed the headlines. At the same time, two quiet 'noisy' revolutions were taking place on both sides of the Atlantic: the first based on the advent of house and techno music and the associated social practice known as 'clubbing'; the second based on the emergence of the internet as the primary information medium of the modern age, and the threat it came to pose to the popular music industry's established economic infrastructure. Both these phenomena were facilitated to a large extent by technological developments (cheaper hardware and MP3 being probably the most significant) that made home recording and music downloading common practices, and that altered for ever not only the ways in which popular music could be made, but also the ways in which it functioned to create meaning in a variety of social, political and cultural contexts.

Without doubt, the band that most fully represented Irish popular music in the 1990s was The Corrs. This fact may well come as a disappointment to all those artists and acts who have worked hard to extend the perception of Irishness in a modern musical context; but the fact is that this spectacularly successful sibling group has done its bit for extending the musical perception of Irishness, albeit in directions that many people on the domestic scene might not appreciate.

Despite occasionally looking and sounding like the result of an early 1990s New York marketing seminar, The Corrs phenomenon grew from fairly inauspicious, and frankly much less glamorous, roots. The band's home town of Dundalk has not traditionally been regarded as one of the more active of Ireland's pop scenes, although like most other medium-sized towns throughout the island it produced its fair share of showbands. The group formed around the time of Alan Parker's *The Commitments*, with which film all four members were involved to a greater or lesser extent (although it was the youngest sister, Andrea – then as after – who featured most prominently). Under the guidance of its manager John Hughes, the band spent the next few years honing its undoubted instrumental and vocal skills, developing a sound that was deeply unfashionable for a number of years but that had the advantage of distinguishing it from the great variety of music that was being produced in and out of Ireland during the early 1990s. A couple of lucky breaks found The Corrs in New York, pitching to Michael Jackson's sometime producer David Foster, and the rest is history.

Forgiven, Not Forgotten, the band's debut album from 1995, featured a number of Irish tunes incorporating 'traditional' instruments – fiddle, whistle and *bodhrán* – into recognizable 'rock' arrangements which included electric guitars, keyboards and drums. This juxtaposition of old (Irish traditional) and new (pop-rock) had the effect of altering the sound (and thus the meaning) of both these discourses at various points and in various ways. A typical example would be 'Toss the Feathers', a traditional tune that became the band's signature and concert-closer for a long time; although the 'original' melody remains more or less intact throughout the track, the arrangement provides harmonic and rhythmic effects that are clearly derived from a rock idiom. By the same token, many of the album's original 'pop' compositions, such as the track 'Runaway', for example, incorporated sounds and effects which were recognizably 'Irish' (which is to say, traditional). It was this blend of traditional and pop, the modern and the new, that won The Corrs iconographic status as *the* sound of the new Ireland. Here were four glamorous, attractive young people writing, singing and playing popular music that was aimed at an international market, but that was at the same time clearly indebted to a musical tradition that was itself grounded in a local cultural context. No better example of President Robinson's vision of an Irishness open to the world and yet confident of its roots could be found.

As we've seen in earlier chapters, Ireland has produced a number of popular artists since the 1960s who have attempted in one way or another, and with greater and lesser degrees of success, to fuse different musical traditions – Sweeney's Men, Van Morrison, Horslips, Moving Hearts, The Pogues. None of these artists enjoyed the advantage of working in a vibrant, confident culture that was itself supported by a strong economic base. The Corrs exploited their situation brilliantly, producing mainstream, radio-friendly pop with enough of a 'traditional' edge to signal their 'Irishness' and to differentiate them from the lumpen pop mass who are attempting to break into the business during any given period. It's interesting in this respect that the 'traditional' element in the music of The Corrs became less of a feature on their next two albums, *Talk On Corners* (1998) and *In Blue* (2000). As they went on to conquer the world (including the UK, previously impervious to their charms), and as their 'Irishness' became established in the attendant media, the songs gradually grew less 'Irish' in terms of any conventional sonic signifiers. Apart from one or two self-conscious nods to the sound that established them, most of the songs on the two later albums clearly emanate from pop's universalizing 'human' space, a space that is always more or less non-affiliated in any national or ethnic terms.

The Corrs rode to success on the crest of a Celtic wave that would in time be felt around the world. As so many Irish people had been doing for so long, the band came to the US in pursuit of a dream. These representatives of the latest generation succeeded in taking Manhattan, however, in ways that that were unimaginable to their emigrant forefathers, such as the denizens of the Five Points as depicted in Martin Scorcese's *Gangs of New York* (2002), yet another product of the Celtic cultural revolution. Meanwhile, back in the old world, change was also on the agenda.

'. . . THEN WE TAKE BERLIN': U2–II

Nineteen ninety one was one of the most significant years in the history of guitar-oriented rock music. In the UK, Primal Scream's *Screamadelica* (September) offered a definitive statement on the fusion of acid house and indie that bands such as The Happy Mondays and The Stone Roses had been pursuing over the previous two to three years. Critics raved over the album's inspired melding of contemporary dance culture, classic psychedelic and 'traditional' Rolling Stones-style rock. *Screamadelica* was regarded (and in fact became) a touchstone of authentic, independent rock for the 1990s (although both adjectives require serious qualification). The same is true of an album released in November, also on Creation Records: My Bloody Valentine's *Loveless*. Also demonstrating (on tracks such as 'Soon') the influence of contemporary acid house, Kevin Shields' studio *tour de force* justified the faith of the indie rump, and was cited throughout the following decade by rock music-makers worldwide as a primary inspiration.[1]

In the US in September, a little-known band from Seattle called Nirvana released *Nevermind*, a record that was to surpass both *Screamadelica* and *Loveless* in terms of influence (if not originality). The reasons behind the emergence of that kind of music in that kind of place are many and varied, but one clear motivation seems to have been the attempt on the part of young, guitar-wielding white men to respond to the advent of two developments: on the one hand, hip hop, and its effortless relevance to the African-American community, and on the other, dance music and its replacement of rock as music of choice amongst many who would once have gravitated naturally towards the latter. There was a feeling abroad that rock had entered one of its periodic adult-oriented slumps, and that the form needed to rediscover its original 'noisy' identity if it were not to become embarrassingly *passé*, and if the range of pleasures and effects it traditionally afforded were not to disappear entirely. In this context, Nirvana was touted as yet another in the long line of rock 'n' roll saviours. Its 'noisy' music and the part rebel / part slacker iconography of the band's charismatic leader, Kurt Cobain, impacted heavily upon the international musical imagination. Throughout the 1990s, grunge in general and Nirvana / Cobain in particular came to represent an important alternative to the dance and pop discourses that dominated popular music-making practices during that time.

It was against this backdrop that U2 released its sixth studio album in November of 1991: *Achtung Baby*. The story of that album's painful evolution has been told by the American journalist Bill Flanagan in his book *U2 At The End of the World* (1995). That book opens with band and crew regrouping after the cool critical response to *Rattle and Hum* and holing up in a Berlin studio in desperate search of some reason to continue. As Flanagan points out, the choice of location was portentous, both for its historical associations (Berlin had been the ultimate symbol of Cold War antagonism, and was at the centre of the changes that were about to overtake Europe as the Soviet empire first crumbled and then, in September of 1991, collapsed), and for its musical associations (the Hansa studio in Berlin used by U2 was where David Bowie had embarked upon one of his periodic career relaunches, recording the classic albums *Low* and *Heroes* there with Eno in the mid-seventies). Change – political, cultural, technological – was in the air; given their background and their sense of themselves as musicians and as people, it was clear to the individual members of U2 that the band must change or die.

It's a testament to the intelligence and the courage of the U2 team that at that particular stage in its career it managed to make a record that was locked into, but not overcome by, the musical *Zeitgeist*.[2] The introduction of noises, rhythms and attitudes related to contemporary dance culture left the group vulnerable to accusations of bandwagoning of the worst kind. U2's achievement on *Achtung Baby*, however, was to engage with the issues raised by those sounds, rhythms and attitudes, but to do so in relation to the formal and conceptual issues that had exercised it from the beginning. The result was a record that was both unfamiliar and familiar, totally unlike anything it had attempted before, and yet at the same time uncannily connected with everything it had ever recorded. The personae and situations introduced by Bono, no less than the sounds and rhythms introduced by the rest of the band, were clearly locatable along the trajectory that had been emerging ever since *Boy* over a decade before. Critics and fans alike recognized this, and were prepared to accept and engage with the music on those terms.[3] This was not a case of old rockers chancing their arms, but a serious response to a new cultural phenomenon – an examination of what would happen when the traditional U2 rock protagonist encountered the alternative mental, physical and emotional demands of dance culture and the technology that facilitated its emergence.[4] It was a fascinating prospect, brilliantly conceived and executed.

The heavy voice distortion on 'Zoo Station' (the opening track of *Achtung Baby*) is an obvious example of this familiar / unfamiliar dialectic: it clearly *is* Bono singing (this is a U2 album, after all), but singing in a way that, and about things with which, up until that point, we wouldn't normally associate him. *The Joshua Tree* had been heroic, politically confident and morally unambiguous, and this was reflected in the pure tones and textures of the music and in the 'natural' desert environment which was that album's informing metaphor. From the opening few minutes it's immediately clear that this new record will be about the claustrophobia of the city streets and the ambivalent moral choices that arise there, as reflected in the urgent, hustling rhythms and 'dirty', noisy textures of the music. 'Zoo Station' combines the metaphor of a train moving through the city at night – with conventional connotations of speed, power and glamour – with that of a car which is at once gridlocked and careering out of control. Intentional or not, the confusion ensuing from this array of images sets the tone for an album that is specifically all about confusion, about what happens to the hero of *The Joshua Tree* when he confronts the alternative environment of the city with its attractions (speed, glamour etc.) and its dangers (frustration, loss of control etc.).

On a collection of memorable songs, it was perhaps 'The Fly' that best encapsulated U2's new / old identity. The protagonist is one with whom live audiences across the world would become familiar over the next few years – the louche, slightly camp, wise-cracking 'Fly', whose personality combined stereotypical elements of European decadence and American chutzpah. A figure further from the various heroic, 'grounded' Bono personae of the 1980s is hard to imagine. The lyric dramatizes the end of a relationship, with the Fly casually dumping his lover by telephone so as to enable him to pursue a new conquest who will, no doubt, be dumped in turn. All the values that had characterized U2 during the 1980s – passion, honour, honesty, integrity, fidelity – are invoked only to be rejected. The body, once merely the material vessel for the conscience, has become dominant, demanding satisfaction and amusement, and dismissing the conscience as a pest.[5] In terms of the drugs that were to dominate the dance music scene throughout the 1990s, the Fly's attitude here might be described as typically cocaine- rather than ecstasy-driven: egocentric, paranoid, self-deluded and exploitative (Robb 1999: 55–60).

Changes in U2's studio identity precipitated changes in the organization's attitude towards live performance. Bolstered by the commercial and critical success of *Achtung Baby*, and with its reputation as the 'biggest' band on the planet intact, U2 was in the fortunate position of being able to fund the technology that would meet its creative vision for a new kind of 'gig'. The result was Zoo TV, an amalgam of sound, vision and atmosphere that represented a revolutionary assault upon the received parameters of live rock music (Cunningham 1999: 147–90; Scrimgeour 2004: 84–124).

Whilst touring Zoo TV throughout the world over the following months, U2 began to write, rehearse and (during flying visits home to Dublin in the spring of 1993) record material for a new album that would eventually be released in July of that year under the title *Zooropa*. Although some members of the band were unhappy with the rushed nature of the project and, as a consequence, dissatisfied with the final version, the album topped the charts on both sides of the Atlantic. In formal and conceptual terms, *Zooropa* continued where *Achtung Baby* had left off. The music was far removed from the traditional 'rock' format with which U2 had become identified during the 1980s: solid rhythm section, chiming guitars, soaring vocals and an overall energy and direction that became characteristic of the U2 'sound'. A typical song such as 'Where The Streets Have No Name' – in many ways the epitome (both musically and lyrically) of U2's career up to that time – represents an identifying statement by the collective identity that is the band: this is *our* vision of the world, expressed in *our* idiom. On *Zooropa*, however, a sort of confused, jaded atmosphere permeates the album; the music becomes a noise amongst other noises, part of an overheard contemporary soundscape rather than (as on *The Joshua Tree* and previous albums) some kind of meaningful discourse plucked from the surrounding cacophony.

Thematically, likewise, *Zooropa* reveals a protagonist coming to terms with his ambivalent inheritance rather that attempting to dominate or overcome it in some way. In this sense, 'Zooropa' is both a place and a set of values. On the one hand, it connotes excitement, exhilaration and freedom from constraint and tradition – this is U2 the international rock group with its collective finger on the pulse, its roots left far behind, its command of state-of-the-art technology affording full access to the pleasures of global culture. The concomitant of this, however, is that 'Zooropa' also connotes homelessness, estrangement, lack of community and loss of identity. Of course, there had been uncertainty and anxiety on *The Joshua Tree*; but whereas both the music and the heroic lyrical content of that album suggested that the hero would eventually find what he was looking for, for the protagonist of *Zooropa* there can be no such certainty – no return to the past, no home within the present, no resolution in the future. 'Faraway' may be both exhilarating (not far enough) and alienating (too far); 'so close' may be both reassuring (close enough) and stifling (too close). The only sensible response to this situation is the characteristically post-modern one which claims that 'uncertainty can be a guiding light' – which is to say, when there are no acceptable solutions, no answers that won't lead you back down a blind alley or forward to a false dawn, it is better to embrace contradiction rather than to fret over it.[6]

From the heroin-chic minimalism of 'Numb', through the suffocating disco of 'Lemon', and on to the American gothic of 'The Wanderer' (guest-sung by the late Johnny Cash), U2 offered its listeners an aural blueprint for survival in the post-modern world. This blueprint would become particularly relevant to an Irish audience, for in many ways the predicament that the band was dramatizing was the one faced during the 1990s by a generation of Irish people (in Ireland and amongst the enormous diaspora) that had been propelled into the future before the past had, so to speak, been properly finished. During the 1990s (as mentioned in the intro-duction to this chapter) the values and practices which had sustained Irish life since the revolution of the early twentieth century began to come under severe pressure in the face of rapid economic and social change. Because they were themselves implicated in this process, the traditional institutions of the public sphere, such as the Catholic Church, the political system, and the media, proved unequal to the task of formulating adequate discourses to enable subjects to cope with these changes to their lives and to the society they shared. In this context, the music of U2 was not so much a *reflection* of society as an *anticipation* of it; before change – in the form of the Celtic Tiger – impacted upon Irish society itself, both *Achtung Baby* and *Zooropa* described the interpersonal crises and socio-political dilemmas precipitated by rapidly changing circumstances. And they did it in a way you could dance to.

If U2's first two albums of the 1990s succeeded in winning friends and influencing people, there was a general feeling abroad that on *Original Soundtracks I* (1995) and *Pop* (1997) the band had overstepped the mark. So far had the music on the former album departed from the 'real' U2 sound that a new 'band', Passengers, also featuring Brian Eno and Luciano Pavarotti, was formed so as to placate a worried Island label management, and so as not to alienate the fan base that the band had worked so long and so hard to build. In any case, the music was uneven, with little of the animating passion of *Achtung Baby* or of *Zooropa*'s restive spirit. Fan devotion and another mammoth global tour helped to send *Pop* to the top of the charts around the world, but it had become clear to the band and their association that, just as a decade earlier, a turning point had been reached and either a viable new direction or a graceful retirement was the order of the day.

U2 was treading water in the late 1990s with a compilation album of material from the first decade of its career. Although a success, it was further fuel for the critical talk about the band having reached the end of *the*, as opposed to *a*, line. But in 1999 rumours began to circulate of a new U2 album, one that would signal the band's return to the pop-rock fold after the musical adventures of the 1990s. Rather than the much-vaunted return to a classic U2 sound circa *The Joshua Tree*, however, *All That You Can't Leave Behind* (2000) was another 'Greatest Hits' album, albeit with new songs. Deferring to the pop nous that had always enabled them to stay one step ahead of prevailing fashion, U2 forsook its extended flirtation with dance music and re-ignited the old love affair with classic rock. It was as if the Fly had returned home to his flat after a night's debauchery where, finally perceiving the moral vacuum at the centre of his life, and in an effort to purify his spirit, he began to listen to all the classic songs that had inspired his younger self.

The album opened with 'Beautiful Day' (also the first single), a track that could function as a master class in U2 for anyone unfamiliar with the band's history. Peppered with religious and environmentalist allusions, the song had all the panoramic sweep, the proselytizing intensity and the dogged optimism of their output during the 1980s. The music and the production likewise harked back to a pre-*Achtung Baby* era, recapturing the texture and colour that had provided U2 with such an immediately recognizable sound. The Edge had rediscovered his fascination with the guitar, while the rhythm section seemed content to provide the rock-steady chassis that held everything together. The 'real' Bono had likewise returned, albeit with some obvious scarring left over from his days as the Fly. A clear sign that U2 wished to 'matter' again was the fact that 'Beautiful Day' was (like many of its 'bigger' songs) mixed by Steve Lillywhite, a proven 'hit' producer with whom the band had kept faith since *Boy* (1980), despite the dominating influence in the intervening period of the more expansive sonic imaginations of Daniel Lanois and Brian Eno.

With the wisdom won only through long nights and hard experience, 'Beautiful Day' insists on the necessity for hope in a hopeless world. It's also (as references to the lack of 'space to rent in this town' and to the gridlocked traffic system suggest) a song about Dublin, which is to say, a song about 'home'. (A song with that title was apparently omitted from the album.) Of course, you don't *have* to get these references to appreciate the music. Like much of the material here and throughout the U2 canon, meaning operates on the interface between local and global experience. Identity is not a matter of the codes and practices identifiable in relation to Irish life; rather, it inheres in the ways in which Irish life (and what is that?) is modified by, but also modifies, off-shore discourses and practices. In typical postmodernist fashion, the point is to travel, to be 'on the road' (or, as the album cover depicts, to be at the airport getting ready to travel), not to arrive at a specific 'destination'. The home for which U2 has been searching since 'I Will Follow' is not a geographical location – not Dublin nor Berlin nor New York – but an existential state in which identity would be capable of acknowledging its absolute reliance upon otherness. The residual religious imagery may continue to grate, but one way of describing that state is a 'beautiful day'.

It's difficult to get an idea of the shape of an artistic career while it's still ongoing, and even more difficult to assess the function of that career in relation to the societies upon which it has impacted. After they had split, one critic observed that the music of The Beatles might be considered in terms of the same age conceit that he observed informing Beethoven's *oeuvre*, in which the passion of youth gave way to the maturity and responsibility of middle age, before old age arrived bringing an array of ironic, multi-faceted perspectives (Mellers 1973: 101). This analogy may be applicable to any artist whose career stretches over a significant period of time; and even though what might count as a 'significant' period in popular musical discourse is constantly changing, it's interesting to take an overview of U2's career to date in the light of this conceit. From the wide-eyed, youthful energy of *Boy*, *October* and *War*, through the growing maturity of *The Unforgettable Fire*, *The Joshua Tree* and *Rattle and Hum*, and on to the 'been there, done that' attitudes of *Achtung Baby*, *Zooropa* and *Pop*, the music of U2 has reflected the band's own aging process while also charting the emergence and development of the post-modern subject and his her response to the world. It's unusual (even in the art tradition) for an artist to get beyond this model, which is why *All That You Can't Leave Behind*, with its creative meshing of discourses from all the band's previous incarnations, was such an impressive achievement.

While on the one hand U2's extended career has obviously been an index of the musicians' own lives, on the other it has also always been closely locked in to the country with which they are so readily identified – reflecting changes in Irish life in the period on either side of the millennium, anticipating shifts in attitude and practice, and filling in the gaps left by other socially salient narratives. Despite the mini-industry that emerged in the wake of the band (Mother Records, the Clarence Hotel with its ultra trendy Kitchen nightclub), its regular live performances, culminating in two huge outdoor gigs at Slane Castle in the Summer of 2001 and so on, and despite Bono's high profile as an intelligent sponsor of peace in Ireland and elsewhere, U2's true contribution to Irish life since 1980 has been largely to do with intangibles such as attitude, self-confidence and atmosphere. It started off in a country where failure was endemic; they soundtracked the emergence of a country where success came to be worshipped. Perhaps the band's greatest achievement has been to encourage people to consider the relationship between these two countries, these Irelands of the mind – what was left behind when the old Ireland was jettisoned, and what was gained (and lost) when the new Ireland was embraced.

THE GIRL WITH THE THORN IN HER SIDE

The 1990s witnessed the emergence of what became known to commentators on popular culture as 'laddism'. As with any modern cultural phenomenon, it's difficult to track the chain of cause and effect that underpinned 'laddism', but certainly some of its associated manifestations included the economic revitalization of soccer in the UK, the success of post-feminist magazines such as *Loaded* and *Q*, a backlash against the 1980s model of intellectualized, emasculated masculinity, and (of most concern to us here) the revival of guitar-based indie rock in the wake of the Oasis circus. If 'laddism' was on the one hand a positive reclamation of core male values in what seemed to many to be an increasingly androgynous world, it was at the same time an answer to the fantasy of all those sexists driven underground by political correctness and the feminist advances of previous generations. Removed from its innocuous sit-com context, the idea of 'men behaving badly' could function in much more troubling and offensive ways, providing a licence for the indulgence of many suspect attitudes and practices.

'Laddism' was predominantly a British phenomenon, and should be considered as a response in large part to that culture's complex post-war gender politics. The same period also witnessed (for the most part in the US) the emergence of the underground phenomenon known as 'Riot Grrrl', a subcultural affiliation of young women playing a kind of music that took its sonic references from punk and its ideological references from a form of 'radical' feminism (Kearney 1997; Miles 1998: 52). Too challenging for even the more indie fringes of the mainstream, 'Riot Grrrl' nevertheless was an important and influential response to the continued male hegemony of the music business. The British response was 'Girl Power', a watered-down version of feminism forever to be associated with The Spice Girls. Deliberately manufactured for blanket market coverage (although with special appeal for prepubescent consumers), 'Girl Power' masked its deeply reactionary gender politics behind a veneer of female 'empowerment'; as the band member Geri Halliwell (Ginger Spice) put it: 'It's like feminism, but you don't have to burn your bra' (quoted in Davies 1999: 163). That former British Prime Minister Margaret Thatcher was cited by some of The Spice Girls as one of their chief inspirations gave a clue as to the band's true orientation.[7]

Again, the provenance of both 'Riot Grrrl' and 'Girl Power' are convoluted, and the 'movements' (such as they were) should be approached as parts of an evolving history of gender relations. But of all the many factors which informed women's engagement with modern popular music, one was quite clearly the politics of a cultural form that throughout its history had (with a few notable exceptions) systematically deferred to a range of received, stereotypical gender identities.[8] With its roots in the blues and country music, perhaps it's not surprising that the cluster of genres derived from rock 'n' roll is culpable in this regard; but the fact is that the greater mass of post-Elvis popular music was inherently masculinist and implicitly sexist, and this includes not only the routinely vilified 'mainstream' but also those acts and genres widely celebrated even today as more 'progressive', sub- or counter-cultural, including The Beatles, hippy and punk.[9] This led in time to the curious situation in which (as Barbara Bradby describes it) feminists were

> suspicious of pop music as typifying everything that needs changing for girls in society, and of rock music as a masculine culture that excludes women. Conversely, those who wished to celebrate the political oppositionality of rock music have often had to draw an embarrassed veil around its sexual politics (1993: 155).

Modern Irish popular music emerged in a society that was deeply conservative with regard to traditional gender roles, and this coloured the development of the practice at every level. Irrespective of 'political' bent (which, by and large, meant class or ethnic provenance), island culture was predicated on a core male / female binary division and its many stereotypical connotations: public, active, intellectual / private, passive, body-oriented. Such a division was indeed famously inscribed in the southern Constitution of 1937, in which document Irish women were encouraged to embrace their 'natural' roles as child-bearers and housewives.[10] This meant that the scope for female engagement with any aspect of popular culture – especially one so suspiciously 'foreign' as modern musical entertainment – was extremely limited. Thus, the idea of a female showband musician was more or less totally unknown during the 1950s and early 1960s. As Vincent Power says: 'The business was a bastion of male supremacy' (2000: 21). Where, after all, would such a woman have found the time or the motivation to learn an instrument? And if she had, wasn't there something decidedly vulgar – dangerous, even – about her participation in this overwhelmingly male preserve?; dangerous for herself, certainly, when one thought about the rigours of life on the road, but also, insofar as exposure to a young, glamorous woman could lead the men (including the showband musicians) of Ireland astray, dangerous for the institution of marriage, and thus the fabric of society.[11]

When Eileen Reid recorded 'I Gave My Wedding Dress Away' with The Cadets in 1964, she touched a nerve amongst Irish people all across the country; the song – in which the protagonist sacrifices her man and her chance of happiness through marriage for a beloved younger sister – became one of the biggest Irish hits of the decade. Thereafter, women singers became more common[12], although the material they sang more or less exclusively concerned fulfilling themselves through the acquisition of a man, marriage and children. Female musicians remained extremely rare on the showband scene throughout the 1960s and 70s, their role being based around the provision of 'glamour' rather than of any peculiar musical effect or element. The boys in the band did the real 'work', providing the musical accompaniment that itself was based on long hours of practice and the camaraderie of ensemble performance. The contradictions inherent in this discourse – 'glamorous' women singing about the need to become housewives, male musicians pursuing shared experiences based on skill and finesse – was rarely remarked.

This situation was mirrored in the folk-trad. revival towards the end of the 1960s, in which there was also a dearth of female singers and almost a complete absence of female musicians. Even in the supposedly more liberated world view of this ethnic-hippy hybrid, men were still regarded as the primary influence, the ones who would decide on musical direction, who would have (and take) the time to master an instrument and learn new material, who would organize the practicalities of gigging and touring and arrangements and recording and so on. Women musicians there were, but this was considered a bonus or a novelty; principally, performers such as Adrienne Johnston, Gay Woods and Alison O'Donnell could only become accepted as song 'interpreters', a specialized 'feminine' role which (as we'll go on to see) women have continued to play in one form or another down to the present day.

Pop and folk-trad. managed to find some roles – albeit of a restricted variety – for women. The same cannot be said of the Irish rock scene, the major figures in the development of which all articulated strongly male-centred perspectives, albeit in a variety of forms. The mystic soul music of Van Morrison, Rory Gallagher's bluesman persona, Philip Lynott's bifurcated rocker-romantic, the punk-inspired anger of Bob Geldof, the evolving hero of the U2 canon – all these depended to a greater or lesser extent upon that traditional model of gender relations described above, in which male desire is predicated upon a range of stereotypical female characteristics and attributes. From song protagonist to intended consumer, from senior band and label management to lowly roadie, Irish popular music was – as elsewhere – almost exclusively a male domain.

The first cracks in the male monopoly of Irish rock began to appear during and after punk's somewhat belated impact upon the domestic scene. All-female band The Boy Scoutz appeared in 1977, and although they left no recordings for posterity (in which sense they were truer to the punk ideal than most of their contemporaries), their importance lay as much in what they represented as in what they sounded like.[13] The classic rock ideal that had been formulated during the middle years of the 1960s, and that drew on a range of American popular genres (most centrally the blues family) from earlier in the century, made little or no provision for female contributions, other than that of singer-interpreter. Thus, the image of a guitar- or drum-wielding woman – let alone an entire band of them – was an affront to many people's perception of what rock music should be, especially in a country such as Ireland where women were traditionally so disabled *vis-à-vis* the national cultural imagination.

Despite the widening opportunities created by the appearance of international female stars such as Debbie Harry, Chrissie Hynde and Patti Smith, the immediate post-punk era failed to produce a credible Irish female popular music figure. In 1980, Gay Woods emerged from folk obscurity (and from the shadow of her husband Terry) to form Auto da Fé. Tracks such as the Phil Lynott-produced 'November, November' combined the folkiness of Woods' earlier career with a sound and a look associated with the British New Wave. The result was attractive and interesting – especially for those familiar with her former incarnation as 'authentic' folk singer – but hardly compelling. Other performers of note included Leslie Dowdall, the vocalist with 'Celtic' rock band In Tua Nua, and Flo McSweeney, the vocalist with one of the later versions of Moving Hearts – both of whom remained active in the Irish popular music scene in the years that followed.

Two of the more independently minded women to emerge during the 1980s were Cait O'Riordan, bass player and occasional singer with The Pogues, and Galway-based blues singer Mary Coughlan. For a number of years O'Riordan kept pace with the male Pogues, both in musical and extramural leisure pursuits, before bailing out in August 1986. Slightness of body, a punky look and a traditional 'male' instrument combined to create a complex iconography that had never been encountered in Irish popular musical discourse up until that point.[14] This complexity is encapsulated on 'I'm a Man You Don't Meet Everyday' from 1985's *Rum, Sodomy And The Lash* album; in her sweet, melodic female voice, O'Riordan sings a song in the persona of a boastful, assertive man, and the effect is both unsettling and disorienting.

Released in the same year, Mary Coughlan's debut album, *Tired And Emotional*, also made play with generic and personal boundaries. Coughlan hailed from Galway and was already a separated mother of three by the time she turned to the possibility of making music for a living. Espousing strong feminist views at a time when more and more Irish women were joining the fight for rights, Coughlan sang a form of 'Irish blues', a genre adopted to suit her own circumstances and experiences.[15] Such an obvious identification between the kind of person Coughlan *was* and the kind of music she *made* was, again, something relatively new on the Irish popular music scene, and it paved the way for future interventions that would also draw on this blurring of textual and autobiographical discourses. In fact, taking the careers of O'Riordan and Coughlan together, we see how these two cleared a path for undoubtedly the most important female figure ever to emerge from the Irish popular music scene: Sinéad O'Connor.[16]

To appreciate fully both the nature and the force of O'Connor's impact upon Irish popular musical discourse, it's necessary to consider the ways in which women traditionally figured in that discourse. Because of the peculiar cultural conditions noted in Chapter One, acoustic-related music remained important in Ireland, even as rock and other related forms have developed. One of the effects of this was that a kind of adult-oriented, easy-listening, acoustic-based folk-pop emerged as a major form on the Irish popular music. During the same period, women (as remarked above) continued to be regarded principally as singers, interpreters who could successfully 'play' the persona in the song, adding glamour and drama while the boys in the band took care of the real business. During the 1970s and 1980s these two trends came together, the result being the emergence of a number of female artists who specialized in a kind of music that incorporated elements of folk, traditional and pop music. Some of the performers associated with this broad school include Mary Black, Frances Black, Dolores Keane and Maura O'Connell.[17]

All these trends and traditions were united on a record that became a phenomenon in modern Irish popular culture. Besides the performers mentioned above, *A Woman's Heart* (1992) also included material by trad. sensation Sharon Shannon, and the woman who conceived of and organized the project, Eleanor McEvoy (who also wrote and performed the title track). *A Woman's Heart* was a huge seller on the Irish market and went on to become something like a franchise, with other albums appearing that also featured a variety of female performers. At the same time, it generated much debate over the role and representation of women in contemporary Ireland, and especially within the music industry. While some regarded it as entirely positive evidence of the emergence of Irish women to a sense of their own power and the validity of their experiences, others saw it as part of their continued ghettoization, a combination of special pleading and victimhood that confirmed received thinking regarding gender divisions in Irish society.

As an instrument-playing musician, McEvoy had experienced the sexism that was endemic within the Irish music industry (Rowley 1993: 80–1). Her response, however – a kind of reverse sexism in which supposedly 'essential' female characteristics are singled out for celebration – was vulnerable to co-option by those oppositionalist discourses upon which sexism, in Ireland as elsewhere, depends for its survival.[18] This was in marked contrast to the work of O'Connor, whose representation of an Irish female identity was altogether a more challenging prospect.

O'Connor was already an international pop star by the time of *A Woman's Heart* appeared in the summer of 1992. Most commentators note that after spells with In

Tua Nua and Ton Ton Macoute in the mid 1980s, she signed a solo deal with the Ensign label of London, but this early decision to forsake ensemble performance and strike out on her own is more significant than is perhaps generally understood. So strongly has O'Connor's iconography as a solo artist become established that it's difficult to imagine her as part of any permanent collective, yet it was neither always nor naturally so. But there is a marked difference, as suggested above, between the band-fronting female singer (such as Leslie Dowdall, who eventually took over vocal duties with In Tua Nua) and the individual female artist backed by a collection of more or less anonymous session musicians. From an early point in her career, O'Connor disdained the former and embraced the latter – and the independence and loneliness that are its corollaries. The decision to 'be' Sinéad O'Connor also helps to account for another of the distinguishing characteristics of her career: constant collaboration with other artists with whom in her loneliness she wishes to express some form of solidarity, and who in their turn wish to benefit from her independent iconographic values.

O'Connor's challenge lay not in the outright rejection of traditional narratives, but in unsettling and reworking them in new contexts and in new combinations. From the beginning of her career, for example, O'Connor fostered a close identification between her personal image and the music she made. In musical terms, she deliberately mixed traditional 'feminine' qualities – melody, sweetness of voice, an extraordinary purity of tone – with 'unfeminine' associations – the uncompromising power encoded into early tracks such as 'Mandinka', for example, or the assertive sexuality of 'I Want Your (Hands on Me').[19] This was mirrored at a personal level, as the beauty, innocence and vulnerability suggested by O'Connor's slight figure was offset by her shaven head (suggestive since the 1960s of the violent skinhead subculture) and confrontational dress style (including Doc Marten 'bovver' boots). The flexible economy of desire created by this enigmatic iconography proved fascinating for both male and female consumers; O'Connor's first album, *The Lion and the Cobra*, appeared in November 1987 and sold well in both the UK and the US.

The groundwork of the first album was brilliantly exploited on 'Nothing Compares 2 U', O'Connor's version of a relatively obscure song by the American artist Prince that turned her from promising newcomer into worldwide superstar. The key to the single's success (and to the album *I Do Not Want What I Haven't Got* which it catapulted to number one on both sides of the Atlantic) was the remarkable video that accompanied it. Its simplicity – an uncut black and white shot of the artist's (still shaven) head and shoulders as she performed the song to camera – only served to accentuate the emotional drama of the lyric, while the apparently genuine tears shed by O'Connor during the performance not only challenged the established boundaries between life and art, but also exposed the contradictory values upon which her image was built. She is alone (with connotations of strength and independence) but tearful (showing her vulnerability and weakness), unconventional with her shaved head and her black polo-necked sweater, but absolutely recognizable insofar as she is a woman crying (apparently) because of a man. The fundamental contradictions which this famous video performance reveals is linked to O'Connor's wider career, and also at a deeper level to her inheritance as an Irish female musician.

Keith Negus noted that a recurring feature of O'Connor's music was

> the use of two distinct voices: a more private, confessional, restrained, and inti-
> mate voice; and a harsher, declamatory, more public and often nasal voice that
> she frequently slides into a snarl or shout. There is often a tension present
> throughout many of Sinéad's vocal performances, between a more vulnerable
> and uncertain voice, and a more imperative and assertive voice (1995: 221).

This oscillation between 'voices' may be heard, for example, on 'Nothing Com-pares 2 U', with lines such as the repeated 'since you took your love away' from the first verse representing the former, while the later section beginning 'I went to the doctor' represent the latter. These contrasting styles – arising from O'Connor's image as both vulnerable *and* aggressive – can create recording problems, for whereas the 'confessional' voice tends to be closely miked, contributing to the impression of intimacy and close proximity to the listener, the 'more imperative and assertive voice' is less breathy and can, if not handled correctly at both record-ing and mixing stages, create specific sound and level anomalies.

The strategies which make O'Connor's identity as a woman problematic serve also to make her identity as an *Irish* woman equally problematic. As Noel McLaughlin and Martin McLoone point out, 'what makes her challenging is the way in which she employs a range of performance strategies deliberately to unset-tle and disturb traditional notions of Irishness' (2000: 193). Again, this challenge arises from a combination of image and sound: the way she looks, the way she acts in a media context and the way she sings. The music, as remarked above, did not conform, in either its recording practices or its performance values, to estab-lished discourses of Irish womanhood. On tracks such as 'I Am Stretched on Your Grave' and 'You Have Made Me the Thief Of Your Heart', O'Connor blends tradi-tional song styles, and their traditional notions of femininity, with different music styles possessed of different gender imagery. At the same time, not only did O'Connor *sound* different, she *looked* different; the skinhead image (arising in the first instance from an English subculture) was sending a number of contradictory messages when transposed onto the body of an Irish woman. The fact was that this Irish woman looked like none ever had, with the result that the critical insti-tutions struggled to 'make sense' of her and her music.

Added to this was O'Connor's public criticism of the role and representation of women in Irish society and her willingness to engage in public controversy, especially with regard to religion and politics. Her music makes common cause with the downtrodden and the underrepresented everywhere, whether they be children, black boys on mopeds, or nineteenth-century famine victims. It's unclear the extent to which this self-elected public role derived from her personal experience as daughter, partner and mother, or from the inheritance provided by pioneering Irish feminists from the 1960s and 1970s. In any event, O'Connor's willingness to intervene contributed to her notoriety and was in marked contrast to the *Woman's Heart* artists whose ostensible 'feminist' agenda in fact colluded at a deep level with received images of Irish femininity.

O'Connor continued to 'keep it real' throughout the 1990s, with the albums *Am I Not Your Girl?* (1992) and *Universal Mother* (1994) revealing her range and ambition. The thing about 'established discourses' and 'received images', however, is that they have the force of time and tradition behind them, insinuating their way into every-day practice so that they become natural, obvious, just the way things are. At the same time, it became increasingly clear as the 1990s progressed that O'Connor's stance – or rather people's response to her stance – was making intense personal demands upon the artist herself. As her genuine vulnerability became apparent, what McLaughlan and McLoone refer to as the 'complexity and contradiction' of O'Connor's music was swept aside. Her appearance on the second volume of *A Woman's Heart* contributed to her reclamation for 'a familiar discourse about nature' (2000: 193), while the radical force of her original 'bolshy' identity began to be lost as she was increasingly co-opted for a traditional narrative of Irish femininity.[20] The release in 2002 of *Sean-Nós Nua* represented a further (and perhaps final) stage in O'Connor's negotiation of an Irish female musical identity.

O'Connor's music revealed another side to popular music's obsession with sex and sexuality. At the same time, she helped to open doors in Irish life through which many women would pass. It's always difficult to recognize after the fact (com-placency may be the one universal human attribute), but Ireland was a different place when Sinéad O'Connor broke onto the popular music scene towards the end of the 1980s, with more restraints on intellectual freedom and fewer opportunities to explore and / or express one's sexual identity. Building on the efforts of those who had been kicking against the official pricks since the foundation of the southern state, O'Connor brought her anger, her energy and her high public profile to bear upon issues that have passed into history, fighting for rights that a subsequent generation has come to regard as obvious.

IRISH POP – THE RETURN OF THE REPRESSED?

Rock musicians have always considered themselves to be much more subversive than their pop counterparts in respect of prevailing socio-cultural mores and prac-tices. Tracing its genealogy back through jazz and the blues, rock began to develop its characteristic countercultural identity as it was emerging during the 1960s. The many and varied subgenres to which rock gave rise have, by and large, subscribed to the same notion. Successive generations have reinvented the mythology of rock as a form of outsider, outlaw music, the performance and consumption of which supposedly implicates its adherents in a long and celebrated renegade tradition.

Pop music, on the other hand, was clearly on the side of law. Formulaic and manufactured, pop colludes (so the story goes) with the establishment – a form of standardized machine music that systematically robs you of your individuality. Its insistent hooks and melodies have more in common with advertising than with art, while its lyrical obsession with love lost and found has been responsible for some of the most inane doggerel ever to emerge from the human mind. If rock is an adult male music – hard and complex – then pop is an adolescent female music – soft and simple. In short, for many people in the modern world, rock and pop represented opposed attitudes to music, life, the universe and everything.

In its modern rendition, this model derives from Adorno's mid-twentieth-century critique of popular music, in which he characterized the practice as formulaic and (although he wouldn't have used the term) soulless. Drawing on his experiences of wartime America, the famous Frankfurt critic had no doubt that popular music was a mechanism of institutional state repression. The music itself was always 'pre-digested' (1994: 206), characterized by patterns that were both technologically determined and (as a consequence) relentlessly standardized, patterns that obviate any original or creative response to the music. This, from Adorno's Marxian perspective, was the real tragedy; and despite his contempt for what he described as 'all the swarming forms of the banal' (1978: 274), his real ire was reserved for the listeners, those traitors to music's radical potential, whom he described in the most vitriolic terms:

> They are not childlike . . . [but] they are childish; their primitivism is not that of the undeveloped, but that of the forcibly retarded. Whenever they have a chance, they display the pinched hatred of those who really sense the other but exclude it in order to live in peace, and who therefore would like best to root out the nagging possibility . . . The assent to hit songs and debased cultural goods belongs to the same complex of symptoms as do those faces of which one no longer knows whether the film has alienated them from reality or reality has alienated them from the film, as they wrench open a great formless mouth with shining teeth in a voracious smile, while the tired eyes are wretched and lost above (1978: 286–7).

Unusually for so 'scientific' a critic as Adorno, cultural critique seems here to have slipped over into some form of pathological response – he *really* hates the music and those who are gulled by it – and the pathology should be recognizable to anyone who has ever heard a rock devotee discoursing on the subject of pop music. This response, we might speculate, is caused by guilty repression, for when it first began to emerge as a discrete form in the late 1960s, rock music was also a form of *popular* music; but it attempted to dissociate itself from pop's regressive character by emphasizing the distance between itself and *pop* music that, in the critical discourse of the time, took on all the weight of the Adornian critique.[21]

Attitudes may have softened somewhat during the prevailing post-modernist critical climate of the late twentieth century in which 'pop' took on new, supposedly 'radical' resonances. In all sorts of locations and amongst all sorts of music consumers, however, the base line remains the same: pop music is unreservedly *bad*, implicating its adherents – and the rest of us, whenever we catch ourselves absentmindedly humming along to the latest hit – in a politically regressive, personally *carceral* regime.

It's interesting to bear all this in mind when watching some famous footage from 1994 that shows a number of young men dancing on *The Late Late Show,* Ireland's premier entertainment forum since the early 1960s. The boys – clearly primed to make as much impact as possible – gyrate and writhe and strut in a variety of highly sexualized poses while the audience and presenter Gay Byrne looks on nervously, obviously caught between amusement and bemusement. The young men were the band Boyzone, a pop project conceived and commissioned by Irish media figures Louis Walsh and John Reynolds.[22] Few would have guessed it on the night, but from this platform Boyzone would go on to unprecedented international success, on the way kick-starting a renaissance in Irish pop, and thus precipitating a renegotiation of the meaning and function of contemporary Irish popular music.

It's salutary to consider that no Irish 'rock' band (Therapy? or The Cranberries, for example, both riding high in 1994) that might have appeared on *The Late Late Show* during this period could have made the same impression. The reasons for this are complex; one might be that rock's so-called 'revolutionary' identity had, a decade and a half after punk, become clichéd, and its range of musical and lyrical languages exhausted. More than this, however, is the fact that we *expect* rock to be oppositional and are in some senses reassured when it is; we *expect* it to be located (as least nominally) outside mainstream society and are disposed to respond to it on those terms. This is, indeed, one of the ways whereby rock music has traditionally been 'contained' in the *soi-disant* 'liberal democracies' (such as the UK and the US) where it has been most successful: rock claims to offer a dissenting voice, but one which is categorically silenced with regard to the dynamics of the social process.

Pop music, on the other hand, has no such anti-social aspirations. As part of the warp and woof of everyday life, pop is institutionally and informally 'inside' society – in the media, the offices, the pubs and the streets in ways upon which rock has, paradoxically, turned its back. For the fact is, of course, that for all its dissenting identity, rock secretly envies pop's commercial success. This was the paradox built into all the great rock 'moments' – prog., punk, indie – in their turn. In this sense, we might say that pop is rock's repressed unconscious, that which it *really* desires at a deep structural level but which (like other illicit desires) it violently eschews at a conscious level. This also helps to explain the rigorous policing practices that have traditionally attended rock discourse at every level, as any indication of 'pop' is ruthlessly exposed and censured.

In the light of the prevailing mythology we might also say that, precisely because of its location *within* mainstream society, and precisely because it is widely regarded as a soft and simple form, pop music is in fact in a much better position than rock music to challenge established social mores and practices. Something of this nature may have been occurring the night Boyzone appeared on Irish television for the first time. Here were five handsome clean-cut boys, clearly working within a recognizable pop aesthetic, yet introducing a self-conscious, highly sexualized ele-ment that ran counter to traditional pop discourse. The sheer *excess* of the perform-ance, with no deference to anything approaching 'authenticity' (not even the traditional mime), was a surprise; so too was the fact that the music was somehow incidental to the real attraction: the boys themselves and both their ability and their willingness to manipulate their bodies. The confused response on the part of the presenter and the audience was evidence of the fact that there were no established genres or narratives with which to make sense of this phenomenon.

The situation is complicated still further insofar as this episode occurred in a country in which, as we have seen, rock music emerged in part as an effect of, and in part as a response to, a unique form of pop music: the showbands. The latter were not 'pop' in the Anglo-American sense, but they certainly functioned as a convenient local example of it for the first generations of Irish rockers. And as we saw at length in Chapter One, Irish rock's relationship with the showband scene was essentially Oedipal, that is to say, obviously connected with it in some crucial senses, but anxious at the same time to cast off the influence of the showbands and to assert its own identity. That the pop values to which the showband subscribed had been repressed but not killed off entirely was evidenced year after year by the country's enthusiastic embrace of the Eurovision Song Contest, the annual competition to find the continent's 'best' new song. And in retrospect, it's hardly coincidental that Ireland won this competition in each of the three years (1992–4) leading up to the formation of a young, attractive Irish pop group designed to appeal to a similar audience.

The emergence of a new form of Irish 'pop' during the 1990s was, therefore, an extremely sensitive issue in terms of the island's popular cultural history. The original showband scene had been 'repressed', in a material sense, insofar as it had restricted access to performance and recording opportunities after the advent of rock during the late 1960s but more significantly in an aesthetic sense, insofar as the values to which it subscribed were rejected out of hand by a large percentage of the target demographic. Ireland's young musicians had spent the best part of three decades forging a rock aesthetic, one crucial element of which was its distance from what was widely represented as an undeserving domestic music. The showbands were the embarrassing skeleton in the family cupboard, the dodgy old uncle who could spoil any party with his misbegotten musical tastes. With first the appearance, and then the success, of Boyzone, that secret was out: the repressed had returned with a vengeance, and a lot of people were decidedly unhappy about it.

In some senses, Boyzone was a vindication of all those showband artists who for whatever combination of aesthetic and / or infrastructural reasons had been denied a shot at international mainstream success during the 1960s. What would Brendan Bowyer or Butch Moore or Dickie Rock have given for the material and the management enjoyed by Boyzone? Would Joe Dolan have traded all those hits in South Africa and France for a sustained assault upon the UK or US charts? But if Boyzone represented the return of a repressed showband aesthetic on the one hand, on the other it represented a significantly new take on pop music, one that benefited from the long hard years of experience in between 'The Hucklebuck' (1964) and 'Love Me for a Reason' (1995). And despite any passing similarities between the showband heroes of old and the new dispensation, it's fair to say that Boyzone was ultimately far more influenced by latterday boy bands such as New Kids On The Block and Take That than it was by The Royal or The Bachelors.

One thing that obviously set Boyzone apart from the vast majority of its show-band ancestors was its ability to contribute to the composition process. Although it began its career with two covers ('Working My Way Back To You' and 'Love Me For A Reason') and would continue to cover other people's songs throughout its career, with the commissioning of former Take That writer Ray Hedges, each band member was encouraged to be an active participant. This may be seen on the debut album *Said and Done* (1995), where they have writing credits on seven of the thirteen tracks. It's not clear if this credit is for lyrical or musical contribution or for vocal arrangement (although Ronan Keating and Stephen Gately dominated the singing, the others had to have *something* to do to justify the band's identity as a quintet). But in any event it was clear from the outset that the entire Boyzone organization – band members, musicians, management – was fully familiar with the conventions and clichés of the pop industry with which it so closely identified, and could produce passable variations on its classic themes and styles.

Take That broke up in 1996, leaving the way clear for the five young men from Dublin's northside to dominate the rest of the decade. With a string of number ones and Top Ten hits, Boyzone's success at home and abroad (although not the US) was unprecedented for an Irish popular music act until solo projects and other developments overtook the enterprise and it faded from view. The group had introduced a radical pop aesthetic into the island's soundscape, and had demonstrated that Ireland possessed the talent and the imagination to achieve international success in the volatile, cut-throat world of early teen-targeted pop music, which is to say that, from our perspective, Boyzone's chief interest lies in the fact that it *was* Irish, in conception, management and personnel, rather than that it *engaged with* any recognizable conventions of Irishness in sound. If you read the reviews or the interviews or the album notes you would of course come across some reference to Boyzone's national identity sooner or later; but it wasn't really possible to tell if it was from Dublin or London or Los Angeles just by listening to its records, as there were no sonic clues in the music or the vocals.

That was not the case with the next pop phenomenon to emerge from Ireland. B*Witched's first single, the irresistible 'C'est La Vie' (1998), managed to incorporate some 'Irish' fiddle playing and some Dublin chat, while on video and in live performance the four band members spiced up an otherwise standard dance routine with some moves derived in spirit (if not in tenor) from *Riverdance.* 'To You I Belong', another No. 1 in the UK (although only making No. 2 on the Irish charts) features a tin whistle that revisits in both sound and atmosphere the huge Celine Dion hit, 'My Heart Will Go On' (1997), from the hit movie *Titanic.* All in all, in fact, B*Witched was a much more obviously Irish prospect than Boyzone. Although using many of the same personnel (including Ray Hedges and Martin Brannigan), and although the Lynch family had members in both groups, it's fair to say that the girl group tapped into a peculiarly 1990s 'Celtic' vibe in a way that the boy band never particularly did. Theirs was not the Ireland of Enya or *Riverdance,* however – of mysterious maidens singing ethereal melodies; it was, rather, an Ireland of fun and youthful energy, of happy cultural hybrids – above all, it was an Ireland (and an

Irish music) emblematic of one of the few words (and fewer concepts) that the island
has given to the modern world: the craic.

'C'est La Vie' was a classic pop debut, and went straight to the top of both the
Irish and the UK charts. B*Witched's target audience was very similar to that of The
Spice Girls (with whom its career significantly overlapped), although as individuals
Edele, Keavy, Sinead and Lindsay were, and certainly *seemed*, younger than the
members of the English five-piece. Like their friends and family in Boyzone,
B*Witched got writing credits on many of its songs, including 'C'est La Vie' and two
of its other three chart-toppers ('To You I Belong' and 'Rollercoaster'). 'Blame it on
the Weatherman' (January 1999) brought the remarkable run of four consecutive
chart-toppers to an end. As so often happens, the attempt to 'break' the US
interrupted its European run, and by the time it returned in the autumn of 1999
with a new album its moment had already passed to some extent. Diminishing
chart success and internal legal wrangles were an unfortunate – although not in
the least untypical – way for the B*Witched adventure to end.

The success of Boyzone and B*Witched paved the way for a veritable pop
revolution in Ireland. Once again, Dublin became a Mecca for A&R personnel, as a
series of names now consigned to the archives (The Carter Twins, Chill, Kerri Ann,
OTT) rolled off the production line with their more or less indistinguishable songs,
dances and haircuts all neatly prepared. But the next great pop act to break from
Ireland would eclipse the achievements of both Boyzone and B*Witched.

IOU emerged in the late 1990s when six teenage boys formed a group to sing
pop cover versions around their local town of Sligo. After some personnel changes
they morphed into a vocal quintet called Westside on the advice of the ubiquitous
impresario Louis Walsh. The boys had sent a demo of an original song to Walsh,
who with his unfailing pop nous had spotted potential not shared by any of the
contemporary Irish acts. He immediately hired the Sligo group to support visiting
US boy band Backstreet Boys whose Dublin concert he was promoting. Eventually
settling on the name Westlife, the group was quickly groomed for the British teen
and pre-teen market, with Boyzone's Ronan Keating (sensing perhaps the transitory
nature of the industry) getting involved on managerial duties. Westlife's debut
single, 'Swear it Again', was released in May 1999, and was the first of a remarkable
(and record-breaking) string of UK No. 1 hits.

For many people, Westlife represents the point at which any show of tolerance
or indulgence towards the modern Irish pop phenomenon has to cease. The highly
professional focus of Boyzone was offset to some degree by a kind of naïve
enthusiasm and the impression of vulnerability beneath the bravado. B*Witched,
meanwhile, managed to retain a winning air of goofy amateurishness throughout
its brief period of success. In both instances, there was a sense that the category of
national identity could mitigate, at least to some degree, the groups' encounter
with the world of modern international pop music, with Ireland's traditional
marginality from the mainstream Anglo-American pop world creating some kind
of space for reflection and irony. With Westlife, however, from the outset there was
an impression (however unjustified) that the deal had already been done, and that

the masterplan was in action. Try as they might, the five young singers couldn't fully shake the aura of saccharine, clinical hit-making that trailed them.[23] To some, it was as if Irishness had become yet another reified part of the pop world – a brand in itself, with its own cash equivalent transfer value – rather than an exterior position from which to make raids upon that world. Of course, Westlife and its management maintained that this kind of industry cynicism mattered little to it as it continued to rack up hit after hit well into the new century.

In terms of talent, orientation and focus, Irish pop finally seemed to have found the artist it deserved with the emergence of yet another Louis Walsh project: Samantha Mumba. The product of Irish / Zambian parentage, the Dubliner Mumba had been training to perform since the age of three; she was spotted and signed during her mid-teens by Walsh. Her debut album, *Gotta Tell You* (2000), featured a clutch of self-penned songs that were produced and performed to a high musical standard and sung by Mumba with a maturity that belied her youth. This maturity also managed to lift her clear of the pop quagmire to which, with a naturally affable personality and the Walsh association, she was in danger of succumbing. The music itself existed in a place where a number of genres (teen pop, UK garage, American R 'n' B) faded into each other – radio-friendly songs of love found and lost, of desire, of the hopes and pains and dreams of youth. Instant success in the UK and the US charts, followed by a creditable Hollywood movie debut and an even better second album, set up a glittering career.

Mumba is the first high-profile black Irish popular musical artist since Philip Lynott.[24] Like Lynott, she speaks in interview with a recognizable Dublin accent, and her experiences reflect a late twentieth-century Irish upbringing. Unlike Lynott, however, Mumba's music makes no lyrical or sonic allusion whatsoever to the fact of her Irishness, and this seems surprising given the emphasis she places upon the latter. Based fairly and squarely on the American soul tradition, her music is aimed at the anonymous, largely context-free teenage audience which constitutes such an important element of the Anglo-American marketing complex. What's equally surprising is that Irish audiences responded so positively to Mumba's music, seemingly expecting no, and demanding no, musical signals of a shared experience between artist and listener. The fact is that this particular artist's success is measured precisely by the degree to which she can reproduce cosmopolitan styles *without* any trace of the 'home' culture. Irish popular music has always produced a kind of artist whose work exists at a significant remove from traditions based upon either purism ('real' Irish music) or hybridity ('real' Irish music fused with music derived from some other tradition). Mumba's success, however, may be prescient of a new stage in Irish cultural discourse (one precipitated by changes in the economic and political spheres) characterized by more or less complete identification with international marketing categories.

In the early years of the new century, Ireland continues to produce pop performers hopeful of emulating the success of Boyzone and B*Witched, Westlife and Samantha Mumba. For every apologist for the likes of Bellefire, Six or Mickey Harte, however, there is always someone else ready and willing to attack these artists and their music for its banality, its complicity with 'the man', its complaisance, and above all for its existential poverty, however that may be defined. It's unlikely that such criticisms cause many sleepless nights for Louis Walsh, a man whose vision remains one of the most potent influences on the evolution of modern Irish popular music.

'COME AND DANCE WITH ME IN IRELAND'

The story of modern popular music could be told by tracking the ways in which the form's three principal elements – rhythm, melody and lyrics – have combined in various ratios at different times and in different places. For reasons that are ultimately impossible to calculate, one or more of these elements may dominate in a particular place or at a particular time, while the others become greater or lesser side-effects of the music – there but not there, present but not fully meaningful, or meaningful only to the extent that they offset the principal signifying element.

Rock 'n' roll emerged during the 1950s as a form of music that emphasized rhythm – it was first and foremost a form of dance music – but the connection between rhythm and the family of styles descended from rock 'n' roll was gradually lost over the years. Various rock and pop subgenres continued to pay occasional lip service to the dance connection, but as a general rule it's true to say that Western popular music witnessed a general drift away from rhythm during the 1960s and 1970s and a concomitant emphasis on melody and lyrics. Both rock and pop became suspicious of flagrantly body-oriented music, and that attitude seemed to have been confirmed by the advent of the 'disco' phenomenon towards the end of the 1970s – one of the most vilified and despised popular musical scenes of the modern era, as well as one of the most divisive. Many of the prejudices that pertained to pop in relation to rock were transposed wholesale to disco, so that from the time of its first appearance it came to be branded as (amongst other things) soft and soulless. Indeed, there was a sense in which disco wasn't really 'music' at all, as the ruling criteria of value did not encompass the musician's traditional command of an instrument or the singer's interpretation of a lyric, or even the listener's considered empathy with these; rather, value in disco was rooted predominantly on the dance floor and was a function of the dancer's body in relation to a 'song's' prevailing rhythm.

The dance floor was to have its revenge a decade after disco, with the emergence of a kind of music that was unashamedly body-oriented, that flagrantly fetishized rhythm and deliberately downplayed traditional popular musical discourses of authenticity and musicianship: music that was itself attached to a kind of lifestyle the impact of which on *fin de siècle* culture would eclipse that of any other popular cultural scene, including rock and pop. This music bifurcated into two main genres, house and techno, while the early rave lifestyle slowly segued into the more acceptable and much more available practice of clubbing.

Modern dance music has its roots in the work of a range of artists (James Brown, Parliament, Kraftwerk), DJs (Larry Levan, Frankie Knuckles, Paul Oakenfold), and in a number of different locations – some American (New York, Chicago, Detroit), some European (Ibiza, London, Manchester). From these pioneers and these locations, house and techno would go on to conquer the world in a remarkably short period, producing the local scenes and the myriad of subgenres which characterize international dance culture in the new century. As with any culture, this one possesses its own specialized codes and practices, as well as its own peculiar participant roles and relationships. Amongst the more obvious instances of this specialized culture have been the rise of the superstar DJ, and the development of a rich argot to describe the culture's prevailing values and practices. Again, as with any modern popular culture, international dance music is riven by opposing tendencies, some oriented towards preservation and protection, some towards dissemination, innovation and fusion.

Like just about every other trend in the world of popular music, both dance music and its accompanying clubbing culture got to Ireland later than many other places. When they did finally arrive sometime in early 1990, both were an immediate underground success. One of the scene's participant-historians reckons that Sides, a gay venue opened in the 1980s and located off Dame Street in central Dublin, was the first genuine dance club in the Republic to play the new house music (Braine n.d.); another ventures that Sir Henry's in Cork was the first dedicated venue, but suggests that Dublin's Temple of Sound was the first true club in the sense of providing proper sound and lighting systems, as well as demarcated dance and chill zones.[25] The Olympic Ballroom off Camden Street was also a popular contemporary venue, attracting (as dance culture always has) fellow travellers and scene-tourists as well as those who were preparing to make a lifestyle commitment to the music. Some of the DJs who went on to become synonymous with Irish dance music, such as Johnny Moy, Billy Scurry and Mark Kavanagh, were involved at this early stage. Thereafter the scene built slowly and steadily amongst a small but growing cognoscenti.

There are a number of reasons why house and techno emerged and became successful in the ways they did and in the places they did. One inescapable fact, however, is the close association between the music, the culture and the mood-altering drug known as Ecstasy. The substances traditionally linked with popular musical discourse – such as alcohol, hashish, LSD, cocaine, speed and heroin – were of limited use in relation to the new dance music, because each produced either side or core effects that militated to a greater or lesser degree against the music and / or its consumption contexts. The two major effects of Ecstasy, however – empathy and energy – rendered it extremely suitable for use in a clubbing context.[26] Part of the success of this particular popular culture during the 1990s (in Ireland as elsewhere) must be put down to the dogged pursuit on the part of consumers of a re-enactment of their first Ecstasy experience; an experience in which, as many accounts testify, the subject is integrated into a community of similarly disposed drug-users each of whom participates in a quasi-religious unity of physical, mental and emotional gratification.

The peculiar forms of pleasure associated with clubbing meant that it was unlikely to stay a secret for very long, and greater numbers began to attend Dublin's few dedicated clubs as well as special occasional events such as the Mansion House raves in the city centre. As its profile began to rise in the UK, so the Irish media and authorities became concerned with the impact that house music and its associated activities might be having on the country's youth. In a country in which alcoholism is endemic, and in which underage smoking and drinking are apparently routine and acceptable activities, many regarded the moral panic that emerged in relation to the advent of Irish club culture to be typical of the double standards that character- ized the conservative, authoritarian state. The police continued to harass Irish club- bers throughout the decade and into the new century, while the licensing laws both north and south seemed specifically designed to *prevent* rather than *encourage* club- bing (Marshall 2002). Allied to a growing realization on the part of aging clubbers that early Ecstasy experiences represented for the most part an unrecoverable Eden, such pressure led in time to the re-emergence of alcohol as a factor on the Irish dance scene, although that scene's continued success means that there are always new consumers in pursuit of the unique experience afforded by the right combination of drug, venue and music.

With success came controversy and resentment, however. The unexpected popularity of dance music in Ireland during the 1990s led to the appearance of a number of large, high-profile venues dedicated to the music and the associated lifestyle. Moreover, these venues required 'big' name DJs to fill them, who in turn needed big cheques, much of the time facilitated by big-brand sponsorship, to lure them over to Ireland from the UK, Europe and the US. While some welcomed all this activity as a sign of the scene's health, others regarded it as evidence of its inevitable decline and submission to a non-scene agenda – promoters and venue managers more concerned to cash in on the temporarily 'cool' rather than to invest in the development of indigenous talent and resources over the longer term.[27] In other words, dance culture in Ireland very rapidly succumbed to a more or less universal popular cultural pattern in which successive generations of consumers – sometimes separated by no more than a year or so – come to resent the usurpation of 'their' values and practices by younger consumers who are initially attracted to the scene because of those values and practices but who, once involved, invariably modify it in order to suit their own peculiar requirements and perceptions.

Perhaps one of the most surprising aspects of Irish dance culture has been its success outside the major conurbations. While Dublin and Belfast remain the twin centres of activity, more or less every other city and town across the island has developed its own scene in which dedicated club nights (or pub nights, when more suitable venues aren't available) are supported by select local communities. Much of the time, these local dance scenes may be intensely genre-focused, so that whereas one town may specialize in hard house or trance, for example, another not so far away may display a preference for progressive house or drum 'n' bass. The reasons for such differences are difficult to pinpoint, influenced as they are by various patterns in age, gender and other demographic factors. One interesting aspect, however, is their recollection of the phenomenon of regional style in traditional music, and the manner in which genre and technique are determined to a significant extent by a set of inscrutable historical and geopolitical influences (Sommers-Smith 1996). Also worth noting in this context is the manner in which the large rural super-clubs recall the ballrooms of old, where the showbands used to perform regularly for upwards of 3,000 dancers.[28] Despite the significant gap in perception and intention between the two musics, they share a fundamental desire to encourage large amounts of people to escape both the rigours and the banalities of everyday life through the suspension of 'normal' rules regarding body use and body space.

Almost as soon as some Irish people began to *consume* house and techno music, others began to *produce* it.[29] The great cultural revolution that occurred during the 1990s in the production of Irish popular music was facilitated by a technological revolution in home computer-aided recording. This revolution had been brewing throughout the twentieth century, with especially rapid developments being made in the 1970s and 1980s; it was during the last decade of the century, however, that programmes began to be developed that would enable a whole generation of people who, because of a lack of instrumental skill or training, would otherwise have been marginalized from the practice, to realize their musical visions (Théberge 1999). The usual prejudices and accusations – lack of soul, lack of talent, lack of authenticity – were routinely wheeled out in response to this new phenomenon, but this didn't stop young people from all across the island acquiring and experimenting with the technology.[30] Not only is there a lot *more* music in modern Ireland as a consequence; there is also a far greater *variety* of music, a variety for which the term 'dance music' is totally inadequate.

Such has been the exponential growth in 'dance' culture in Ireland during the 1990s, in fact, that the scene has become highly stratified in terms of its different forms and subforms. Although all its constituent styles are more or less descended from techno and house – the Adam and Eve of modern international dance music – the scene at the outset of the new century comprised a bewildering array of deviations and derivations which even the most engaged participants have problems in tracking. And as the music itself has diversified, so also have its audiences and its consumption contexts. Each new style has its devoted cell (sometimes comprising a relatively tiny proportion of the wider dance community) and its dedicated DJs, some of whom find it financially expedient to combine a subgeneric specialism with a broader appeal.

Beneath all this diversification, of course, non-scene commentators (especially those with affiliations to rock music) discern a level of standardization – rhythmic, melodic, harmonic, structural, technological – and a degree of atomization which appears fully to vindicate Adorno's mid-century critique of popular music as a deeply reactionary social form. To take just one example, the advent of multi-tracking has led to a situation in which traditional effects – say, the idea of ensemble performance and everything that such a performance connotes – may now be created by an individual working alone in a studio. In his profoundly influential critique, Adorno rejected the idea that popular music could (or would if it could) say something new, radical or revolutionary; instead, it duped consumers into thinking they had a choice between a range of fundamentally similar styles. With choice, moreover, comes the illusion of identity, as if opting for *this* rather than *that* (which is always more or less *this* in any case) somehow makes you an autonomous, discerning, fully-present subject:

> The types of popular music are carefully differentiated in production. The listener is presumed to be able to choose between them . . . The listener is quickly able to distinguish the types of music and even the performing band, this in spite of the fundamental identity of the material and the great similarity of the presentations apart from their emphasized distinguishing trademarks. This labelling technique, as regards type of music and bands, is pseudo-individualization, but of a sociological kind outside the realm of strict musical technology. It provides trademarks of identification for differentiating between the actually undifferentiated (1994: 209).

One problem with this account is that people (now, as in Adorno's day) are not routinely disposed to think of themselves as 'identity-less', and that his model has no purchase with subjects for whom the subtlest of details can represent significant musical and lifestyle choices.[31] In any event, Adorno met his theoretical match in the work of Attali, whose model of a new noise, a new popular music – or rather *'a new way of making music'* (1977: 134, original emphasis) – based on a hugely expanded community of 'composers', expressed through 'the body' and oriented towards 'festival and freedom' (133) clearly anticipated the emergence of the early rave scene.[32]

The production of Irish dance music was initially a fairly amateur, *ad hoc* affair, with DJs (such as François, who is credited with producing the first) recording a set to make 'mix CDs' for friends. Such a practice was related in some ways to the long established 'compilation tape' custom, that had been ubiquitous amongst rock and pop fans since the advent of cheap recording technology in the 1960s. A more significant factor, however, was the idea that, to the extent that they could imprint a peculiar style of mixing on a specific collection of musical texts, thereby creating specific effects and an atmosphere that was peculiar to them, a DJ could both create and control the 'meaning' of the music, therefore becoming to all intents and purposes a 'performer' in his own right. This association between name and meaning – you attend to *this* DJ in order to witness *these* effects and experience *this* atmosphere – became one of the principal ways in which the new dance music accommodated some of popular music's established discourses, which themselves were based on an older, specifically bourgeois ideology of art.[33]

As the scene continued to expand throughout the 1990s, and as the technology became cheaper and more flexible, the boundaries between different roles (DJ, mixer, composer, musician, producer, distributor etc.) became less defined. Ronan O'Ciosoig, for example, uses Apple Mac technology both to write and to reproduce dance music – in other words, using computers as other DJs use vinyl record decks – and tours the country under the moniker 'Ron's Mobile Disco'. Another typical example of this trend is Mark Kavanagh who, besides being involved with the scene since its inception as both DJ and journalist, also formed his own label (Baby Doll) specializing in 'hard house' – an up-tempo, specifically club-oriented genre – thus providing both a creative outlet and a source of material for himself and like-minded DJs. The biggest Irish hit to emerge from the dance scene in the Republic was a remix of 'Maniac' (2000), a 'cheesy' disco-ish hit from the 1980s, by DJ Mark McCabe, whose re-creation of a club atmosphere won crossover success for a small domestic dance label. The two most successful Irish exponents of 'dance' music, meanwhile, David Holmes and Fergie (Robert Ferguson), also fulfil a number of different roles; and again this is indicative of both the success and the uncertain generic bases of contemporary dance music.

David Holmes began his career as a DJ, a role with a certain (limited) author function attached to it, but at some stage he adopted a different role, that of composer / producer. Holmes emerged from an incredibly vibrant and creative Northern Irish scene that, in terms of clubs, DJs and artists, seemed to respond particularly well to the advent of the new music.[34] Insofar as his career has witnessed a gradual metamorphosis from club-oriented styles to a less rhythm-driven, more frankly cerebral music, Holmes also exemplifies another trend within Irish (and international) 'dance' music: the development of a self-conscious avant-garde which operates at some distance from the concerns of the DJ with a dance floor to entertain. (This is also related to the trend remarked above, in which greater age and experience encourages a more reflective engagement with the music.) Although all parties would probably disavow the connection, there are in fact significant overlaps between the 'popular' electronica produced by Irish artists such as Decal and Donnacha Costello and 'serious' Irish art composers such as Roger Doyle. In a debate that echoes the emergence of post-*Pepper* progressive rock (Smyth 2001), some regard the music produced by the likes of Decal and Costello as a decadent departure from the dance ideal while others see it as an indication of the form's strength and adaptability.

Dance music is patently no longer an underground form, in Ireland or elsewhere. This is reflected in the willingness of rock and pop acts to engage with it in a variety of ways (Haslam 1998: 160). We've already remarked U2's attempt to develop a rock-dance fusion on albums such as *Achtung Baby* and *Pop*; with conviction, luck, talent and the proper help it just about managed to pull off this potentially embarrassing move (established rock stars attempt to 'keep it real' with the kids). Part-time DJ and full-time singer-songwriter David Kitt entered the fray with more credibility, deploying loops and other electronic effects to offset the deep romanticism of his songs. Zrazy and The Afro-Celt Sound System has attempted to fuse 'dance' rhythms and 'Celtic' music in a variety of ways, although as the scare quotes indicate, neither term is engaged straightforwardly. On another tack, Sinéad O'Connor introduced dance elements into some of her own material (as we saw in the previous section) while also guesting as 'diva' for a number of frontline international dance artists such as Moby and Massive Attack. A more common trend is the employment of 'name' DJs and / or producers to produce 'dance remixes' of otherwise straightforward songs by artists such as The Corrs and U2. Again, such a practice may be regarded as an indication of the form's decadence – a dilution of dance's radical energy by bandwagoning 'pop' stars – or as a symptom of its own success – evidence that the principle of rhythm remains a fundamental element within modern popular musical discourse, despite the prolonged hegemony of melody and lyric.

Despite panics regarding periodic fall-offs in the number of clubbers, the re-emergence of guitar-oriented pop music, and the vulnerability of the form to 'corporatization', dance music has managed to retain its popularity in Ireland, a sign (there as elsewhere) that it represents a moment in popular cultural history at least as significant as the advent of rock 'n' roll. The sheer number of venues, festivals, DJs, collectives, producers, artists and labels is a clear indication of the very noisy revolution that has overtaken Irish popular music-making practices in recent years. Despite the odd 'Irish' tune or act[35], dance music in Ireland is for the most part aspirationally internationalist, pursued and practised not for what separates it *from*, but specifically for what connects it *with*, dance culture in other parts of the world. As such, it is perhaps the most typical popular cultural manifestation of Celtic Tiger Ireland: absolutely self-assured as to the right, the talent and the wherewithal to engage with this international phenomenon.

At the same time, it's interesting to observe the way in which the stereotype of the hospitable, craic-loving Celt migrated from more familiar discourses into this seemingly new and unrelated cultural dispensation. Stories abound of non-Irish DJs, journalists or clubbers who 'just love' Ireland for reasons – friendliness, mysticism, mad-for-it behaviour – that clearly echo the Celticist discourse of the nineteenth-century British ideologue Matthew Arnold (Byers, Fitzpatrick and Fowler 2001). This is not a reflection on the Irish clubbing community (although the inclination to pander to international opinion is just as prevalent there as it is elsewhere in Irish society), but on the ways in which dance music in Ireland, like every other form of cultural activity, is subject to meaning-making discourses beyond its immediate influence.

ARE YOU A 'SINGER-SONGWRITER' OR A 'SOLO ARTIST'?

Because of its simplicity and relative lack of expense, the genre of the solo, guitar-playing singer-songwriter was always popular with the blues, folk and country singers of the US during the earlier twentieth century. In time, this genre accumulated a number of conventional associations – instrumental techniques, vocal qualities, subject matter, and so on – that in turn produced its specific aura of authenticity. It was this aura that the young Bob Dylan encountered and adapted so brilliantly when, with the release of *Another Side of Bob Dylan* in November 1964, he subtly metamorphosed from 'protest singer' to 'singer-songwriter'. Probably no one realized at the time how significant and long-lasting would be his invention of that new popular music category.

The singer-songwriter genre has been thriving since then, and nowhere more so than in Ireland. At the same time, it's fair to say that, before the current boom in singer-songwriting, one doesn't find too many pure examples of the basic Dylanesque model: the acoustic guitar-player singing original ballads that reflect his her experience of love and life. Various Irish musicians (Andy White, Luka Bloom, Christy Moore and Freddie White, for example) have from time to time referenced the Dylan iconography, tapping into the power of the 'three-chords-and-the-truth' myth that he was so successful in remaking for the modern era. More frequent is the singer-songwriter who (like Dylan himself since 1965) employs a backing band of greater or lesser size to fill out his her sound and to borrow musical and other discursive effects from ensemble playing. Popular Irish musicians such as Van Morrison, Chris de Burgh, Brian Kennedy and Pierce Turner are now regarded as 'solo artists'[36] in the Dylan sense, responsible for the ensemble music created in their names.

Ireland's most typical 'solo performer' in this regard (and certainly one of its most successful) is Paul Brady. Originally from Strabane in Co. Tyrone, Brady began his musical career in the 1960s by playing small gigs in northern holiday towns. On moving to Dublin to attend university he became involved with the burgeoning beat scene. He soon forsook rock music to indulge his love for the other great musical scene that was invading the Irish sonic landscape at the time: acoustic folk-trad. Hooking up in the first instance with The Johnstons, Brady spent over a decade researching, exploring and performing this kind of music, during which time he revealed himself as a consummate musician and ballad interpreter of enduring classics such as 'The Lakes of Ponchartrain' and 'Arthur McBride'. The two albums Brady recorded in the latter part of the 1970s, *Andy Irvine and Paul Brady* (1976), and the award-winning *Welcome Here Kind Stranger* (1978), represent the culmination of his interest in the musical genre that he had helped to develop and in which he excelled.

Brady had become associated with a particular style of music and with a particular style of performance. Yet he was a 'natural' folk musician neither by technique nor by temperament, and even at the height of his folk-trad. career he always operated at somewhat of a tangent to its main concerns. His leanings towards rock music were suppressed but not extinguished. It was not as surprising as some claimed, then, when in 1981 he released *Hard Station*, an album of original material written and performed in the rock idiom. With songs such as 'Nothing But the Same Old Story' and 'The Promised Land' Brady revealed that he was capable of putting as much effort into song-writing – structure, lyric, arrangement and so on – as he had once put into producing 'definitive' folk-trad. classics. Reflecting his experience and his ambitions, Brady's songs tend to be thoughtful, mature, melodic and complex. In the years since 1981 he has become one of Ireland's most celebrated 'solo performers', each song reflecting his developing response to life, each album keeping pace with the concerns of his similarly aging audience.

Besides being a charismatic performer in his own right, Brady has also become known as a supplier of songs for other artists. The fact that many of his songs have been picked up and performed by international artists is on one level a clear indication of the changing trajectory of Brady's career and the widening currency of his themes. Put in the simple financial terms that pop music seems to understand most readily: folk-trad. music = small audience = small money; rock music = bigger audience = bigger money. At another level, however, Brady's turn to 'universal' themes capable of being covered by artists such as Santana and Tina Turner reflects the extent to which his career functions as a microcosm of Ireland's changing cultural sensibilities in the modern era. Brady's infatuation with ethnic tradition during the 1960s and 1970s led him deep into the Irish cultural condition as he became attuned to its rhythms, its inflections, its complexities, above all, to its uniqueness as a response to the natural world and the human condition. At a certain point, however, he came to regard that uniqueness as a limitation; Irish acoustic folk-trad. represented a restricted musical language whose beauty was always in danger of tending towards a form of self-obsessed provincialism. Realizing that the Irish cultural condition represented only one amongst many possible responses to life, Brady (re)turned to rock music as a means of (re)connecting with the wider world and as a way of exploring what made him *the same* as non-Irish people, as opposed to what made him *different*.

This move anticipated a wider tendency within Irish culture during the last decades of the twentieth century, as more and more people across the island seemed to become less and less fixated with their supposedly unique identity. This tendency (which had its roots in the 1960s) did not represent an outright rejection of Irishness, however, but a mitigation of the propensity to reduce issues of cultural meaning to a single question of identity. Just as the rock note was never entirely absent during his folk-trad. days, so Brady imported into his new career a number of reminders of his time as one of the foremost practitioners of that genre – a feel for melody and phrasing, a penchant for story-telling, a vocal style evolved from 'ballad' performance and so on. Irishness, in other words, was neither fully jettisoned (as with the uncritical adoption of rock), nor was it fully embraced (as with the uncritical reversion to a supposedly pristine 'ethnic' tradition); rather, it was brought into a fructifying relationship with *otherness*, thereby offering a new way of being Irish in the modern world.

Singer-songwriting has always been a particularly popular choice for women, as the great number of high-profile international examples attest – so much so, in fact (and despite Dylan's pivotal status), that the genre is sometimes regarded as inherently feminized. In the late 1960s, as Sheila Whiteley points out, 'the de-escalation in group consciousness (as evidenced by the break-up of such influential groups as The Beatles and Cream), and the general shift from activist rage to a more introspective examination of the self provided a specific space for women singer songwriters' (2000: 75–6). As popular music developed after the 1960s, a general rule seemed to obtain: the louder the music, the more 'masculine' the meaning. 'Quiet' artists such as Joni Mitchell, Janis Ian, Carole King and so on became particularly associated with the articulation of finely observed meditations on life and love. These artists also learned, however, how to exploit the association between volume, iconography and meaning in ways that were not readily available to those who trafficked in sounds at the other end of the volume scale. Following this model, singer-songwriting offered on one level a straightforwardly popular option for Irish women who wished to engage with popular musical discourse. At the same time, it provided these women with a space in which to play with the discursive connotations of the genre, and with their own 'meaning' in relation both to the music and to the society from which the music emerged.

As we observed in a previous section, Sinéad O'Connor is a solo artist who occasionally references the iconography of the singer-songwriter; some of the most effective performances of her career ('Three Babies' and 'Black Boys on Mopeds', for example) are those that have been stripped down to a minimum of instrumentation, featuring only acoustic guitar and the artist's startlingly expressive voice. The music of Sinéad Lohan and Juliet Turner is possessed of a more folky feel, and in their frequent recourse to a perennially familiar persona – one who is by turns reflective, poetic and wistful – both are closer than O'Connor in focus and in sound to the singer-songwriting ideal. In recent years the female performer who has engaged most creatively with the linked discourses of singer-songwriter and solo artist is Gemma Hayes. Exploiting (somewhat in the manner of O'Connor) received sound–mage connotations, Hayes offsets her fragile personal beauty with muscular ensemble music that suggests a much more proactive engagement with the world.

Hayes is one of the more successful of a great number of Irish solo artists who emerged during the late 1990s. Contemporary Ireland (and especially Dublin) is possessed of a superabundance of singer-songwriters / solo artists who play small gigs and record albums for a scene that tends to make little impact on mainstream popular music. A range of factors have contributed to the rise of the modern singer-songwriting scene, the most significant of which are the greater availability of cheap computer technology and the consequent growth in home-recording. All you need is a quietish room, a microphone and a computer with studio software and you are ready to make your own 'album'; with any one of the great number of inexpensive, poly-functional keyboards currently on the market, you can at the same time bring a limitless number of noises within your ambit – noises which, handled sensitively, can recreate the impression of sympathetic ensemble performance. The result is that more or less anyone with a leaning in that direction can now make high-quality domestic recordings.

In this regard, it might be instructive to consider, in passing, the commonalities between singer-songwriting and rap music, a genre which began to develop a small but dedicated network throughout Ireland during the 1990s. The interest in rap music in Ireland (as elsewhere) during this time was inspired in large part by the sustained success of the white American artist Eminem. Poles apart in some obvious ways, modern singer-songwriters and rap artists are nonetheless related in certain technological, formal and conceptual aspects that probably would not be acknowledged by any of the involved parties. Indeed, you wouldn't want to push the point too far, but to hear modern Irish rappers such as Exile Eye, Creative Controle or Rí-Rá engaging with various aspects of modern Irish life is to appreciate how much they have borrowed from a Dylanesque discourse so fundamental to popular music as to be more or less invisible.

Of course, technology would signify nothing without the people to wield it. More music and more artists led to more venues and more gigs, the result being that contemporary Ireland has probably more solo artists per capita than any other comparable country. As always, it's difficult to decide whether the quality led to the confidence or the confidence to the quality, but the fact is that the singer-songwriting scene in Ireland exploded because more people felt that they possessed both the *right* and the *ability* to formalize – and thereafter to disseminate – their response to the world. In this regard, singer-songwriting is perhaps the quintessential genre of the Celtic Tiger era. The particular combination of talent, technical expertise and cultural self-assuredness that the genre encompasses reflects more or less perfectly the profile of a generation that has come to maturity during a period of extended economic success.

The major Irish solo artists who have emerged in recent years tend to fit this profile of technological and cultural confidence. Artists such as Paddy Casey, Damien Rice and David Kitt write and perform sophisticated musical meditations that reflect their cosmopolitan cultural experiences. The pattern tends to be the same in each case: although all are capable of engaging with the traditional guitar-playing, singer-songwriting mode, each of these solo artists also has experience of group performance, and each is associated with the production of ensemble music of greater or lesser complexity, depending on the performance context. Kitt, for example, initially writes and records alone but is obliged to employ a backing band for live shows. Having achieved considerable success on the domestic scene, all three are faced with the perennial pop challenge of bringing their musical visions before a wider international audience. These artists are facilitated in this endeavour insofar as the Irish cultural experience that they are attempting to articulate is year after year bearing a greater resemblance to the experience of the international audience they are attempting to access. Unlike many of the artists we've looked at throughout this book, there is practically nothing in the formal and / or conceptual content of the music of Rice or Kitt or Casey that would lead a listener to suspect any setting other than that vacant Anglo-American zone wherein so much of the world's pop music is located.

The same is not true of Damien Dempsey, a modern singer-songwriter who appears to affiliate his music (if not his persona) with veteran Irish solo artists such as Luke Kelly, Shane MacGowan and Christy Moore. The songs collected on Dempsey's sophomore album, *Seize the Day* (2003), all speak to the Irish condition, both historical and modern, indicting injustice, privilege and hypocrisy wherever they are encountered. Dempsey sings of these issues, moreover, in a clearly audible Dublin accent, a sound that has its own special connotations (mostly comic or criminal) in Irish cultural history. In 'Ghosts of Overdoses' he draws a parallel between the tuberculosis epidemic that assailed Ireland throughout the early twentieth century and the heroin epidemic that ravaged Dublin during later decades, while in songs such as 'Celtic Tiger', 'Industrial School' and 'Marching Season Siege' he confronts some of the island's thorniest political issues. The political is pulled back towards the personal on 'Negative Vibes' and 'It's All Good' (the album's stand-out track), songs in which the modern 'young Paddy' refuses to be victimized as previous generations of Irish people were. The irreducible national identity of *Seize the Day* is confirmed by the provision of a glossary of terms and phrases in common use in Ireland, designed to explain references that would perhaps be unfamiliar to a non-Irish listener. However, whether this (allied to the accent and the subject matter) will aid or impede an international breakthrough for Dempsey remains uncertain.

Dempsey is a key figure in contemporary Irish popular music, a solo artist with a band sound whose material is both musically and lyrically attuned to Irish cultural history and to the country's present condition. His anger towards the past and his scepticism towards the present offers a judicious corrective to the triumphalism of the Celtic Tiger. Of course, not everyone expects (or indeed desires) so much from their pop music, and one can envisage a dispensation in which the 'seriousness' that is one of the traditional attributes of the singer-songwriter goes out of fashion again. In the meantime, solo artists like Dempsey exist alongside various pop and dance acts in the Irish soundscape, part of the noisy soundtrack of the modern island. But what of rock music itself, the genre around which so much of modern popular music coalesces? And what of the rock band, for so long the basic unit of popular group music-making?

The new Irish rock

As we move closer to the present, the sheer number and variety of Irish popular musical acts threatens to become overwhelming. There's no simple or satisfactory way to categorize the many different guitar bands that emerged from the Irish rock scene during the 90s and early noughties – some were louder than others, some were faster, wordier, funnier, dancier, punkier, poppier – some, in the unfathomable terms this book has tried to fathom, were *better* than others. What may be said with a reasonable degree of certainty is that, although each of these bands drew (to a greater or lesser extent) on a heritage of Irish popular music, each also benefited from developments in media technology and from Ireland's greater openness to that technology and to the world that produced it.

One of the most successful Irish bands of the period was The Cranberries which hailed from Limerick, a city and a county with no remarkable pop pedigree.[37] This band's metamorphosis from backwater obscurity to international pop stardom tells a classic rock 'n' roll story. Removed from the intensities of the Dublin scene and the overpowering influence of U2, The Cranberries developed a customized variation on the 'indie' sound – crisp, clean, guitar-driven pop that served as the perfect backdrop for one of the most unmistakeable voices in the modern pop idiom. A bidding war amongst a number of British record companies helped to raise The Cranberries up the pecking order during the early 1990s, at which point a successful US tour and American college radio did the rest. Rapid mainstream success ensued, with the band's first three albums achieving phenomenal record sales. Critics were agreed, however, that although it was its highest charting release on both sides of the Atlantic, the third album, *To the Faithful Departed* (1996), displayed a marked decline in quality. It seemed clear that a loss of musical inspiration was linked to the increasing exhaustion of Dolores O'Riordan and the other members of the band.

Against record company advice and good rock 'n' roll sense, the band took an extended sabbatical throughout much of the late 1990s, before returning in 2001 with the generally poorly received *Wake Up and Smell the Coffee*.

O'Riordan's idiosyncratic vocal technique is as recognizable as that of O'Connor; indeed, in the face of the largely anonymous men who provide the music, her voice represents the band's 'identity' to a great extent. A Cranberries song without O'Riordan's trademark singing would be an artistically (and commercially) compromised prospect. In fact, these two singers have often been linked as examples of some kind of distinctive Irish female singing style with roots in earlier cultural traditions and practices. Certainly, O'Riordan's voice is (like O'Connor's) some way removed from most contemporary popular Irish female singers who tend to 'interpret' their material with reference to a more or less universal international singing style; and certainly strains of *sean-nós* and the ancient Irish practice of 'keening' (crying) for the dead may be heard occasionally in the angularity and robust intonation of their voices. Ultimately, however, the singing style of O'Riordan – no less than that of any modern, media-consuming subject – incorporates local 'traditional' factors alongside a range of 'modern' influences at large in the soundscape, all more or less unconsciously adapted to suit her own physiological capabilities.

There's no knowing what elevates a particular group of musicians out of the great amorphous mass of would-be stars into the realms of genuine pop success; there are many ingredients but no precise formula, and that in itself constitutes one of the perennial attractions of the practice. Nobody in 1990 could have predicted that a band such as The Cranberries would achieve the success it did later in the decade. The same is true of both Ash and JJ72, two of the most successful acts to emerge from the island during the 1990s.

Ash was formed in the historic Northern Irish town of Downpatrick by school friends Tim Wheeler and Mark Hamilton. They were famously still studying for their A-level examinations when they released an EP (actually an album in all but name) called *Trailer* on Infectious Records in the autumn of 1994. The band's brand of melodic punky pop was a hit with both critics and fans, and its first proper album – *1977* (1996), apparently named in honour of the year in which the film *Star Wars* was released – made it to the top of the British charts. With guitarist Charlotte Hatherley added to the line-up, they released the less commercial *Nu-Clear Sounds* (1998), a reaction in some ways to the image of tearaway teenage punks that had trailed the band since its breakthrough. Like The Cranberries, Ash then took time out to recover from the rigours of constant touring and to rethink the band's strategy. The result was the brilliant *Free All Angels* (2001), an album that achieved the rare trick of recapturing past values while at the same time revealing a clear musical and lyrical development.

JJ72 were also in their teens when they emerged towards the end of the decade. Formed by Dubliners Mark Greaney (guitar) and Fergal Matthews (drums), the line-up was completed by bassist Hilary Woods (who was replaced by Sarah Fox in 2003). In the late 1990s JJ72 was just another band trying to crack the Dublin scene when a record deal with Lakota and a 'Single of the Week' slot – for 'October Swimmer' (1999) – on BBC DJ Mark Radcliffe's radio show turned them from local also-rans into hot contenders. If Ash gravitated towards the punk-pop end of the rock spectrum, JJ72 were apparently much more influenced by a strand of 'progressive' rock (dominated in recent years by Radiohead) concerned to articulate a more cerebral, less body-oriented response to the world. Greaney's early songs were quirky, angst-ridden observations from the limited perspective of an Irish teenager, yet sung with absolute conviction in a tremulous falsetto that was as unmistakeable as any voice in the entire contemporary popular musical spectrum. The band's eponymous debut album (2000) was accompanied by high-profile media and festival appearances, and once again it appeared that Ireland had produced a winning pop product from unlikely materials.

With reference to an earlier section, one interesting thing shared by Ash and JJ72 is their inclusion of low-profile female musicians. It may initially appear that the incorporation of Hatherley and Woods (and latterly Fox) into these successful bands represents a further stage in the de-masculinization of Irish rock music, but matters are not as straightforward as that. In fact, the role played by these women connotes a complex gender politics, for although they are not foregrounded (Wheeler and Greaney remain the respective band leaders, as is clear from publicity photographs and interviews), it's clear that the inclusion of attractive female personnel both alters the semiotic resonance of the music itself whilst simultaneously widening the bands' appeal. This in itself represents a subtle development from earlier stages in Irish popular music's gender economy, one that is not necessarily progressive but that is clearly an indication of changes within the wider national culture.

If popularity and commercial achievement are the relevant criteria, then Irish rock music of the 1990s may be likened to a pyramid with the likes of U2 and The Corrs at the top followed by a number of decreasingly successful bands. Therapy? continued the tradition of loud aggressive Ulster acts; its music was in the vanguard of the indie-punk-metal hybrid that was so successful throughout the decade, and won a Mercury Prize nomination in 1994 for the album *Troublegum*. Just when the stereotype was becoming too entrenched, along came The Divine Comedy and That Petrol Emotion, the first (led by Neil Hannon) playing music that referenced a wide range of popular traditions – cinema, big band, chanson – the second (led by former Undertone John [Sean] O'Neill) playing politicized *avant-la-lettre* indie-dance. Thereafter things begin to get a little sketchier. Cork's Rubyhorse bucked the long-established cultural trend by trying to break from the US rather than the UK. Two other Cork bands, The Sultans of Ping FC and The Frank and Walters, continued the city's tradition for pop eccentricity; the former scored an unlikely UK hit with 'Where's Me Jumper?' in 1992, while the latter continued to plough a resolutely independent furrow from their London base throughout the decade.

Further down this commercially defined pyramid we find the likes of My Little Funhouse, The Devlins, The 4 of Us, An Emotional Fish, The Stunning (latterly reformed as The Walls) and Picturehouse – all producing variations of greater or lesser distinction on a core rock aesthetic. No precise relationship may be described, but it's instructive to observe that the further down this pyramid one gets, the greater the deviation from that core aesthetic, and the more critical credibility groups tend to garner. Bands such as A House, Engine Alley and The Pale were certainly more left-field, and in Dave Couse, Canice Kenealy and Matthew Devereux they possessed key personnel whose distinctive vocal styles complemented the quirkiness of their visions. Although reproducing the conventions of guitar-led popular music at some level and to some extent, these bands were also clearly engaging with an experimental tradition that challenged the formal and conceptual limitations of mainstream popular music.

Every place and every era produces a number of 'if only' bands; for Ireland in the 1990s it was Whipping Boy and Something Happens. The first was a purveyor of apparently straightforward rock (vocal, guitar, bass, drums) but with a deceptively dark undercurrent. Few songs succeed as well as 'We Don't Need Nobody Else' (from the stunning *Heartworm* album of 1995) in expressing a type of bemused resentment towards the kind of society into which modern Ireland was evolving. Something Happens was cursed with the stigma of 'intelligence', but that didn't stop it from writing and recording some of the most memorable Irish pop-rock songs of that or any period. One might think that the failure of bands of this range and quality to achieve an international profile would be discouraging to subsequent generations, although the continued popularity of rock music amongst the island's youth clearly proves this not to be the case.

Probably the two most interesting modern bands in the context of this study are Aslan and The Frames. Amongst their undoubted other qualities, these two Dublin groups focus certain trends and tendencies within the domestic cultural arena: the possibility of an 'Irish' sound, for example, or the limits of local 'success' or the role and function of longevity in cultural production. Aslan was formed in the northside working-class suburbs of Finglas and Ballymun in the early 1980s. Its first single, 'This Is' (1986), was a massive Irish hit and won the band a reputation (which has remained intact over two decades) for no-nonsense, melodic rock. Aslan also began to make inroads into the UK scene at this time, winning positive reviews for its recordings and live shows. A hit album, *Feel No Shame* (1988) followed, at which point, torn apart by stress and substance-abuse of various kinds, the band split. After a series of more or less uninspired and unsuccessful side projects, the band reformed five years later during a supposedly one-off charity gig on its home patch of Finglas. Another hit single, 'Crazy World' (1993), followed, since when Aslan has moved from strength to strength within the Irish musical consciousness, with hit records, successful tours, and a high national cultural profile.

The Frames were formed in 1990 by Aslan's fellow northsider Glen Hansard, a man who is best known (or at least most readily recognized) as the actor who played guitarist Outspan Foster in *The Commitments* (1991), Alan Parker's cinematic version of the novel by Roddy Doyle. Highly successful though it was, this film was but a passing diversion from Hansard's true 'commitment', which was to writing, recording and performing his own music. Albums, record labels and personnel came and went throughout the 1990s, during which time Hansard remained true to

his musical vision, a sort of customized indie aesthetic through which he could articulate his own passionate responses to the world. The band achieved a creative peak
with the brilliant *For the Birds* (2001), recorded in Kerry and Chicago and produced
in part by American 'name' Steve Albini (the second ex-Pixies producer, after Gil
Norton, with whom the band had worked). The Frames have always toured exten-
sively, but it's their regular home shows – invariably played to their adoring fans
and usually well supported by the national media – that have turned the band into
something of a national institution.

Aslan and The Frames have both achieved about as much success as it is
possible to do in Ireland. They have identifiable styles, appealing to established
sections of the music-consuming public; they play well-advertised gigs and release
records that sell comparatively well amongst the island's limited population; they
have a recognizable profile within the domestic (print and electronic) media.
Neither band produces music that is particularly 'Irish' in any of the conventional
senses associated with that term (although the violin, as played by Colm Mac Con
Iomaire of The Frames, is unusual is a rock context).[38] Despite support from prestigious niche audiences in various international locations, neither band has 'cracked'
the world of mainstream popular music. What they do represent, however, are two
dominant facets of the modern Irish rock imagination – Aslan with its mixture of
blokishness and vulnerability, The Frames with their staunch 'into-the-music' ethic.

Not every modern Irish band would necessarily wish to be located on any scale
that measured 'success' in terms of finance or popularity. The island supports a
small but determined underground scene, the adherents of which disdain any
dealings with the mainstream media. The feeling tends to be mutual. As a rule you
won't hear, for example, any representatives of Ireland's metal scene (which
incorporates a number of subgenres such as thrash, death, hardcore, crust, Celtic
and punk) on any television or radio station, nor will you be able to read feature
articles or gig reports about them in any mainstream magazine or newspaper. The
music produced on this scene is so extreme, so 'noisy', that there are very few
opportunities for it to be heard in any wider sonic context. The scene itself
comprises a relatively small community of fans and musicians who share certain
values and codes which (self-) identify them as 'misfits' with regard to the mainstream Irish institutions. You don't really have to hear bands such as Brutal,
Nappyrash, Jobbykrust or Blood Red Dolls to have some impression of the kind of
music they play, or to guess that you won't be hearing it on national radio. Some
bands and musicians are obviously going to be more serious than others – some
record and tour and promote their music with the clear aim of dissemination – but
Ireland's underground metal scene is for the most part enthusiastically amateur,
run by and for people who share a set of lifestyle options, and who have no wish
to 'make it' in conventional terms.

Meanwhile back in the 'overground', at the absolute base of the Irish popular
musical pyramid we find the thousands of musicians who make up the hundreds of
bands who make up the lifeblood of the community. Week by week these bands continue to engage in the scene's core activities – rehearsing, gigging, recording

demoes, breaking up and reforming, all hoping to hit upon the formula that will propel them further up the pyramid and give them a chance of breaking through. In 1992 Tony Clayton-Lea and Rogan Taylor referred to Dublin as a 'city of 1000 rock bands' (88); in 2005 that seems like a significant underestimation. At the same time, every regional town and city can now also boast its own local scene, each with their dedicated fans, venues and pools of musicians. All in all, and despite the success of clubbing and the singer-songwriter genre, it's fair to say that ensemble, guitar-oriented rock music thrived in Ireland throughout the 1990s. The factors responsible for this are many and various, although (as remarked at the opening of this section) it seems clear that the island's enthusiastic embrace of advances in electronic media must surely count as the most important. And as the media have changed, so too has the music, which is not to say that one drives the other, but rather that medium and music are locked in a symbiotic relationship whereby even slight variations in the one can have major ramifications for the other. Amongst its many attractions, perhaps the most beautiful thing about popular music is that although everyone knows this, no one knows how or why it happens.

Conclusion
Rock 'n' Roll Can Never Die?
The Industrialization of Irish Rock Music

When the London Fleadh was cancelled in the summer of 2003 due to what the promoters described as the lack of a suitable headline act, there was much speculation regarding the current and future condition of Irish popular music. 'Irish acts in doldrums as festival is axed: annual Fleadh in London falls by wayside as Celtic music's vitality wanes' ran the headline in the *Observer* (Wazir 2003). The festival had started in the optimistic atmosphere of 1990 when the Republic battled its way to the quarter-finals of the World Cup in Italy. Throughout the following decade it had shadowed the reversal in Irish fortunes at home and abroad, providing a high-profile arena for the performance of 'Irish' values amongst the diaspora and sympathetic others. As the festival grew into a major annual event, however, the Mean Fiddler organization found it more and more difficult to book credible Irish acts; some were too big or too familiar, most were too small to draw viable numbers. While commercially successful, headline performances by Crowded House and Neil Young around the turn of the decade undermined the Fleadh's tacit mission, to showcase and celebrate 'Irish' popular music talent. Although disappointing, it came as no great surprise to many commentators when the Mean Fiddler's Vince Power announced the event's cancellation.

The 'failure' of the Fleadh should be set in the context of Ireland's amazing success in the sphere of modern popular music; indeed, it's precisely *because* the island has been so successful at producing artists with enduring international appeal that the latter-day dearth of suitable acts is considered to be remarkable. 'Ireland', write Rob Strachan and Marion Leonard, 'is a nation with a minuscule domestic record industry in terms of per-capita sales and yet in terms of artist origin the country is one of the largest exporters of music in the EU . . . Moreover,' they continue,

in 2001, Irish artists sold over 56 million albums accounting for 2.3% of worldwide CD sales. Ireland is actually the fifth highest provider of international hit records in the international rock / pop market with acts such as U2, Sinéad

O'Connor, Chris de Burgh, Enya and Van Morrison having sold 124.5 million records between them (2004: 39–40).

If there is a crisis in Irish popular music, it's one that any similar (in terms of size and population) territorial unit anywhere in the world would be happy to experience.

The problem, such as it is, does not lie with some supposed dearth or drop in quality of new acts; the decade since 1995 has witnessed the emergence of more (and more original) Irish popular musicians than at any other time since the advent of rock 'n' roll.[1] Rather, it concerns what might be described as the *industrialization* of the discourse during the 1990s and its conversion from a set of codes and practices located *at a tangent to* the mainstream economy, to a set of codes and practices formalized *within* the mainstream economy (a process that in turn is linked with a more fundamental reorganization of cultural practices both within Ireland and globally). Strachan and Leonard trace the emergence in Ireland during the 1990s of a series of initiatives in which government and business worked together to try to manage the production of Irish popular music. The plan was effectively to convert the field from a set of *ad hoc* customs and traditions to a regulated 'industry' possessed of very specific procedures designed to cover every aspect of the popular music-producing process. This plan culminated with the establishment in 2001 of the Music Board of Ireland (MBI) by the Republic's Minister for Arts, Heritage, Gaeltacht and the Islands, Síle de Valera, 'with a brief to assist in the development of the music sector and to work toward policies to increase its contribution to the national economy' (Strachan and Leonard 2004: 39).

It would be foolish in the extreme to romanticize a practice that has always been so dependent upon financial considerations. Popular music is not – has never been – some kind of naturally occurring phenomenon; rather, it's the result of a series of economic processes that function at both a micro and a macro level to bring the musical text and the consumer into meaningful conjunction. By the same token, it would be invidious to criticize attempts to professionalize some aspects of the discourse. A standard critique of 'the Celts' was that they were always far too engrossed with the dream, temperamentally indisposed to engage with reality, which itself was better off left to those (mainly British and American) with an understanding of such matters. For too long (ran the argument), Ireland had swallowed that romantic racist guff, remaining content to see culture as *expression* rather than as *product*; for too long, it lacked a professional management sector capable of capitalizing on the native predisposition towards cultural production. The recognition on the part of various bodies of Irish popular music's economic dimension is then simply an acknowledgement of an ineluctable condition for the practice, while the attempt to bring policy to bear upon it is yet another sign of the island's growing maturity after its long exile in the land of the past.

At the same time, for many artists and commentators there is something fundamentally contradictory, perhaps even unwholesome, about the attempt to marshal creativity in this manner. Of course, there is a form of popular music practice in which financial considerations are paramount; its name is 'pop', and many of the acts and artists invoked throughout the course of this book make no bones about their subscription to that form. But along the continuum from the pop ideal other models of musical production begin to come into force, ones that are less easily reconcilable with an economically driven understanding of popular musical discourse. Again, this is not to deny the inescapable presence of money as a determining factor in all aspects of the field; but it *is* to question the distribution of motivating and enabling factors behind the production of modern popular music. Taking this another step, it becomes necessary to question the amenability of certain cultural forms to the manipulations of a centrally organized institutional policy that is itself designed to expedite a particular economic system.[2]

The international 'branding' of Irish music, and more specifically of a kind of music assumed to be in some way naturally or essentially 'Irish', has been, at the very least, an ambivalent development. Irish popular music may be in the process of becoming a victim of its own success, in other words, planned into obsolescence by those whose ostensible project it is to 'nurture', 'develop' and 'protect' it. This is an unlikely scenario in the short to medium term, however, as the music always seems to find a way to remake itself in the image of the new generations; indeed, it's always been in the interest of corporate policy-makers not to over-manage the bottom end of the market, for it's only in that way that 'new' sounds can develop and emerge.[3] But it's clear, nevertheless, that change is afoot within the field of Irish popular music and that a number of different trends are evolving, some of which will be more significant than others. One has only to consider the 'breakthrough' of acts such as The Thrills, Snow Patrol, Damien Rice and David Kitt to appreciate how established systems are being adapted and replaced by new models based upon the radically altered socio-cultural dispensation that now obtains throughout the island of Ireland.

For good or ill, Irish popular music has ceased to be a dance in the dark; it's now largely a matter of training, grants and gear, pitches, plans and sector-specific knowledge. There are at least two paradoxes here: firstly, Irish popular music has finally acknowledged what it always was: a business; and secondly, the perennial one that attends the conjunction of economics and art, in this case, money and music. It's the nature of the business that only an extremely tiny proportion of the artists who continue to seek success will in fact 'make it' – that is, produce a product that sells in enough quantities to recoup initial investment and subsequently sustain an acceptable lifestyle. Most people who get involved in playing popular music know that the odds against them are unfavourable, but they carry on just the same. At the same time, the greater the number of people involved in any activity, the greater the chances of those with real talent and originality coming through. It's the ratio between its huge base and its narrow pinnacle that has informed rock 'n' roll music over the years, and that has allowed it to survive despite the levels of corporate over-management that have dogged it since its inception.

Then there are the tens of thousands who, while not engaged in *making* rock music, consume it in one form or another on a regular basis, and incorporate it as a fundamental part of their evaluating and sense-making activities. That so many young people should still wish to engage with these activities, that so many older people should still wish to invest (both financially and sentimentally) in these activities, is a testament to the power of the rock 'n' roll imagination. Amongst its many different qualities and attributes, this particular form of music has clearly been meeting some deep desire amongst certain sections of the global population in the half century or so since its first appearance. Contrary to reports, rock 'n' roll *can* and *will* die; at the very least it will cease to function in the ways it has during its first fifty years. But today it is still here, still relevant, still impinging significantly upon our aural negotiation of the world, and still providing us with some of the most accessible means to make sense of that strangest of human adventures: life.

NOTES

INTRODUCTION

1. The full text of this speech is reproduced at *http://www.imro.ie/speeches.html>*.

2. Much has been written about Irish rock music (see the bibliography accompanying this volume), some of it scholarly but most of it speculative. Only two full-length studies have appeared: Mark J. Prendergast's *Irish Rock: Roots, Personalities, Directions* (1987), and *Irish Rock: Where It's Come From, Where It's At, Where It's Going* (1992) written by Tony Clayton-Lea and Rogan Taylor. Although informed and informative, neither text engages systematically with the cultural-historical contexts out of which Irish popular music has emerged. In 2000, RTE screened a six part series on Irish rock music, *From a Whisper to a Scream*, made by Little Bird productions of London. The series was written by *Hot Press* editor and long-time Irish rock music champion Niall Stokes. A promised volume to accompany the series never materialized, although a DVD version (entitled *Out of Ireland*) of the TV series did appear in 2003.

3. Although, as Lavinia Chang points out, '[the] creative sector . . . is impressive relative to the size of the population', at the same time '[the] indigenous entrepreneurial sector of the Irish music scene is relatively small, the market being dominated by a handful of giant multi-national record companies and publishing houses' (1995: 244). Strachan and Leonard reiterate the point: '[Although] Irish artists have enjoyed enviable levels of worldwide commercial success, often the money accruing from the popularity of these acts has not flowed back into the Irish music industry' (2004: 42). This raises serious questions as to the 'Irishness' of Irish popular music, and also as to the motives underpinning its recent economic re-orientation.

4. The brief given to FORTE by the Minister for Arts, Culture and the Gaeltacht was 'to examine the potential for employment in the music industry and to identify and review any factors that might be inhibiting the development of the industry' (1996: 8).

5. Some of the institutions attending the production of music in modern Ireland include the Federation of Music Collectives, The Irish Business and Employers Confederation Music Industry Group, the Irish Music Rights Organisation, the Music Board of Ireland etc. See Leonard and Strachan (1999, 2004) for an attempt to map the interrelations between these different institutions and initiatives.

6. We should also note the influence of the Italian Marxist thinker Antonio Gramsci on the emergence of Cultural Studies generally, and Popular Music Studies in particular, especially in his emphasis of popular culture's anti-hegemonic tendencies.
7. Attali's theory runs contrary to traditional analyses which see culture as *reflecting* the underlying social, political and economic realities. In *The Best of Decades* (1984), for example, Fergal Tobin sees the revolution in Ireland in the 1960s as a classic top-down phenomenon, led by middle-class liberals working within the established institutions; the idea that popular music could be anything other than a symptom or a reflection of that revolution is nowhere entertained.

CHAPTER ONE

1. The Republic of Ireland joined the World Bank and the IMF in 1957, and made its first application to join the EEC in 1961.
2. Although see the materials gathered on Ian Gallagher's Showband Memories website (at www.iangallagher.com), especially the BBC Northern Ireland interview from 1989 with Belfast band leader Dave Glover who claims to have invented the 'showband' moniker, and who dates the onset of the phenomenon to 1956 (the same year, incidentally, as Elvis's breakthrough single, 'Heartbreak Hotel'). Glover explains that the 'show' element developed out of musicians' play-acting and on-stage humour, which in time became as much a draw for audiences as the band's ability to provide dance music; as Hugo Quinn of The Clipper Carlton explained: 'We gave people something to watch as well as to listen to' (quoted in Power 2000: 38).
3. Perhaps it's not coincidental that the Republic's most successful showband was The Royal.
4. Whereas most Irish politicians welcomed the social and cultural changes brought about by economic reform during the 1960s, the Catholic hierarchy remained critical and suspicious. Fergal Tobin quotes Bishop McNeely of Raphoe from his pastoral letter of 1961: 'What passes for amusement and pastime is not always the harmless thing it was a generation ago' (1984: 39); while in 1962, 'the Bishop of Derry stressed the moral dangers of dances after midnight and urged "moderation" in the number of dances attended' (40). In this respect, the cessation of showband activity during Lent (the period running up to Easter, traditionally a time of fasting and self-denial for Catholics) recalls Jacques Attali's analysis of Brueghel's famous painting *Carnival's Quarrel with Lent:* '[It] is a battle between two fundamental political strategies, two antagonistic cultural and ideological organizations. Festival, whose aim is to make everyone's misfortune tolerable through the derisory designation of a god to sacrifice; Austerity, whose aim is to make the alienation of everyday life bearable through the promise of eternity – the Scapegoat and Penitence. Noise and Silence' (1985: 21–2).

5.   Although he never cracked the US, Joe Dolan did emerge as a truly inter-national singing star whose success (including British chart penetration) in retrospect rivalled that of Bowyer and The Royal.

6.   'The Hucklebuck' also made the Irish charts when it was re-released in 1976 (No. 4), and again in 1981 (No. 10).

7.   When the showband bubble burst in the early 1970s, its Country and Western wing – represented by acts such as Big Tom and the Mainliners – managed to survive, mutating over the years into the thriving 'Country and Irish' scene.

8.   Although there are some fundamental differences between the two scenes, the showbands' drive to reproduce the music of original British and American acts might be compared with the contemporary vogue for tribute bands, whose concern is not only to *sound* like, but to *look* and *act* like – in effect, temporarily to *be* – the real thing. The continuing appeal of karaoke amongst British and Irish audiences is also suggestive.

9.   Phil Coulter wrote songs for Butch Moore and The Capitol; other showband musicians such as Billy Brown (of The Freshmen) and Tommy and Jimmy Swarbrigg (of The Times) composed some original material. Although they never managed fully to escape their showband inheritance, The Freshmen represented the most attractive aspects of the scene, and indeed for many commentators remain amongst the best popular musicians of any genre to emerge from Ireland during the 1960s.

10. As Bourdieu goes on to say: 'The refusal of what is easy in the sense of simple, and therefore shallow, and "cheap", because it is easily decoded and culturally "undemanding", naturally leads to the refusal of what is facile in the ethical or aesthetic sense, of everything which offers pleasures that are too immediately accessible and so discredited as "childish" or "primitive" (as opposed to the deferred pleasures of legitimate art). Thus people speak of . . . the too insistent, too predictable charm of what is called "light" music (a word whose connotations virtually correspond to those of "facile")' (1984: 486).

11. Gracyk argues that popular music is subject to both *external* and *internal* aesthetic evaluation; the first from a high cultural élite who regard it is a culturally impoverished form with appeal to only the most basic of human instincts, the second from an educated cognoscenti (comprising fans and a range of media types) with sentimental and / or material investment in the idea of a popular musical hierarchy.

12. The concept of a modern 'folk' music is anomalous in one central respect, as described by Malcolm Chapman: '"Folk" music now exists, as a genre, recorded, performed, published, sung and listened to, in the nearly complete absence of any "folk" to provide the full social context that once (in whatever arguable and murky sense) might have existed; the social context of "folk" music today is one of vinyl and magnetic tape, recording studios, published works, media performance and specialist gatherings. "Celtic" music is going

the same way, and has always been closely related to "folk" music in these respects' (Chapman 1994: 42–3).

13. While Nuala O'Connor (1991: 103–18) and June Skinner Sawyers (2000: 192–216) offer speculative sketches of the relations between Irish / British and North American folk music, tracking the genealogy of individual tunes and songs is a standard research technique amongst academic folklorists.

14. For some impression of the extent of Dylan's influence in Ireland during the 1960s see the index to *My Generation: Rock 'n' Roll Remembered* (1996), edited by Antony Farrell, Vivienne Guinness and Julian Lloyd.

15. It's indicative of the fluidity of modern musical influence that Carthy should be responsible for a particular form of guitar tuning known widely in folk circles as 'Irish'. As an instrument, the guitar itself is caught up in the controversies attending the meaning of, and relationships between, 'traditional', 'folk', and various other kinds of acoustic music.

16. Terence Brown quotes a speech to a Dublin music festival by Thomas Derrig, Minister for Education, from March 1937: 'That set of values which makes the Irish mind different looks out at us clearly from our old music – its idiom having in some subtle way the idiom of the Irish mind, its rhythms, its intervals, its speeds, its build have not been chosen arbitrarily, but are what they are because they are the musical expression, the musical equivalent of Irish thought and its modes' (1985: 147). This was a repetition of the official line promulgated by de Valera himself in a radio speech from 1933, in which he claimed: 'Ireland's music is of singular beauty . . . It is characterised by perfection of form and variety of melodic content . . . Equal in rhythmic variety are our dance tunes – spirited and energetic, in keeping with the temperament of our people' (quoted in Kennedy 1990: 31–2).

17. At the same time, institutionalization, even of a liberal ilk, fosters a hierarchy of musical taste and value. As Edward O. Henry writes: 'Governments promote those kinds of music favoring the desired image. This music *can* become a kind of ethnic, regional, or national show business – entertainment for people outside more than for those inside the community in which the music was originally performed. The music persists, but sometimes in an altered form with a different ethos. Those types or styles of music selected for presentation acquire an implicit seal of official approval, and those which are not selected suffer neglect and less chance of survival' (1989: 68).

18. As Thérèse Smith has shown, this tension is at least as old as the modern interest in Irish music as an expression of national identity. In comparing the activities and practices of two early activists, Edward Bunting and Thomas Moore, Smith writes of 'a fundamental philosophical difference: Bunting was interested in collection and preservation, Moore in reinterpretation. It was inevitable that Bunting would be the loser,' she goes on, 'for it is a truism of anthropology that virtually the only thing that is constant about culture is change: cultural elements that are no longer perceived as useful are discarded if not re-interpreted' (2000:154).

19.   Not everyone considers Ó Riada's embrace of traditional music to have been the great leap forward for twentieth-century Irish music it is widely represented to be. From the perspective of art music, as Harry White writes, 'The more nearly he encountered the ethnic tradition, the more difficult it became . . . to integrate that tradition within the language of the European aesthetic . . . The significance of Ó Riada [is that] he silenced the claim of original art music as a tenable voice in the Irish cultural matrix: he silenced it too in its address upon the Irish mind. In its stead, he advanced the claim not of original composition but of the ethnic repertory itself' (1998: 149).

20.   Also worth mentioning in this respect are Emmet Spiceland (including Donal Lunny and Leo O'Kelly) who had a string of Irish hits during 1968, including a No. 1 with 'Mary from Dungloe'.

21.   The Irish acoustic 'scene' during the late 1960s was typical of most modern popular musical scenes which, as described by Sara Cohen, tend to be 'created through . . . [local] people and their activities and interactions. Many forge close relationships with each other and form clusters or cliques, while others are part of looser networks or alliances' (1999: 240). For example, Irvine regularly guested (alongside future guitar hero Gary Moore) with progressive folkies Dr Strangely Strange before going on to play with seminal 'trad.' groups Planxty and Patrick Street. Woods contributed with his wife Gay to the classic *Hark! The Village Wait* album by influential English folk-rockers Steeleye Span, before forming The Woodsband, and eventually joining (after an extended sabbatical) The Pogues. In a long and eventful career, Henry McCullough played guitar with Joe Cocker and Wings amongst others. It's also interesting to note that many of these folkies had close connections not only with beat and rock musicians (Moore and Philip Lynott, for example), but also with the showbands: Joe Dolan and Leo O'Kelly (of progressive folk act Tír na nÓg), for example, played in minor outfits The Swingtime Aces and The Tropical Showband, respectively; McCullough started with showband The Skyrockets before going on to play with showband-cum-beat group Gene and the Gents, while Des Kelly, former leader of showband heroes The Capitol, was manager of Sweeney's Men. On the complex process of interaction between different musical scenes see Olson 1998: 279ff.

22.   The change in Irish cultural values since the 1960s is evident, as Marie McCarthy suggests, 'in the ongoing and extensive debate concerning the meaning of "Irish music", and in increasing efforts to provide access to a variety of musical genres' (1999: 171). 'In no other period', she continues, 'did mass media have as great an impact on the way music is known and transmitted' (172).

23.   As the vogue grew after 1964, the number of Dublin venues – both city-centre and suburban – catering for beat music increased, including the Caroline Club, Club A Go-Go, Club Arthur, the Crystal Ballroom, the Moulin Rouge, the Five Club, the Flamingo, the Seventeen Club, the Apartment, the

Scene Club, the Barn and the Stella in Mount Merrion, and the tennis clubs at Terenure and Templeogue.

24. As Allan F. Moore explains, the beat bands of the early 1960s introduced a set of stylistic norms which were 'clearly conceived in terms of metre and the approach to the beat, vocal tone, the structural role of harmony and, pre-eminently, the setting-up of a musical texture stratified through specific instrumental functions or roles'(1993: 59) – in other words, they had a sound that was identifiable, and identifiably different from other popular music styles.

25. The Clipper Carlton's somewhat awkward and spiritless version of The Beatles' 'I Wanna Hold Your Hand' (1963) is indicative of the gap that was emerging not only between the showbands and the beat groups, but between different generations of showband.

26. Mark J. Prendergast describes how beat group The Chosen Few was 'killed off' when two of its members – Fran O'Toole and Paul Ashford – were poached by The Miami Showband (1987: 49). Ashford went on to play bass in 70s outfit Stepaside; O'Toole was murdered in the Miami Massacre of 1975.

27. As Paul Brady recalls of the burgeoning beat scene: 'There seemed to be about fifty bands in Dublin, including The Black Eagles, The Gnumphs, all mostly doing covers' (Hayden 2001b: 3).

28. Hence, the fear – as well as anger and derision – animating the oft-quoted lines from Skid Row's 'Un Co-op Showband Blues': 'Got a job in a showband / Working like a slave / Six nights and every Sunday / C'mon and put me on a weekly wage'.

29. Prendergast 1987: 12; Clayton-Lea and Taylor 1992: 7–8. As with the folk and traditional scenes, the Irish beat scene of the 1960s was typical in that it was made up of a centralised pool of musicians who tended to cluster together in temporary combinations as different musical ends were refined and rejected. Cohen's theory (1999) of 'the scene' as simultaneously local and global – as both responsive to, and productive of, local factors, whilst remaining closely identified with wider musical developments – is highly suggestive for the Irish beat scene of the period.

30. See also Cohen (1991) who, in her ethnographical analysis of the Liverpool rock music scene in the 1980s, found that different musical allegiances 'were encapsulated by the band's name, which was carefully chosen not only to attract attention but to symbolize the band's character, aspirations, and ideology. Consequently, band names often fell into certain genres and fashions, perhaps indicating the bands' politics, image, or style of music' (36–7).

31. Modern Ireland's oscillation between the values of Eurotrash and Americana may be traced through the work of U2.

32. After Whitcomb left for the United States, Bluesville split into two groups: The Chosen Few and The Action (featuring Peter – son of Larry – Adler), both of which played music heavily influenced by African-American styles

such as soul, jazz and rhythm 'n' blues. Although energy was still a key factor, the emphasis upon image and virtuosity in these (and other similar) groups shows that beat music was itself developing rapidly at this time, and that its adherents were unlikely to stay satisfied for long with its limited (in terms of space and musical vocabulary) range.

33.	I am grateful to Gerald Dawe for this information, and for the opinion that insofar as rhythm 'n' blues (as opposed to rock 'n' roll) was the principal inspiration behind the anti-showband ethos, Belfast, rather than Dublin, can justly claim to be the centre of Irish popular music discourse during the 1960s. See *The Rest is History* (1998).

34.	David Hatch and Stephen Millward argue that the difference between those British groups (such as The Beatles) influenced by rock 'n' roll and those (such as The Rolling Stones and Them) influenced by rhythm 'n' blues was determined by age, with the former being on average about four or five years older than the latter.

35.	As Noel McLaughlin and Martin McLoone suggest: '[Morrison], more than any other Irish (or British) rock musician, has maintained a strong sense of his roots while at the same time exploring – and extending considerably – the international rock idiom. His art is an art of the periphery, soaking up the influences of the centre, adapting them to its own designs and then offering them back to the centre in a wholly unique form' (2000: 184).

36.	An anonymous Cork journalist at the time wrote: 'The three have got together to form a new group and they're calling themselves The Taste (well by now we're used to odd names, bad or good, in the group world)' (quoted in Coghe n.d.: 29).

37.	Bell played in various showband and beat outfits, including Shades of Blue and a late version of Them; later he played in The Noel Redding Band and a range of other low-key projects. After The Black Eagles (a band which opened for many of the showbands), Downey played in Dublin blues band Sugar Shack before joining Lynott in Orphanage (which also included ex-Sweeney's Man Terry Woods) and eventually Thin Lizzy.

38.	Although Lynott was not the first non-white popular musician in Ireland – Earl Jordan (of The Derek Joys and The Caroline Showband) was black and Gene Chetty (of Gene and the Gents) was Asian – he was the first high-profile black Irish rock performer, and this at a time when, apart from the extraordinary example of Jimi Hendrix, rock music was an overwhelmingly white pursuit.

39.	See Hicks (1999: 1–11) for an analysis of what he terms the 'against-the-grain of the voice', by which he means the development during the 1960s of particular ways of articulating 'tough' and 'tender' personae in rock vocalization, and more interestingly of creating tension between them, occasionally within the same song.

40.	Carr and Fean had already collaborated (with the poet Peter Fallon and scene stalwart Declan Sinnott) in an avant-garde ensemble called Tara Telephone.

41.   One of the reasons why Horslips was able to perform successfully in the ball-rooms was that it had a spectacular stage show (influenced in part by the contemporary British trend for 'glam-rock') and thus provided more of a 'show' than the showbands themselves. In the light of this, consider Foucault's dictum: 'Rules are empty in themselves, violent and unfinalized; they are impersonal and can be bent to any purpose. The successes of history belong to those who are capable of seizing these rules, to replace those who had used them, to disguise themselves so as to pervert them, invert their meaning, and redirect them against those who had initially imposed them; controlling this complex mechanism, they will make it function so as to over-come the rulers through their own rules' (Rabinow 1984: 85–6).

42.   A contemporary review of *The Book of Invasions* in Britain's *New Musical Express* describes Horslips as 'Irish, crazy and well versed in the musical lore and pre-history of their native patch. Which is where the sorcery starts' (MacKinnon 1977).

CHAPTER TWO

1.   In preamble to a 1981 interview with Paul Brady, Niall Stokes wrote that it was 'in reaction to [David Bowie's] image-manipulation and theatricality that so many Irish musicians retired, confused and alienated, to traditional music in the early Seventies'.

2.   The legislation referred to any 'original and creative work, whether written, composed or executed, as the case may be, before or after the passing of this Act, which falls into one of the following categories – (a) a book or other writing; (b) a play; (c) a musical composition; (d) a painting or other like picture; (e) a sculpture', and which has been determined 'to be a work having cultural or artistic merit.' A successful applicant would 'be entitled to have the profits or gains arising' from her his work 'disregarded for all purposes of the Income Tax Acts' (www.irishstatutebook.ie/front.html).

3.   In his essay 'Getting to know Dublin 4', the journalist Desmond Fennell described the 'liberal agenda' which he believed to be active in Ireland since the 1960s, and which was organized around the 'the proposition that progress for the Republic of Ireland means removing every taint of Catholicism and of Irish nationalism from its public life and institutions and accommodating itself to Britain, the Northern Unionists and EC Europe, while retaining a state apparatus in Dublin. This boiled down to divorce, more condoms, easy on abortion; support the EC, unionists' demands, British policy in the North and revisionist history-writing; bash Charles Haughey, Fianna Fáil, the Catholic Church, the Constitution, the IRA, Sinn Fein, the GAA, Irish Americans, and all those ignorant, deluded people in north side Dublin and "rural Ireland" (the rest of the Republic) who support that sinister man or one of those benighted organisations.' He then characterized 'Dublin 4' (a term which came into wide usage after 1982) as 'the large and powerful segment of the middle and upper-middle class in South

Dublin that is committed to the liberal agenda, and which acts as mobiliser, mouthpiece and platform for all who share this commitment' (1993:197).

4.   The poet and critic Patrick Kavanagh first used these terms in the 1950s to describe different Irish cultural modes; the *provincial* (which he believed most Irish art to be) always defers to the metropolis (London), whereas the *parochial* (the novelist James Joyce being his key example) has faith in 'the social and artistic validity of his parish' (quoted in Smyth 1998: 108).

5.   Despite frequent claims that it appeared *ex nihilo* in the autumn of 1976, Jon Savage (2001: *passim*) has excavated the extensive roots of British punk, while also revealing the extent to which it was influenced by a number of contemporary popular musical genres, of which the most potent were 'glam' (especially David Bowie and Roxy Music) and rhythm 'n' blues-based pub rock.

6.   What enables the Rats' credentials to be regarded as suspect is the almost religious air of authenticity which developed around punk rock from an early stage. Despite its self-proclaimed inclusiveness – Jon Savage (2001: 220) quotes Sid Vicious: 'You just pick a chord, go twang, and you've got music' – fans and musicians were and remain fiercely protective about punk's meanings and boundaries.

7.   On the advent of pub rock and its role within the pop / rock world of the early 1970s see Bennett (1997). One of the first pub-rock bands was Bees Make Honey, which included Deke O'Brien, Mick Molloy and Barry Richardson of 1960s' Irish beat group Bluesville. O'Brien provided the link between beat and punk in Ireland, in fact, as he went on to form Nightbus, a band which toured the country with The Boomtown Rats on the infamous Falling Asunder tour in 1976 – a project which did as much as anything else to introduce a modern rock sensibility into Ireland. On the tour itself, the formation of The Boomtown Rats, and the general socio-cultural climate of Ireland in the mid-1970s, see Geldof 1986: 121ff and *passim*.

8.   Despite the obviously different musical aesthetics to which these groups ostensibly subscribed, there was, as in any small cultural formation, much overlap and influence. The Radiators from Space came to the Chiswick label in London (part owned by ex-pat Dubliner Ted Carroll, a major figure on the nascent punk scene) on the recommendation of Horslips' Eamon Carr, with whom a youthful Philip Chevron had collaborated on a project back in Dublin, and whose band Chevron particularly admired. Carroll also managed Thin Lizzy and (for a time) prog-folkies Mellow Candle. In August 1977, The Radiators from Space and The Boomtown Rats played a one-day festival in Dublin's Dalymount Park headlined by Thin Lizzy, and personnel from all three groups consorted widely over the next few years. Indeed, for many, the latter group was 'the missing link' between garage and punk; certainly, Lynott's collaboration with punk musicians such as Rat Scabies, Johnny Thunders, Steve Jones and Paul Cook show that Lizzy was one of the few established 'rock' bands to share some common ground with punk.

9.   Elsewhere Chevron has said: 'Suddenly we were part of this thing, punk rock. To be fair, it did become obvious to us that we were not part of it. We didn't wear spiky hair, we didn't have safety pins through our noses. We were aware that we had something different to offer which, alluding back to Horslips, was that we were an Irish rock band. That's something we expressed on *Ghostown*, but by that stage it was too late' (McCann 1988).

10.   O'Neill and Trelford 2003: 88–94. According to Sara Cohen, music stores such as Good Vibrations (and, of course, Sex, birthplace of British punk in London's King's Road) provide '[central] locations for interaction between scene participants', a place where they may 'share the jokes, jibes, and jargon, the myths, hype, and bravado surrounding bands and band-related activity' (1999: 241).

11.   Besides Good Vibrations, some of the more successful independent Irish or Irish-related labels to appear during the punk and post-punk period included Danceline, Hotwire, Mother, Mulligan, Reekus, Scoff, Setanta and Solid.

12.   The Northern Irish punk scene continues to be regarded as a largely non-religious movement, as may be seen from the many disavowals recorded in *It Makes You Want to Spit! The Definitive Guide to Punk in Northern Ireland* (2003) by Sean O'Neill and Guy Trelford. Hooley himself has claimed that 'the punk thing was the first time in over 10 years that all the kids came from all the ghettos and it didn't matter whether you were a Protestant or a Catholic as long as you were a punk' (quoted in Clayton Lea and Taylor 1992: 29).

13.   Rolston 1999: *passim*. See also McCann 1995, and Stokes 1994a: 9–10.

14.   The Undertones released one record – the 'Teenage Kicks' EP (September 1978) – on Good Vibrations. Having been turned down by CBS and legendary London independent label Rough Trade, they signed to American label Sire. Stiff Little Fingers released 'Suspect Device' (March 1978) on their own Rigid Digits label before becoming Rough Trade's first band in October of that year. They eventually signed to major label Chrysalis. The story of The Sex Pistols' adventures with EMI, Time Warner and Virgin over the course of their brief career, as described by Jon Savage (2001: *passim*), provides an illustration of punk's contradictory attitude towards the popular music industry, to which it is both ideologically opposed and commercially attached.

15.   Jon Savage quotes Feargal Sharkey from 1990: 'We were extremely angry young men, and it was a way of getting it out. We lived in Northern Ireland and the option was to go and join the IRA. It was an option that lots of friends of ours took. I didn't want to join up, out of simple fear. The Undertones was a way of getting out of that situation. People used to ask early on why we didn't write songs about the troubles: we were doing our best to escape from it' (2001: 619). After the demise of The Undertones, the O'Neill brothers took up the 'social realist' challenge with the resolutely political That Petrol Emotion.

16.   Although not as blatantly as some, such as their contemporaries and fellow Good Vibrations band Ruefrex.

17.   Swiss, Sloop and Herman (1998: 3). See also Street (1995), Breen (1995), and Berland (1992). The latter argues that '[in] theoretical terms, we need to situate cultural forms within the production and reproduction of capitalist spatiality . . . [The] production of texts cannot be conceived outside of the production of diverse and exacting spaces . . . much of the time we are not simply listeners to sound, or watchers of images, but occupants of spaces for listening who, by being *there*, help to produce definite meanings and effects' (39). 'The production of texts', she maintains, 'cannot be conceived outside of the production of spaces' (42).

18.   This was still the case in 2001 when Jessica Fuller, manager of the IRMA (Irish Recorded Music Association) Trust Instrument Bank, claimed that 'aside from social and economic disadvantage, geographic location is one of the main obstacles to music development here, with many organisations and services operating from the larger cities and towns. This inhibits the growth of some music' (30).

19.   Both Prendergast (1987: 249) and Clayton-Lea and Taylor (1992: 115) refer to the 'musical lunacy' of assorted Cork bands.

20.   On Donnelly and the post-punk scene in Cork see the documentary by McDermott, Hurley and O'Toole (no date).

21.   This is not to deny the vitality of local scenes such as Carlow, for example, a town which – in Deirdre O'Brien's lively account to the author (2003) – functioned as an important centre of popular music activity in the midlands throughout the 1980s. The point is that the local scene provided a limited forum, and that the more ambitious artists would eventually have to advance to the next tier of activity, which in the case of Ireland meant Dublin.

22.   On the mutual musical suspicion between Dublin and the rest of the country see 'Ireland's gone west' (1990: 102–6), an essay by journalist Fintan O'Toole which develops an earlier piece, 'Going west: the country versus the city in Irish writing' (1985).

23.   The road song is, of course, seminal to rock discourse, and as such seems to tie in with Olson's point that popular music may be less about identity – who you are – than about migrancy and movement – 'a continual reorientation toward new sites, new scenes, new homes' (1998: 284).

24.   Of course, Planxty's willingness to combine different styles and traditions may not have been the trail-brazing, high-concept package it was widely perceived to be, but the result of much more pragmatic, and much less romantic, developments. As Paul Brady said in interview in 1981: 'it was basically a whole load of people with varying, different views and attitudes towards life and music, desperately trying to find some common way – some direction to go in. Some wanted to stay there, others wanted to get out – and I wanted to get out' (Stokes 1981).

25.   In the same 1981 interview with Niall Stokes, Brady claimed that he didn't

'find many messages coming through to me from that area', and that 'there is a bottom to the well'. 'I think probably people are arriving at that same opinion,' he went on, 'that there's an end to what people can do with traditional music without it no longer being traditional music. Whether or not that's been reached yet is a matter of opinion.'

26.   The influential American *Billboard* magazine introduced its world-music chart for the first time in 1990; five years later, as June Skinner Sawyers points out, 'two-thirds of world-music chart toppers were Celtic' (2000: 270).

27.   Ernest Renan, *The Poetry of the Celtic Races* (1859), quoted in Storey 1988: 54–60.

28.   Skinner Sawyers' study is not a scholarly book, and might therefore be seen as somewhat of a soft target for the current analysis. Yet as a popular text looking to engage with and contextualize a set of highly popular contemporary musical and economic practices, it does contribute to a pervading discourse in which 'Celtic' music circulates as ideological currency, impacting upon all manner of social, cultural and political contexts.

29.   Skinner Sawyers 2000: 5, emphasis added. Although Clannad had been travelling the road since the debut in the early 1970s, 'Celtic' music as an international phenomenon might be dated from the release of Enya's soundtrack album for the BBC television series *The Celts* (1987).

30.   It's an interesting fact that the name 'Shane MacGowan' translates into English as 'John Smith'. One wonders if the man in question would have garnered the same reputation, or indeed pursued the same career in the same manner, had he been so tagged.

31.   On the controversy excited by The Pogues amongst members of the Irish folk scene see Scanlon 1988: 75ff. Woods reflected in a later interview: 'Irish music had become very precious to a number of people, and it was kept in a precious sort of way. I wanted to take Irish music into rock back in the sixties. One of the things The Pogues gave me was being able to be a lot freer about the music' (Bellamy 2001/2002: 26).

32.   *My Magpie Eyes are Hungry for the Prize* (2000) is David Cavanaugh's compelling account of Alan McGee's Creation Records label, offering a fascinating history – sometimes inspiring, sometimes depressing – of the emergence of indie, and the practical and theoretical problems faced by the successful independent label.

33.   See Prendergast (1987: 235–62) and Clayton Lea and Taylor (1992: 104–26) for annotated lists of artists from the period. Although formed during the 1980s, some bands (such as Aslan, The Frames, A House and Something Happens!), made their biggest impacts during the 1990s, and will be dealt with in Chapter Three.

34.   This was the context within which the Field Day Theatre Company was formed in Derry City in 1980 by Brian Friel and Stephen Rea.

35.   It's interesting to note that more or less around the same time (*c*. 1987) as The Stars of Heaven were at their peak, Roddy Doyle's fictional band, The

Commitments, was converting from a ten-piece soul band to a four-piece Byrds-style country rock group called The Brassers (Doyle 1992: 136–40).

36. Some of the bands that displayed 'shoe-gazing' tendencies were Lush, Moose and Chapterhouse, as well as many Creation acts: Ride, Slowdive, The Jesus and Mary Chain, Wire, and even, for a time, Five Go Down To The Sea?, which proved too maverick for a label devoted to mavericks. My Bloody Valentine is also widely cited as a seminal influence by many subsequent rock acts.

37. Goodge and Butcher had little to do with My Bloody Valentine as a studio proposition, and insofar as most of O'Ciosig's drums were pre-recorded into a sequencer on *Loveless*, that album is predominantly the work of Shields.

38. In retrospect, any number of factors might be adduced to account for the emergence of 'raggle-taggle', but some of the more obvious influences included U2's interest in Americana; Van Morrison's collaboration with The Chieftains on *Irish Heartbeat* (1988), and his re-emphasis of a 'Celtic' sensibility on albums such as *No Guru, No Method, No Teacher* (1986) and *Poetic Champions Compose* (1987); and the culmination of The Pogues' fusion of punk and trad. on *If I Should Fall From Grace with God* (1988). Murphy also cites the contemporary work of Leonard Cohen, Elvis Costello, David Byrne and Patti Smith as contributing to the advent of this new sensibility.

39. Murphy 2003a: 17. Other Irish acts routinely described as part of the 'raggle-taggle' mode include The Black Velvet Band, The Frames and Kila – the latter two surviving into (and indeed thriving in) the new century.

40. Although, as mentioned, 'shoe-gazing' and 'raggle-taggle' were very different musical propositions, O'Maonlai and O'Braonain had played with Shields and O'Ciosoig in Congress, an early 1980s precursor to My Bloody Valentine.

41. It's ironic in this context that one of the performers – Maria Doyle Kennedy – associated with Hothouse Flowers also appeared (as singer Natalie) in Alan Parker's adaptation of *The Commitments*.

42. In 'On the fringe', their chapter on the Irish avant-garde tradition, Tony Clayton-Lea and Rogan Taylor claim that 'the face of Irish rock has been, is, and will undoubtedly continue to be, rather one-dimensional. Very enjoyable, often inspirational, occasionally exciting, but generally lacking the innate thrilling adventurism and possibility of failure of many American or British avant-gardists' (1992: 55).

43. It should be noted that The Virgin Prunes are not the 'noisiest' (in Attali's terms) Irish band from the modern era, as their music retains links – however tentative or remote – with the idea of 'the song'.

44. Some of the musicians and collectives frequently cited as part of Ireland's alternative 'rock' tradition include Nine Wassies from Bainne, Toasted Heretic, Five Go Down To The Sea?, Stump and Stano. To this list may be added many other bands – Fatima Mansions and My Bloody Valentine, for

example – whose music, although perhaps more mainstream, still manages to inhabit the borderland between rock music and something else.

45. In his history of Alan McGee's Creation label, David Cavanagh (2000) describes at length the philosophical and commercial bases underpinning the post-punk 'independent' movement. It's clear that, whatever its roots, by 1980 Island was no longer an independent label in the strict sense demanded by the British underground; it's clear also that, whatever *its* roots, U2 never subscribed to the 'indie' ideal in any meaningful sense. This helps to account for the continued widespread antipathy towards the band and its label on the part of certain sections of the British music press. At the same time, Hesmondhalgh (1999) shows that as it was developing during the 1980s and 90s, 'indie' came to connote much more than merely being signed to an 'independent' label.

46. In *Rock: The Primary Text*, Allan F. Moore discusses the link between U2's sound during the 1980s and the aura of 'authenticity' with which it was surrounded at that time. This 'authenticity', he suggests, was itself partially an effect of the 'big', frequently outdoors connotations of its music, which could be created in a variety of ways:

> Aside from the wide registral gaps at the openings to many songs (thereafter the guitar will frequently fall to the vocal register), the great use of digital delay on the guitar (giving very immediate echoes) and the high degree of apparent reverb (the 'atmospheric' background, wherein any textural holes are felt to be only temporary) both seem to contribute greatly to this effect, as if the sound were bouncing around in a great amphitheatre. This, combined with the use of long sustained organ chords / notes and sometimes high sustained guitar pitches, becomes most apparent on *The Unforgettable Fire*. A possible additional factor is the fact that, especially from *The Unforgettable Fire* onwards, textures often progress from an initial guitar (possible combined with voice) though the gradual addition of bass and kit and frequently a second guitar layer. Comparison of U2's *War* and *The Unforgettable Fire* makes this plain – the sense of space is much more apparent on the later album (1993: 144–5).

47. Ironically, it was on *The Unforgettable Fire* that some commentators began to discern the emergence of a more 'Irish' sound. See Stuart Bailie (1990), who claims that 'Eno's methods heightened the atmosphere and introversion in their approach . . Bono's vocals, freed from the clunky restraints of the rock medium, had a fluid, more Celtic drift here . . ."MLK" . . . with its simple, wavering melody, wasn't a thousand miles from *sean-nós* singing' (18–19).

48. In a contemporary interview (entitled 'Bono: The White Nigger') with the Irish philosopher Richard Kearney, the singer discussed U2's ambivalent relationship with the US – and, more precisely, what it might mean to be 'an Irish rock band' in America. He claimed that 'we found the 'Irish Thing' through the American: Gospel, Blues, Robert Johnson, Bob Dylan, these became passports home' (Kearney 1988: 189).

CHAPTER THREE

1.   In latter years Shields has become a semi-permanent member of Primal Scream. In 2004 he was nominated for a BAFTA award for his contribution to Sofia Coppola's film *Lost in Translation.*

2.   The distance Bono and the rest of the band had travelled in a short time may be gauged by his comment in conversation with Richard Kearney in 1988: 'What kind of music will people be listening to in the 1990s? Machine music? Sophisticated noise of a New York dance club? I don't think so. Traditional musics may be reinterpreted by the new technology, but as we are more dehumanised, urbanised, corralled into confusion, surely we will turn to simplicity' (Kearney 1988: 191).

3.   A contemporary reviewer in the *NME* (never a natural ally of U2's music) wrote: 'Necessity is the smotherer of invention in big league pop, yet U2 have just made an LP that's sparky and surprising and sulky, bristling with offbeat effects and guttural noises . . . U2 are not the villain' (Andrew Collins, 'Adam and the Trabants' in Kessler (2003), 106.

4.   Both Atara Stein (1999) and Robyn Brothers (1999) discern an essential continuity between the concerns of the 'real' U2 of the 1980s and the series of personae adopted during and after *Achtung Baby.*

5.   With special reference to the Fly character, Stein writes: 'On both [*Achtung Baby* and *Zooropa*], the band self-consciously deconstructs the love song, revealing how the speaker's love object ultimately serves as a vehicle for his own self-love and self-aggrandizement, a screen or mirror of his own narcissistic self-projection. She becomes his "inspiration", which he must then figuratively "kill" and cannibalize in order to find himself as an artist or poet' (1999: 269).

6.   In general terms, we may say that one influential strand of modernist thought (as exemplified, for example, in the work of Martin Heidegger) insists that the flourishing of any genuine work of art depends upon its roots in a native soil. Deprived of such roots, art is reduced to a meaningless caricature of its former self. The problem, therefore, is to recover a viable homeland in which meaningful roots can be established. Place construction should be about the recovery of roots, the recovery of the art of dwelling. This may be compared with the post-modernist response to space, as described (with reference to U2 and a number of other popular cultural figures) by Kieran Keohane: 'Aesthetic political representations of the Irish spirit currently fluctuate between discourses of communitarian essentialism and the transcendental homelessness of a race of angels. There is a desire for post-national, cosmopolitan identification, to escape from the bonds of tradition to a free, but fearfully lonely, existential condition of rootlessness and, at the same time, a desire to return to, to re-collect and re-live in the tradition(s) of "real" (that is to say imagined) Ireland(s)' (1997: 302).

7.   Although see Whiteley (1997), who in her chapter on 'Girl Power' finds the collusive materialism of The Spice Girls to be mitigated by their presentation of 'a more pragmatic and practical side of feminism' (227).

8.   The subject of women's relation to, and representation in, modern popular music has exploded in recent years, but for extended treatments see Bayton (1999), Burns and Lafranc (2001), Evans (1994), O'Brien (1995), O'Dair (1997), Raphael (1995), Reynolds and Press (1995), Whiteley, (1997, 2000).

9.   In their introduction to *The Sex Revolts*, Reynolds and Press differentiate between a more aggressive male identity – encompassing a variety of martial discourses – such as may be found in various artists (The Rolling Stones, Iggy Pop, The Clash, Thin Lizzie) and genres (heavy metal, techno, gangsta rap), and what they call 'the psychedelic mother's boy' who creates 'idealised images of women and femininity' to facilitate 'the endless expressions of a longing to *come home*, to return to the womb, that often takes the form of cosmic / oceanic mysticism or worship of Mother Nature' (The Byrds, Van Morrison, Pink Floyd, Brian Eno, My Bloody Valentine) (1995: xff). This model is linked to what earlier critics had identified as a bifurcation in rock discourse between 'cock-rock' – 'an explicit, crude and often aggressive expression of male sexuality' – and 'teenybop' – 'based on self-pity, vulnerability and need' (Frith and McRobbie 1990: 374–75, *passim*).

10.   The relevant clauses from *Bunreacht na hÉireann* (*Constitution of Ireland*) runs: '(1.1) The State recognises the family as the natural primary and fundamental unit of Society, and as a moral institution possessing inalienable and imprescriptible rights, anterior and superior to all positive law . . . (2.1) In particular, the State recognises that by her life within the home, woman gives to the State a support without which the common good cannot be achieved. (2.2) The State shall, therefore, endeavour to ensure that mothers shall not be obliged by economic necessity to engage in labour to the neglect of their duties in the home. (3.1) The State pledges itself to guard with special care the institution of Marriage, on which the Family is founded, and to protect it against attack.'

11.   On female rock musicianship see Bayton (1990), Clawson (1999) and Cohen (1991: 201–22), each of whom considers the reasons – sociological, cultural, political – behind the general dearth of female rock musicians and what Clawson refers to as the 'conflation of [rock] music and masculinity' (106). Bayton also offers an ethnographical study of the dynamics of, and the special challenges faced by, all-female rock groups.

12.   Some of the better-known female showband performers from the 1960s and 70s include Philomena Begley, Muriel Day, Bridie Gallagher, Sandie Jones, Eileen Kelly (Kelley), Maisie McDaniel, Tina, and Eleanor Toner. For photographic images and a fuller list see *www.iangallagher.com* and *homepage.tinet.ie/~athenryart/showindex.htm*.

13.   One former member of The Boy Scoutz, Catherine Owens, went on to work for U2 on the designs for its Zoo TV tour – one of a number of women associated with the Principle management company. Flanagan (1995: 135) has discussed the gender weighting within the U2 organization, although he fudges the question of the different kinds of roles (administrative, practical, organizational etc.) assumed by men and women.

14. On the association of women with bass guitar see Clawson (1998), who speculates as to the relationship between the instrument's gender iconography (heaviness, string thickness, rhythmic qualities etc.), the relative ease (compared with the other standard rock instruments, such as drums, guitar, keyboards) with which it may be learned, and the complex job 'queuing' system that obtains within rock discourse. Her description of the 'meaning' of female bass players accords with O'Riordan's profile within The Pogues: 'For aspiring, and often late-starting, women musicians, the bass offered relatively quick and easy entrance into a world that had largely excluded them; for men, both performers and audiences, acceptance of women as bassists provided confirmation of a broad-minded, oppositional identity within a framework that reorganized, rather than totally abandoned, masculine predominance' (202). Female bass players of note include Kim Deal (The Pixies), Jill Emery (Hole), Kim Gordon (Sonic Youth), Maureen Herman (Babes in Toyland), Tessa Pollitt (The Slits), Tina Weymouth (Talking Heads), D'Arcy Wretzky (Smashing Pumpkins), Annette Zilinskas (The Bangles), as well as Hilary Woods of Irish band JJ72.

15. Coughlan has cited Dolores Keane and Gay Woods as influences, describing their music as a form of 'Irish blues' and comparing it with that of Billie Holiday (Farrell, Guinness and Lloyd 1996: 33).

16. Although I consider her principally in an Irish context here, O'Connor was heiress at the outset of her career to over thirty years of female involvement with rock 'n' roll, encompassing the work of many different artists pursuing many different strategies. See Reynolds and Press (1995) and Whiteley (2000), *passim.*

17. In *The Complete Guide to Celtic Music,* June Skinner Sawyers claims that '[women] played a big part in the perpetuation of the ballad' (136), going on to cite contemporary Irish singers such as Mary Black, Maura O'Connell, Eleanor Shanley, Eleanor McEvoy and Dolores Keane as inheritors of a 'Celtic' tradition of female balladry (157).

18. Reynolds and Press describe a female approach that 'attempts to infuse rock with "feminine" qualities: rather than imitate men, it tries to imagine a female strength that's different but equivalent . . . The affirmation of "feminine" qualities consolidates female identity against the attacks of both straight society and rebel counterculture. But, even as it valorises the "feminine", it runs the risk of confirming patriarchal notions of what femininity is (emotional, vulnerable, caring, maternal etc.)' (1995: 233). They go on to cite O'Connor as fitting into this category; and while this maybe true in the wider context of Anglo-American popular music, it's clear that her music functions differently when considered in terms of the contemporary Irish scene – an example of the way in which different contexts (geographical, political and so on) impact upon analysis.

19. As Holly Kruse writes: '[Female] singers who transgress the boundaries of what is considered "nice" singing often encounter hostility from the male-dominated music industry and music press. Powerful, unconventional female

voices evoke profoundly negative and, not incidentally, gendered reactions because of what the signify, both to the singers and to the audience: the visceral expression of female pain, rage, and frustration. This scream of female anger poses a direct threat to patriarchy, which attempts to cover over both the existence of such anger and the structures which engender it' (1999: 90–1).

20. As Keith Negus points out, 'In trying to negate a gender stereotype, her deviation from the conventional was emphasized and this became part of the way in which her gender identity was reinforced in the media' (1995: 222).

21. Adorno never remarked the contradiction whereby his left-wing critique of popular music replicated the essentially bourgeois division of music into specific canons of taste. He was thus implicated in what Tony Bennett describes as 'a highly paradoxical history in which Marxist criticism has functioned largely collaboratively in relation to the distinctions forged by bourgeois criticism: approving of the same body of canonized works but for different reasons, and disapproving of the rest – lumped together as a residue – but, again, for different reasons' (1986: 241). Adorno's category error is then replicated by popular condemnations of popular music which, as David Brackett points out, tend to 'assume a particular definition of music which the new genres do not fit . . . What is interesting is that mass media definitions of "noise" and "music" often rest on the same, unstated assumptions as do musicological definitions. Both privilege Romantic, European-based notions about what music should be; and both tend to undervalue styles and genres originating in social locations outside those of bourgeois, European or Euro-American society' (1999: 128–9).

22. Walsh and Reynolds apparently auditioned approximately 300 hopefuls before choosing the five members of Boyzone: Keith Duffy, Stephen Gately, Mikey Graham, Ronan Keating and Shane Lynch.

23. The spat between members of Westlife and UK hip hop outfit So Solid Crew at the 2002 Brit Awards represented an interesting clash of styles and iconographies.

24. It was around about the time of Lynott's death in 1986 that black footballers – usually the product of mixed-race marriages in the UK – began to play on a regular basis for the national team. In some respects, the prospect of so many black Irishmen in the public eye helped to prepare the way for the emergence of a high-profile black Irish pop singer.

25. Interview with François Pittion, Dublin, 6 April 2002.

26. As Collin and Godfrey say: '[Ecstasy] seemed to help people to open up and really talk, to enable honesty without fear or conditioning intervening. It induced a powerful impression that everything was all right with the world. Yet what no one really hit on at first was that it also had an incredible effect on the body, seeming to free up the spine and limbs. When combined with rhythmic music it hooked the mind into the textures of the percussion and the outline of the melody. Certain sounds appealed intensely to the drug effect' (1997: 28).

27.   On the rise of the 'superstar' DJ see Haslam 1998. On the adulteration of 'authentic' Dublin club culture by a combination of sponsorship, police harassment and various 'corporate' concerns see the article in *The Slate* (Anon., 2002). A disdain for the contemporary Irish scene – with its awards, its business- and drug-orientation, and its general ignorance of the music itself – is a common attitude amongst many older members of the Dublin dance scene.

28.   The recruitment of high-profile British DJs to play non-metropolitan Irish dance venues recalls a similar practice during the 1960s when British band-leaders such as Joe Loss, Sid Phillips and Humphrey Littleton would bring their orchestras to various Irish regional centres.

29.   For some of the names at the forefront of modern Irish dance and electronica see the annual *Hot Press Yearbook*.

30.   This relates to what Paul Théberge describes as 'a persistent tendency among those who regard music as a form of essential and authentic experience to vilify technology as a corrupting force' (1999: 209). A typical example in this context would be the advocation of a 'roots' approach to recording by Christy Dignam of Aslan: 'I find when you do it that way, you might get warts in the music but it retains sincerity and a bit of soul. Whenever you use these new computer packages, it can bleach the soul out of the music' (Walsh 2001: 21). As Théberge goes on to point out, however, '[in] isolating particu-lar technologies in this way, critics and proponents alike tend to ignore the degree to which other (favored) genres of pop music are also technologically based' (211).

31.   Later, in terms especially resonant for this section, Adorno writes:

> To be musical means to them to be capable of following given rhyth-mical patterns without being disturbed by 'individualizing' aberrations, and to fit even the syncopations into the basic time units. This is the way in which their response to music immediately expresses their desire to obey . . . For the machine is an end in itself only under given social condi-tions – where men are appendages of the machines on which they work. The adaptation to machine music necessarily implies a renunciation of one's own human feelings and at the same time a fetishism of the machine such that its instrumental character becomes obscured thereby (212–13).

32.   Attali predicted the emergence of digitalization and the sampler, for example – a prediction which came true with the emergence of house and techno – and he went on to describe some of the implications of this new technology for the ways in which popular music would be made in the future. On the central role of sampling and sequencing within modern dance music see Brown (1998), and Goodwin (1990, 1991).

33.   On the historical emergence of the idea of 'the author', and the changing meaning of what he terms the 'author function' see Foucault (1969). On the evolution of mixing and DJing as modern 'art forms' see Kealy (1990) and Rietveld (1998). It's clear that the initial threat to traditional notions of

authorship represented by dance technology has been gradually overtaken by the re-emergence of various 'author-functions' associated with specialist DJs, producers and labels. On the pursuit of specific personalized 'sounds' by DJs / producers / writers, and what he calls 'a reconsideration of the problems of skill, technology and the role of sound in defining musical style' (275), see Théberge 1995. One of the more disappointing aspects of this return to authorship has been the way in which it has worked to reproduce discourses of exclusion – such as gender – associated with previous dispensations (Bradby 1993).

34.   There is no clear reason why acts from Northern Ireland such as Holmes, Fergie, D:Ream or Agnelli & Nelson should perform better in commercial terms than their southern counterparts although, as with the rhythm 'n' blues movement of the 1960s, the official cultural and political ties with the UK are surely a significant factor.

35.   The first home-produced dance track to make any kind of impression – called 'West in Motion' (1992) by Dublin collective Bumble – incorporated elements of traditional Irish music. This trend was revitalized later in the decade by Dances to Tipperary, which specializes in producing generic dance versions of popular Irish songs.

36.   The Irish singer-songwriter scene during the 1990s became particularly associated with a regular dedicated session at the International Bar in Dublin. The artists who feature on a special compilation album of this session are Pat Barrett, Luka Bloom, Damien Dempsey, Glen Hansard, Gemma Hayes, Nina Hynes, Miriam Ingram, Nick Kelly, Sinéad Martin, Kevin May, Mundy and Dave Murphy.

37.   The city's most renowned pop products up until the advent of The Cranberries were Granny's Intentions and Tuesday Blue.

38.   The use of the violin in a rock context suggests obvious parallels with the music of The Waterboys, who at one stage operated as a fully fledged raggle-taggle band.

CONCLUSION

1.   At the time of writing, some of the most promising of the new Irish acts include The Revs, Melaton, Fresno, Go Commando, Jack L, Jetplane Landing, The Jimmy Cake, Bell XI, Hal, Future Kings of Spain, Relish and Mundy (see the Discography). The Fleadh returned in 2004 with Bob Dylan headlining. Besides Ash, the most serious Irish contenders to headline a future Fleadh are JJ72, The Thrills and Snow Patrol – all of whom, incidentally, have bypassed the domestic scene to some extent.

2.   The British journalist Tom Cox, for example, is in no doubt of the malignant influence of money on music: 'To anyone even vaguely in love with the past, it is clear that the corporate stranglehold of today's music business is siphoning the lifeblood of pop's heart and soul. The difference is the gap between writing what you think the public will perceive as a hit single, and writing

what you think someone in a suit will think the public will perceive as a hit single . . . Musicians are no longer part-time drop outs; they are corporate cogs' (2000).

3. It's interesting in this context to consider an event such as the 'Fuck Witness' festival, held annually as an alternative to one of the island's major popular music gatherings: does it represent a genuine protest again a perceived stranglehold on Irish music held by the multinational corporations, or are the participant acts simply peeved because they haven't been invited to perform at Witness itself? And at what stage, if ever, will the latter become less cool than the former?

Bibliography

(titles published in London unless otherwise stated)

Theodor Adorno, 'On popular music', in Storey (1994), 202–14

Anon., 'Dublin's squeaky clean rave scene', *The Slate* 13 (April 2002), 16–18

Matthew Arnold, *On the Study of Celtic Literature* (1867; Smith, Elder & Co., 1900)

T.G. Ashplant and Gerry Smyth (eds), *Explorations in Cultural History* (Pluto Press, 2001)

Jacques Attali, *Noise: The Political Economy of Music* (1977), trans. Brian Massumi (Manchester: Manchester University Press, 1985)

Stuart Bailie, 'Black velvet: Ireland's finest vinyl', *New Musical Express* (2 June 1990), 18–19

Mavis Bayton, 'How women become musicians' (1988), in Frith and Goodwin (1990), 238–57

——. *Frock Rock* (Oxford: Oxford University Press, 1999)

Seamus Bellamy, 'Down all the days: The Pogues are back in town', *Irish Music* 7.5 (December / January 2001 / 2002), 26–7

Jody Berland, 'Angels dancing: cultural technology and the production of space', in Grossberg, Nelson and Treichler (1992), 38–55

Paul Bew and Henry Patterson, *Seán Lemass and the Making of Modern Ireland, 1945–1966* (Dublin: Gill and Macmillan, 1982)

Andrew Blake, *The Land Without Music: Music, Culture and Society in Twentieth-century Britain* (Manchester: Manchester University Press, 1997)

——. (ed.) *Living Through Pop* (Routledge, 1999)

Dermot Bolger (ed.), *Letters from the New Island* (Dublin: Raven Arts Press, 1991)

Pierre Bourdieu, *Distinction: A Social Critique of the Judgement of Taste* (1979), trans. Richard Nice (Routledge, 1984)

Tara Brabazon and Paul Stock, '"We love you Ireland": *Riverdance* and stepping through antipodean memory', *Irish Studies Review* 7.3 (1999), 301–11

David Brackett, 'Music', in Horner and Swiss (1999), 124–40

Barbara Bradby, 'Sampling sexuality: gender, technology and the body in dance music', *Popular Music* 12.2 (1993), 155–76

John Braine, 'The history of Dublin clubbing' (MS, n.d.)

Marcus Breen, 'The end of the world as we know it: popular music's cultural mobility', in Straw *et al* (1995), 45–53

Robyn Brothers, 'Time to heal, "Desire" time: the cyberprophesy of U2's "Zoo World Order"', in Dettmar and Richey (1999), 237–67

Adam Brown, 'Let's all have a disco? football, pop music and democratization', in Redhead, Wynne and O'Connor (1998), 61–83

Terence Brown, *Ireland: A Social and Cultural History 1922–1985* (Fontana, 1985)

Lori Burns and Melisse Lafranc, *Disruptive Divas: Feminism, Identity and Popular Music* (Routledge, 2001)

Nicole Byers, Rob Fitzpatrick and David Fowler, 'Coming up for Eire', *Ministry* (December 2001), 55–59

David Cavanagh, *The Creation Records Story: My Magpie Eyes are Hungry for the Prize* (Virgin, 2000)

Iain Chambers, 'Review of *Dangerous Crossroads: Popular Music, Postmodernism and the Poetics of Place* by George Lipsitz', *Popular Music* 15.2 (May 1996), 247–8

Lavinia Y.M. Chang, 'Moral rights and the Irish music industry', *Commercial Law Practitioner* 2 (November 1995), 243–50

Malcolm Chapman, 'Thoughts on Celtic music', in Stokes (1994), 29–44

Paula Clancy *et al*, *The Public and the Arts: A Survey of Behaviour and Attitudes in Ireland* (Dublin: The Arts Council, 1994)

Mary Ann Clawson, 'When women play the bass: instrument specialization and gender interpretation in alternative rock music', *Gender and Society* 13:2 (1998), 193–210

——. 'Masculinity and skill acquisition in the adolescent rock band', *Popular Music* 18:1 (1999), 99–114

Tony Clayton-Lea and Rogan Taylor, *Irish Rock: Where It's Come From, Where It's At, Where It's Going* (Dublin: Gill and Macmillan, 1992)

Sara Cohen, *Rock Culture in Liverpool: Popular Music in the Making* (Oxford: Clarendon Press, 1991)

——. 'Scenes' in Horner and Swiss (1999), 239–50

Matthew Collin and John Godfrey, *Altered State: The Story of Ecstasy Culture and Acid House* (Serpent's Tail, 1997)

Tom Cox, 'Pop', *The Guardian* (11 November 2000), 18

Mark Cunningham, *Live and Kicking: The Rock Concert Industry in the Nineties* (Sanctuary, 1999)

Jude Davies, '"It's like feminism, but you don't have to burn your bra": Girl Power and the Spice Girls' Breakthrough, 1996–7' in Blake (1999), 159–73

Gerald Dawe, *The Rest is History* (Newry: Abbey Press, 1998)

Kevin J.H. Dettmar and William Richey (eds), *Reading Rock and Roll: Authenticity, Appropriation, Aesthetics* (New York: Columbia University Press, 1999)

Katie Donovan, A. Norman Jeffares and Brendan Kennelly (eds), *Ireland's Women: Writings Past and Present* (Kyle Cathie, 1994)

Roddy Doyle, *The Barrytown Trilogy* (Minerva, 1992)

Eamon Dunphy, *Unforgettable Fire: The Story of U2* (Penguin, 1988)

Liz Evans (ed.), *Women, Sex and Rock 'n' Roll: In Their Own Words* (Pandora, 1994)

Antony Farrell, Vivienne Guinness and Julian Lloyd (eds), *My Generation: Rock 'n' Roll Remembered – An Imperfect History* (Dublin: The Lilliput Press, 1996)

Desmond Fennell, *Heresy: The Battle of Ideas in Modern Ireland* (Belfast: Blackstaff Press, 1993)

Bill Flanagan, *U2 at the End of the World* (Bantam Press, 1995)

Michel Foucault, 'What is an author?' (1969) in Rabinow (1984), 101–20

Simon Frith, 'The cultural study of popular music', in Grossberg, Nelson and Treichler (1992), 174–86

——. 'Music and identity', in Hall and du Gay (1996), 108–27

Simon Frith and Andrew Goodwin (eds), *On Record: Rock, Pop, and the Written Word* (Routledge, 1990)

Simon Frith and Angela McRobbie, 'Music and sexuality' (1978), in Frith and Goodwin (1990: 371–89)

Jessica Fuller, 'Playing dividends', interview in *Hot Press* 25.21 (October 2001), 30

Bob Geldof, *Is That It?* (Harmondsworth: Penguin, 1986)

Andrew Goodwin, 'Sample and hold: pop music in the digital age of reproduction', in Frith and Goodwin (1990), 258–73

——. 'Popular music and postmodern theory', *Cultural Studies*, 5:2 (July 1991), 174–90

Theodor Gracyk, 'Valuing and evaluating popular music', *The Journal of Aesthetics and Art Criticism*, 57:2 (Spring 1999), 212–20

Lawrence Grossberg, Cary Nelson and Paula Treichler (eds), *Cultural Studies* (Routledge, 1992)

Stuart Hall and Paul du Gay (eds), *Questions of Cultural Identity* (Sage, 1996)

John P. Harrington and Elizabeth J. Mitchell (eds), *Politics and Performance in Contemporary Northern Ireland* (Amherst: University of Massachusetts Press, 1999)

Dave Haslam, 'DJ culture', in Redhead, Wynne and O'Connor (1998), 150–61

Jackie Hayden, 'Interview with Paul Brady', *Hot Press* 25:21 (10 October 2001b), 3–8

Dick Hebdige, *Subculture: The Meaning of Style* (Methuen, 1979)

Edward O. Henry, 'Institutions for the promotion of indigenous music: the case for Ireland's Comhaltas Ceoltóirí Éireann', *Ethnomusicology* 33:1 (Winter 1989), 67–95

David Hesmondhalgh, 'Indie: the institutional politics and aesthetics of a popular music genre', *Cultural Studies* vol. 13, no. 1 (1999), 34–61

Michael Hicks, *Sixties Rock: Garage, Psychedelia, and Other Satisfactions* (Urbana and Chicago: University of Illinois Press, 1999)

Bruce Horner and Thomas Swiss (eds), *Key Terms in Popular Music and Culture* (Oxford: Basil Blackwell, 1999)

Steve Jones, 'Recasting popular music studies' conceptions of the authentic and the local in light of Bell's theorem', in Straw *et al* (1995), 169–72

Edward R. Kealy, 'From craft to art: the case of sound mixers and popular music' in Frith and Goodwin (1990), 207–20

Mary Celeste Kearney, 'Riot grrrl – feminism – lesbian culture', in Whiteley (1997), 207–29

Richard Kearney, *Across the Frontiers: Ireland in the 1990s – Cultural, Political, Economic* (Dublin: Wolfhound Press, 1988)

——. 'Letters on a new republic (three open letters to three presidents, Jacques Delors, Mary Robinson, Gerry Adams)' in Bolger 1991, 302–21

Brian P. Kennedy, *Dreams and Responsibilities: The State and the Arts in Independent Ireland* (Dublin: The Arts Council, 1990)

Kieran Keohane, 'Traditionalism and homelessness in contemporary Irish music', in Mac Laughlin (1997), 274–303

Ted Kessler (ed.), *U2* (NME Originals, 2003) vol. 1, no. 5

Richard Kirkland, *Culture in Northern Ireland since 1965: Moments of Danger* (Harlow: Longman, 1996)

Holly Kruse, 'Gender', in Horner and Swiss (1999), 85–100

Dave Laing *et al*, *The Electric Muse: The Story of Folk into Rock* (Methuen, 1975)

J.J. Lee, *Ireland 1912–1985: Politics and Society* (Cambridge: Cambridge University Press, 1989)

Henri Lefebvre, *The Production of Space* (1974), trans. Donald Nicholson-Smith (Oxford: Basil Blackwell, 1991)

Eamonn McCann, 'Down all the days: an interview with Philip Chevron', *Hot Press* (24 March 1988)

May McCann, 'Music and politics in Ireland: the specificity of the folk revival in Belfast', *British Journal of Ethnomusicology* 4 (1995), 51–75

Marie McCarthy, *Passing it On: The Transmission of Music in Irish Culture* (Cork: Cork University Press, 1999)

R.M. MacIver and Charles H. Page, 'The mark of a community is that one's life may be lived wholly within it', in Worsley (1970), 296–7

Angus MacKinnon, *The Book of Invasions: A Celtic Symphony* (review), *New Musical Express* (15 January 1977)

Jim Mac Laughlin (ed.), *Location and Dislocation in Contemporary Irish Society: Emigration and Irish Identities* (Cork: Cork University Press, 1997)

Noel McLaughlin and Martin McLoone, 'Hybridity and national musics: the case of Irish rock music', *Popular Music* 19.2 (May 2000), 181–200

Ray Mac Sharry and Padraic White, *The Making of the Celtic Tiger: The Inside Story of Ireland's Boom Economy* (Cork: Mercier Press, 2000)

Robert Marshall, 'License to Thrill: Licensing Laws in Southern Ireland' in *BBM* 73.3 (April 2002), 88–90

Wilfred Mellers, *Twilight of the Gods: The Beatles in Retrospect* (Faber, 1973)

Cressida Miles, 'Spatial politics: a gendered sense of place', in Redhead, Wynne and O'Connor (1998), 48–60

Tony Mitchell and Peter Doyle (eds), *Changing Sounds: New Directions and Configurations in Popular Music* (Sydney: University of Technology, 1999)

Allan F. Moore, *Rock: The Primary Text* (Buckingham: Open University Press, 1993)

Peter Murphy, 'The wayward wind', *Hotpress* 27:10 (21 May 2003a), 17–21

——. 'The people's band', *Hotpress* 27:11 (18 June 2003b), 24–26

Keith Negus, 'Sinéad O'Connor: miniature portrait of the artist as an angry young woman', in Straw *et al* (1995), 221–23

Nuala O'Connor, *Bringing It All Back Home: The Influence of Irish Music* (BBC Books, 1991)

Sean O'Hagan, 'Crossing the great divide: The Stars of Heaven', *New Musical Express* (2 May 1987), 22

Mark J. V. Olson, '"Everybody loves our town": scenes, spatiality, migrancy', in Swiss, Sloop and Herman (1998), 269–89

Sean O'Neill and Guy Trelford, *It Makes You Want to Spit! The Definitive Guide to Punk in Northern Ireland* (Dublin: Reekus Muisc, 2003)

Fintan O'Toole, 'Going west: the country versus the city in Irish writing', *The Crane Bag* 9.2 (1985), 111–16

———. *A Mass for Jesse James: A Journey through 1980's Ireland* (Dublin: Raven Arts Press, 1990)

———. *Black Hole, Green Card: The Disappearance of Ireland* (Dublin: New Island Books, 1994)

George Petrie, *The Petrie Collection of the Ancient Music of Ireland*, vols I & II (Farnborough, Hants: Gregg International Publishers, 1967)

Kenneth C. Pohlmann, *The Compact Disc Handbook* (Oxford: Oxford University Press, 1989)

Vincent Power, *Send 'Em Home Sweatin': The Showband Story* (1990: rev. edn. Cork: Mercier Press, 2000)

Mark J. Prendergast, *Irish Rock: Roots, Personalities, Directions* (Dublin: The O'Brien Press, 1987)

Paul Rabinow (ed.), *The Foucault Reader: An Introduction to Foucault's Thought* (Penguin, 1984)

Amy Raphael, *Never Mind the Bollocks: Women Rewrite Rock* (Virago, 1995)

Steve Redhead, Derek Wynne and Justin O'Connor (eds), *The Clubcultures Reader: Readings in Popular Cultural Studies* (Oxford: Blackwell, 1998)

Adrian Redmond (ed.), *That Was Then, This Is Now: Change in Ireland, 1949–1999* (Dublin: Central Statistics Office, 2000)

George Revill, 'Music and the politics of sound: nationalism, citizenship, and auditory space', *Environment and Planning D: Society and Space* 18.5 (October 2000), 597–613

Simon Reynolds and Joy Press, *The Sex Revolts: Gender, Rebellion, and Rock 'n' Roll* (Cambridge MA: Harvard University Press, 1995)

Hillegonda Rietveld, 'The house sound of Chicago', in Redhead, Wynne and O'Connor (1998), 106–18

John Robb, *The Nineties: What the F*** Was That All About?* (Ebury Press, 1999)

Bill Rolston, 'Music and politics in Ireland: the case of Loyalism', in Harrington and Mitchell (1999), 29–56

———. ' "This is not a rebel song": the Irish conflict and popular music', *Race and Class* 42:3 (2001), 49–67

Eddie Rowley, *A Woman's Voice* (Dublin: O'Brien Press, 1993)

Jon Savage, *England's Dreaming: Sex Pistols and Punk Rock* (1991; Faber and Faber, 2001)

Ann Scanlon, *The Pogues: The Lost Decade* (Omnibus Press, 1988)

Diana Scrimgeour, *U2 Show* (Ted Smart 2004)

June Skinner Sawyers, *The Complete Guide to Celtic Music: From the Highland Bagpipe and Riverdance to U2 and Enya* (Aurum Press, 2000)

Thérèse Smith, 'The fragmentation of Irish musical thought and the marginalisation of traditional music', *Studies* 89:354 (2000), 149–58

Gerry Smyth, 'Who's the greenest of them all? Irishness and popular music', *Irish Studies Review* 2 (Winter 1992), 3–5

——. ' "The natural course of things": Matthew Arnold, Celticism, and the English poetic tradition', *The Journal of Victorian Culture* 1.1 (March 1996), 35–53

——. *Decolonisation and Criticism: The Construction of Irish Literature* (Pluto Press, 1998)

——. *Space and the Irish Cultural Imagination* (Pluto Press, 2001)

——. 'I'd love to turn you on: The Beatles' *Sgt. Pepper's Lonely Hearts Club Band* (1967)' in Ashplant and Smyth (2001), 169–98

——. (ed.) *Music in Contemporary Ireland: A Special Edition of the Irish Studies Review* (2004)

Edward Soja, *Postmodern Geographies: The Reassertion of Space in Critical Social Theory* (Verso, 1989)

Sally Sommers-Smith, 'The origin of style: the famine and Irish traditional music', *Éire-Ireland: An Interdisciplinary Journal of Irish Studies* 32:1 (1996), 121–35

Atara Stein, '"Even better than the real thing": U2's (love) songs of the self', in Dettmar and Richey (1999), 269–86

Martin Stokes (ed.), *Ethnicity, Identity and Music: The Musical Construction of Place* (Oxford: Berg, 1994)

——. (1994a) 'Introduction: ethnicity, identity and music' in Stokes (1994), 1–28

Niall Stokes, 'Paul and the road to Damascus: an interview with Paul Brady', *Hot Press* (23 May 1981)

John Storey (ed.), *Cultural Theory and Popular Culture: A Reader* (Hemel Hempstead: Harvester Wheatsheaf, 1994)

Mark Storey (ed.), *Poetry and Ireland since 1800: A Source Book* (Routledge, 1988)

Rob Strachan and Marion Leonard, 'The state, cultural policy and the politicisation of music industry concerns: the case of the Republic of Ireland', in Mitchell and Doyle (1999), 279–83

——. 'A musical nation: protection, investment and branding in the Irish music industry', in Smyth (2004), 39–49

Will Straw *et al* (eds), *Popular Music: Style and Identity* (Montreal: Centre for Research on Canadian Cultural Industries and Institutions, 1995)

John Street, '(Dis)Location? Rhetoric, politics, meaning and the locality', in Straw *et al* (1995), 255–63

Thomas Swiss, John Sloop and Andrew Herman (eds), *Mapping the Beat: Popular Music and Contemporary Theory* (Blackwell, 1998)

Paul Théberge, 'What's that sound? listening to popular music, revisited', in Straw
      et al (1995), 275–83

——. *Any Sound You Can Imagine: Making Music / Consuming Technology*
      (Middletown, CT: Wesleyan University Press, 1997)

——. 'Technology' in Horner and Swiss (1999), 209–24

Fergal Tobin, *The Best of Decades: Ireland in the 1960s* (Dublin: Gill and Macmillan,
      1984)

Mary Trachsel, 'Oral and literate constructs of "authentic" Irish music' *Éire-Ireland:
      An Interdisciplinary Journal of Irish Studies,* 30:3 (1995), 27–46

John Walsh, 'Lionhearts', *Hot Press* 25:23 (December 2001), 18–22

Michael Walsh, 'Emerald magic', *Time* 47:11 (11 March 1996), 78–80

John Waters, *Race of Angels: Ireland and the Genesis of U2* (Belfast: Blackstaff
      Press, 1994)

Burhan Wazir, 'Irish acts in doldrums as festival is axed: annual Fleadh in London
      falls by wayside as Celtic music's vitality wanes', *The Observer* (Sunday 1
      June 2003)

Harry White, *The Keeper's Recital: Music and Cultural History in Ireland, 1770–1970*
      (Cork: Cork University Press, 1998)

Sheila Whiteley (ed.), *Sexing the Groove: Popular Music and Gender* (London and New
      York: Routledge, 1997)

——. *Women and Popular Music: Sexuality, Identity and Subjectivity* (London and New
      York: Routledge, 2000)

Peter Worsley (ed.), *Modern Sociology: Introductory Readings* (Harmondsworth,
      Middlesex: Penguin, 1970)

Henry Wymbs, 'Taking a walk in Clipper Carlton country', *The Irish Post* (17 May
      2003), 13

WEBSITES AND OTHER SOURCES

Bertie Ahern, Speech at formal launch of IMRO, Conrad Hotel (Monday, 2nd March
      1998), reproduced at *<http://www.imro.ie/speeches.html>.*

Breaking the Barricades? The Story of Ulster Rock (BBC Radio 2, Saturday 28 February
      2004), 9.00pm

Bunreacht na hÉireann (Constitution of Ireland) (1937), *www.taoiseach.gov.ie/
      upload/static/256pdf*

John T. Davis, *Shellshock Rock* (punk documentary, 1979)

FORTE Task Force, *Access all Areas: Irish Music – An International Industry. Report to the
      Minister for Arts, Culture and the Gaeltacht* (Dublin: The Stationery Office, 1996)

Ian Gallagher's *Showband Memories, www.iangallagher.com*

www.irishmusiccentral.com/index

www.bbc.co.uk/radio/aod/radi02_aod.shtml?docu3

David Heffernan (dir.), *From a Whisper to a Scream* (Daniel Productions in association
      with Radio Telefís Éireann, 2000, 3 episodes)

IBEC Music Industry Group, *Striking the Right Note,* IBEC (Irish Business and
      Employers Confederation), Dublin 1995

IFPI, *The Music Industry in Ireland* (International Federation of the Phonographic Industries), London 1993

———. *The Music Industry in Numbers* (London: 1998)

Francis Kennedy's *Irish Showband Archive*, *homepage.tinet.ie/~athenryart/ showindex.htm*

Paul McDermott, Kieran Hurley and Conor O'Toole, *Get that Monster off the Stage: A Documentary on Finbarr Donnelly and 5 go down to the sea* (Cork Campus Radio, no date)

Music Board of Ireland (2002a) *Shaping The Future: a strategic plan for the development of the music industry in Ireland*, Music Board of Ireland: Dublin

Music Board of Ireland (2002b) The Economic Significance of the Irish Music Industry, Music Board of Ireland: Dublin

O'Brien, Deirdre, 'My part in Irish rock's downfall!', email correspondence with the author, November 2003

Simpson Xavier Horwath Consulting, *A Strategic Vision for the Irish Music Industry, A Submission to Government*, 1994

INTERVIEWS

Brendan Balfe, Dublin, 5 June 2002

John Braine, Dublin, 2 April 2002

Catherine Casey, Dublin, 6 April 2002

John Fisher, Dublin, 3 April 2002

Killian Murphy, Dublin, 4 April 2002

Mick O'Keefe, Dublin, 5 April 2002

Sheila O'Callaghan, Dublin, 5 April 2002

François Pittion, Dublin, 6 April 2002

Kevin Smyth, Dublin, 6 April 2002

Billy Webster, Dublin, 1 April 2002

Select Album Discography

Full (or at least fuller) discographies of many of the artists cited below already exist in a number of forms and in a number of locations (most readily the internet), and I have no desire to replicate such material here. What follows is a list of key indicative albums by as many as possible of the artists mentioned in this book, plus a selection recordings by various artists.

The Afro-Celt Sound System, *Volume 1: Sound System* (Virgin 1996)

Agnelli & Nelson, *Hudson Street* (Xtravaganza 2000)

A House, *I Am The Greatest* (Setanta 1991)

Alphastates, *Made From Sand* (Magir 2004)

Altan, *The Blue Idol* (Virgin 2002)

An Emotional Fish, *An Emotional Fish* (EastWest 1990)

Anno Domini, *Anno Domini* (Decca 1969)

Iain Archer, *Flood The Tanks* (Bright Star 2004)

Ash, *1977* (Infectious 1996)

—*Free All Angels* (Infectious 2001)

Aslan, *Made In Dublin* (EMI 1999)

The Asteroids, *Moonlight Music For Beginners* (Scientific Laboratories 2001)

The Atrix, *Possession* (Scoff 1981)

B*Witched, *B*Witched* (Sony 1998)

Don Baker, *Miss You* (Record Services 2000)

Bees Make Honey, *Music Every Night* (EMI 1973)

Bellefire, *After the Rain* (Virgin 2002)

BellX1, *Music In Mouth* (Island 2003)

Big Self, *Stateless* (Reekus 1985)

Mary Black, *No Frontiers* (Dara 1989)

Black 47, *Fire of Freedom* (EMI 1993)

The Black Velvet Band, *When Justice Came* (Elektra 1989)

Frances Black and Kieran Goss, *Frances Black and Kieran Goss* (CBM 1992)

The Blades, *The Last Man in Europe* (Reekus 1985)

Blink, *Deep Inside The Sound Of Sadness* (Serene Records 2004)
Luka Bloom, *The Acoustic Motorbike* (Reprise 1992)
The Bogey Boys, *Friday Night* (Chrysalis 1979)
The Boomtown Rats, *A Tonic for the Troops* (Ensign 1978)
The Bothy Band, *After Hours* (Green Linnet 1984)
Boyzone, *Said and Done* (Polygram 1995)
Paul Brady, *Welcome Here Kind Stranger* (Mulligan 1978)
—*Hard Station* (WEA 1981)
Maire Brennan, *Whisper To The Wild Water* (World Records 2000)
Brilliant Trees, *Wake Up And Dream* (Plush Vibe 1998)
Cactus World News, *Urban Beaches* (MCA 1986)
Paddy Casey, *Living* (Sony 2003)
The Chieftains, *The Chieftains 1* (Claddagh 1963)
Mic Christopher, *Skylarkin'* (Loza Records 2002)
Clannad, *Clannad 2* (Gael Linn 1974)
   Magical Ring (RCA 1983)
The Clipper Carlton, *Ireland's Premier Danceband* (Foyle Hospice, no date)
Sonny Condell, *Camouflage* (Mulligan 1976)
The Corrs, *Forgiven*
   Talk on Corners (Atlantic 1997)
Donnacha Costello, *Together Is the New Alone* (Mille Plateaux 2001)
Mary Coughlin, *Uncertain Pleasures* (EastWest 1990)
The Cranberries, *Everybody Else Is Doing It, So Why Can't We?* (Island 1993)
Cry Before Dawn, *Witness For The World* (CBS 1989)
Daemien Frost, *Corpus Daemo* (Alpha Relish 2001)
Dances to Tipperary, *Ride On* (21C 1999)
Danu, *The Road Less Travelled* (Shanachie 2004)
Chris de Burgh, *Spanish Train and Other Stories* (A&M 1975)
Decal, *404 Not Found* (Planet Mu 2002)
De Danann, *Anthem* (Dara 1985)
Damien Dempsey, *Seize the Day* (Clear Records 2003)
Dervish, *Decade* (Whirling Discs 2001)
Desert Hearts, *Let's Get Worse* (Tugboat Records 2002)
The Devlins, *Waves* (Ruby Works 2004)
Cara Dillon, *Cara Dillon* (Rough Trade 2001)
The Divine Comedy, *Promenade* (Setanta 1994)
Dr Strangely Strange, *Heavy Petting* (Vertigo 1970)
Joe Dolan, *Make Me An Island: The Best Of Joe Dolan* (Castle 1996)
Philip Donnelly, *Town And Country* (Dublin Records 1988)
Dorian Mood, *Can't Stand Still* (Big Mood Records 1989)
The Dubliners, *A Drop Of The Hard Stuff* (Major Minor 1967)
The Dudley Corporation, *In Love With The Dudley Corporation* (Scientific
   Laboratories 2003)
Eire Apparent, *Sunrise* (Buddah 1969)

El Diablo, *The Crooked Straight* (Catchy Go Go 2003)
Emmet Spiceland, *Emmet Spiceland* (Hawk 1968)
Energy Orchard, *Stop The Machine* (MCA 1992)
Engine Alley, *A Sonic Holiday* (Mother 1992)
Enya, *Watermark* (WEA 1988)
Fatima Mansions, *Viva Dead Ponies* (Kitchenware 1990)
The Fat Lady Sings, *Twist* (EastWest 1991)
Martin Finke, *Untended Stories* (Parallel Music 2003)
The Fountainhead, *The Burning Touch* (China 1986)
The 4 of Us, *Songs For The Tempted* (CBS 1989)
The Frames, *For the Birds* (Plateau 2000)
The Frank and Walters, *Trains Boats & Planes* (Setanta 1992)
Gavin Friday, *Each Man Kills The Thing He Loves* (Island 1989)
Fruupp, *Future Legends* (Dawn 1973)
Future Kings of Spain, *Future Kings Of Spain* (Red Flag 2002)
Rory Gallagher, *Live in Europe* (Polydor 1972)
Irish Tour (Polydor 1974)
Against The Grain (Capo 1975)
Mark Geary, *Ghosts* (Independent Records 2004)
Bob Geldof, *Sex, Age and Death* (Eagle 2001)
Giveamanakick, *Is It Ok To Be Loud, Jesus?* (Out On A Limb 2003)
The Golden Horde, *The Golden Horde* (Mother 1991)
The Gorehounds, *Semtex* (Big Chief 1989)
Granny's Intentions, *Honest Injun* (Deram 1969)
Hal, Hal (Rough Trade 2005)
Halite, *Courses* (Brassneck 2004)
Mick Hanly, *Happy Like This* (Round Tower 1993)
Ronán Hardiman, *Anthem* (Decca 2001)
Gemma Hayes, *Night On My Side* (Source 2002)
Margaret Healy, *And You Are?* (Medical Records 2001)
David Holmes, *This Films Crap Lets Slash The Seats* (Go! Discs 1995)
Horslips, *Happy To Meet, Sorry To Part* (Oats 1972)
    The Táin (Oats 1973)
    The Book Of Invasions: A Celtic Symphony (Oats 1976)
Hothouse Flowers, *People* (London 1988)
Nina Hynes, *Staros* (Reverb Records 2002)
Interference, *Interference* (Sound Sound 2003)
In Tua Nua, *Vaudeville* (Virgin 1987)
Andy Irvine and Paul Brady, *Andy Irvine Paul Brady* (Mulligan 1976)
Jape, *The Monkeys In The Zoo Have More Fun Than Me* (Trust Me I'm a Thief 2004)
Jetplane Landing, *Zero for Conduct* (Smalltown America 2003)
The Jimmy Cake, *Dublin Gone. Everybody Dead* (Pilatus 2002)
JJ72, *JJ72* (Lakota 2000)
The Johnstons, *Give a Damn* (Transatlantic 1969)

Jubilee Allstars, *Lights Of The City* (Independent Records 2000)

Kaydee, *Stop! I'm Doing It Again* (Lime / EMI Records 1998)

Ronan Keating, *Ronan* (Polydor 2000)

Katell Keineg, *O Seasons O Castles* (Elektra 1994)

Luke Kelly, *Best of Luke Kelly* (Celtic Arts 2004)

Brian Kennedy, *Get On With Your Short Life* (Sony 2001)

Kerbdog, *Kerbdog* (Vertigo 1994)

Kila, *Tog É Go Bog É* (Kila Records 1997)

David Kitt, *The Big Romance* (Blanco Y Negro 1999)

Jack L, *Universe* (Dara 2001)

Large Mound, *Go Forth and Amplify* (Scientific Laboratories 2004)

The Last Post, *Dry Land* (Bright Star 2002)

Light A Big Fire, *Surveillance* (Siren 1987)

Lir, *Magico Magico* (Vélo 1991)

Sinead Lohan, *Who Do You Think I Am?* (Dara 1995)

Lunasa, *The Merry Sisters of Fate* (Green Linnet 2001)

Donal Lunny, *Journey: The Best Of Donal Lunny* (Hummingbird 2000)

Philip Lynott, *Solo In Soho* (Vertigo 1980)

Barry McCormack, *We Drank Our Tears* (Hag's Head 2003)

Eleanor McEvoy, *Yola* (Blue Dandelion Records 2001)

Mama's Boys, *Plug It In* (Pussy 1982)

Mellow Candle, *Swaddling Songs* (Deram 1972)

Messiah J and The Expert, *What's Confusing You?* (Volta Sounds 2003)

Microdisney, *The Clock Comes Down the Stairs* (Rough Trade 1985)

Midnight Well, *Midnight Well* (Mulligan 1977)

The Moondogs, *That's What Friends Are For* (Sire 1981)

Christy Moore, *Ride On* (WEA 1984)

Gary Moore, *Wild Frontier* (10 1987)

Van Morrison, *Astral Weeks* (Warners 1969)

    Moondance (Warners 1970)

    Veedon Fleece (Polydor 1974)

Van Morrison and The Chieftains, *Irish Heartbeat* (Mercury 1988)

Moving Hearts, *Moving Hearts* (WEA 1981)

Samantha Mumba, *Gotta Tell You* (Wild Card / Polydor 2000)

Mundy, *24 Star Hotel* (Camcor 2002)

My Bloody Valentine, *Loveless* (Creation 1991)

My Little Funhouse, *Standunder* (Geffen 1992)

Maura O'Connell, *A Real Life Story* (Warners 1991)

Sinéad O'Connor, *The Lion and the Cobra* (Ensign 1987)

    I Do Not Want What I Haven't Got (Ensign 1990)

Seán Ó Riada *Mise Eire* (Gael Linn 1959)

    Ó Riada Sa Gaiety (Gael Linn 1969)

Gilbert O'Sullivan, *Nothing Rhymed* (MAM 1970)

The Outcasts, *Self Conscious Over You* (Good Vibrations 1979)

Paddy-A-Go-Go, *Keep it Reel* (PAG 1995)

The Pale, *Here's One We Made Earlier* (A&M 1992)

Paranoid Visions, *After The Faction* (AX-S Records 1996)

Peggy's Leg, *Grinilla* (Bunch 1973)

Planxty, *Planxty* (Polydor 1972)

Picturehouse, *Sadmess, Madness and Gladness* (Wacca Wacca 2002)

The Pogues, *Rum, Sodomy And The Lash* (Stiff 1985)

    If I Should Fall From Grace With God (Pogue Mahone 1988)

Power of Dreams, *Immigrants, Emigrants and Me* (Polydor 1990)

The Prayer Boat, *Pollichinelle* (Invisible Records 1998)

Protex, *Strange Obsessions* (Polydor 1979)

Pugwash, *Almanac* (Vélo 2002)

Colm Quearney, *The World's Not Round* (Strange Vibe 2001)

The Radiators, *Ghostown* (Chiswick 1979)

The Redneck Manifesto, *Thirtysixstrings* (Red Flag 2001)

Relish, *Wildflowers* (EMI 2001)

Republic Of Loose, *This Is The Tomb Of The Juice* (Big Cat 2004)

Rest, *Burning In Water, Drowning In Flame* (Out On A Limb 2004)

Revelino, *Revelino* (Dirt 1994)

The Revenants, *Septober Nowonder* (Black Burst Records 1999)

The Revs, *Sonictonic* (Treasure Island 2002)

The Rhythm Kings, *Setting Fire To My Heart* (Scoff 1983)

Damien Rice, *O* (DRM 2002)

Dickie Rock, *The Best Of Dickie Rock And The Miami Showband* (Castle 1998)

Roesy, *Sketch The Day, Paint The Sky* (Schism 2002)

Rollerskate Skinny, *Horsedrawn Wishes* (Warners 1996)

Rubyhorse, *Goodbye To All That* (Brash Music 2003)

Rudi, *Big Time: The Best Of Rudi* (Anagram 1996)

Ruefrex, *Flowers For All Occasions* (Kasper 1985)

Salthouse, *Hanging By A Thread* (Hook Records 2003)

Saville, *Somnambular Ballads* (Reekus 2003)

The Saw Doctors, *All The Way From Tuam* (Solid 1992)

Ann Scott, *Poor Horse* (Raghorse 2003)

Scullion, *Balance And Control* (WEA 1981)

The Sewing Room, *The Sewing Room and Nico* (Dead Elvis 1995)

Sharon Shannon, *Sharon Shannon* (Solid 1991)

Skid Row, *34 Hours* (CBS 1971)

Simple Kid, *SK 1* (2m 2003)

Snow Patrol, *Final Straw* (Black Lion 2003)

Solas, *The Hour Before Dawn* (Shanachie 2000)

Something Happens, *Stuck Together With God's Glue* (Virgin 1990)

Davy Spillane, *A Place Among The Stones* (Columbia 1994)

Stano, *Only* (Mother 1989)

The Starjets, *God Bless The Starjets* (Epic 1979)

The Stars of Heaven, *Sacred Heart Hotel* (Rough Trade 1986)
Stiff Little Fingers, *Inflammable Material* (Rough Trade 1979)
Stockton's Wing, *Light In The Western Sky* (Tara 1982)
Stump, *A Fierce Pancake* (Ensign 1988)
The Stunning, *Paradise In The Picturehouse* (Solid 1990)
The Sultans of Ping, *Casual Sex In The Cineplex* (Rhythm King 1993)
Supply Demand and Curve, *Supply Demand and Curve* (Mulligan 1976)
Sweeney's Men, *Tracks of Sweeney* (Transatlantic 1969)
Taste, *On The Boards* (Polydor 1970)
That Petrol Emotion, *Manic Pop Thrill* (Demon 1986)
Them, *Angry Young Them* (Decca 1965)
Therapy?, *Troublegum* (A&M 1994)
Thin Lizzy, *Shades Of A Blue Orphanage* (Decca 1972)
    Live And Dangerous (Vertigo 1978)
The Thrills, *So Much For The City* (Virgin 2003)
Tír na nÓg, *Strong in the Sun* (Chrysalis 1973)
Toasted Heretic, *Another Day, Another Riot* (Solid 1992)
Tuesday Blue, *Shibumi* (EMI 1988)
Turn, *Forward* (Nurture 2003)
Pierce Turner, *Now is Heaven* (Beggars Banquet 1991)
The Tycho Brahe (Tychonaut), *This Is The Tycho Brahe* (Konstantin Records 2002)
U2, *Boy* (Island 1980)
    The Unforgettable Fire (Island 1984)
    The Joshua Tree (Island 1987)
    Achtung Baby! (Island 1991)
The Undertones, *The Undertones* (Sire 1979)
The Virgin Prunes, *If I Die, I Die* (Rough Trade 1982)
Waiting Room, *Catering For Headphones* (Out On A Limb Records 2004)
The Waterboys, *Fisherman's Blues* (Ensign 1988)
Watercress, *Bummer* (Creeping Herb 1998)
Westlife, *Coast to Coast* (BMG 2000)
Whipping Boy, *Heartworm* (Columbia 1995)
Andy White, *Rave On Andy White* (London 1986)
Freddie White, *Close To You* (Lime 1991)
The Woodsband, *The Woodsband* (Decca 1971)
Wormhole, *Chicks Dig Scars* (Roadrunner 1994)
Zrazy, *Give It All Up* (Vélo 1994)

COMPILATIONS

Allied: Electronic Alliance From ie-dance (Homeburnt Records 2001)
By The New Time (Silverdoor 2001)
Intoxicated Volume 1 (Toxic Records 2001)
Irish Rock – Ireland's Beat Groups 1964–1969 (Sequel 1993)
Irish Showband Years: The Ultimate Collection (Outlet 1999)

It's All Good – The Best Of Irish (Phutloose 2001)
Just For Kicks (Kick Records 1979)
Louis Walsh's History of Irish Pop (Solid 2002)
Eleanor McEvoy *et al, A Woman's Heart* (Dara 1992)
Postmodern (Hot Press 2003)
Psychokinesis (Psychonavigation Records 2002)
Songs From A Small Room: A Celebration Of Ireland's Best-loved Songwriter Night (Self
      Possessed Records 2001)
Synthetic Allsorts (Frontend Synthetics 2001)
Tom Dunne's 30 Best Irish Hits Volume 1 (Solid 2001)
Tom Dunne's 30 Best Irish Hits Volume 2 (Solid 2002)
The Tupelo Tapes: Best of Independent Ireland (Vitaminic 2001)

Index